RUNAWAY GENRES

Runaway Genres

The Global Afterlives of Slavery

Yogita Goyal

NEW YORK UNIVERSITY PRESS
New York

NEW YORK UNIVERSITY PRESS
New York
www.nyupress.org

© 2019 by New York University
All rights reserved

References to Internet websites (URLs) were accurate at the time of writing. Neither the author nor New York University Press is responsible for URLs that may have expired or changed since the manuscript was prepared.

Library of Congress Cataloging-in-Publication Data
Names: Goyal, Yogita, author.
Title: Runaway genres : the global afterlives of slavery / Yogita Goyal.
Description: New York : New York University Press, [2019] |
Includes bibliographical references and index.
Identifiers: LCCN 2019006929| ISBN 9781479829590 (cl : alk. paper) |
ISBN 9781479832712 (pb : alk. paper)
Subjects: LCSH: Slavery—History. | African diaspora. | Globalization—Social aspects—Africa—History.
Classification: LCC HT861 .G69 2019 | DDC 306.3/6209—dc23
LC record available at https://lccn.loc.gov/2019006929

New York University Press books are printed on acid-free paper, and their binding materials are chosen for strength and durability. We strive to use environmentally responsible suppliers and materials to the greatest extent possible in publishing our books.

Manufactured in the United States of America

10 9 8 7 6 5 4 3 2 1

Also available as an ebook

For my father
in memoriam
Madan Lal Goyal

CONTENTS

Introduction: The Genres of Slavery   1

1. Sentimental Globalism   35

2. The Gothic Child   69

3. Post-Black Satire   105

4. Talking Books (Talking Back)   141

5. We Need New Diasporas   171

Epilogue: What We Talk about When We Talk about Slavery   211

Acknowledgments   217

Notes   223

Index   253

About the Author   263

Introduction

The Genres of Slavery

Something new is beginning—or perhaps something old and nasty is reviving.
—Octavia Butler, *Parable of the Sower*

Some twenty-five years ago, Toni Morrison lamented that there was "no suitable memorial" to slavery in the United States—no "plaque or wreath [or] three hundred foot tower," not even a "small bench by the road." Explaining how she wrote *Beloved* to counteract this national amnesia and urge to erasure, Morrison claimed that "because such a place does not exist (that I know of), the book had to."[1] Now, however, slavery is seemingly everywhere, in every form, a fit subject for solemn memorials, irreverent comedy, imaginative reconstruction, an allegory of contemporary racial politics, or an enterprise of painstaking fact finding for historians. In other words, slavery is now the site for the reinvention of form.

That slavery offers immense aesthetic and political resources to contemporary African American writers is not at all surprising. After all, current forms of inequality and race-based discrimination can easily be traced back to slavery, as both institutional and psychic afterlives, as structures and as structures of feeling. And the fields of art, literature, history, and political theory have all been transformed by the study of slavery and its varied afterlives. In literature, especially, the dominance of the neo-slave narrative over the last four decades as the paradigmatic mode for thinking about African American identity and history is now axiomatic. Such writers as Dionne Brand, Octavia Butler, Fred D'Aguiar, Bernardine Evaristo, Marlon James, Charles Johnson, Edward Jones, Gayl Jones, Andrea Levy, James McBride, M. NourbeSe Philip, Caryl Phillips, Alice Randall, Colson Whitehead, and Sherley Anne Williams have satisfied Morrison's call and fully memorialized slavery and its constitutive role in any conception of the nation's past, present, and future. Moreover, philosophies of history derived from slavery, inquiries into practices of archival recovery, studies of racial capitalism, and debates about ethics and affect have assumed center stage in current scholarship. The extensive activism around prison abolition and ending mass incarceration, to take just one example, substantiates a clear understanding of the foundational role of slavery and its incomplete abolition in the discriminatory laws that shape current US carceral regimes. In recent years, debates about reparations, Confederate statues, and antebellum nostalgia, calls for accounting for the university's connection to slavery, and renewed attention to ideologies of white supremacy and antiblackness have all helped shape the volatile afterlife of slavery in the political sphere.

But slavery appears in more than such historical or memorial garb. Slavery, in fact, frames a range of contemporary phenomena across the globe: from human trafficking to illegal immigration, from conscription in war as a child soldier to forced marriage, from debt bondage to domestic servitude. Such parallels to the transatlantic slave trade proliferate in contemporary culture, demanding new ways of understanding racial formation across past and present landscapes, and in relation to new geographies of terror and containment. *Runaway Genres* tracks the emergence of slavery as the defining template through which current forms of human rights abuses are understood in order to rethink race in a global frame. Neo-abolitionist movements to end child labor, human rights campaigns against human trafficking and supportive of the rights of refugees and asylum seekers, feminist efforts to end the exploitation of sex workers, populist advocacy for animal rights, antiabortion efforts, activism against incarceration, discrimination based on caste, and the abuse of migrant labor all make rampant use of slavery to elicit support for their cause. And to do so, they rely on the same power of narrative that abolitionists once did. As one Boston editor put it in 1840, "Argument provokes argument, reason is met by sophistry; but narratives of slaves go right to the hearts of men."[2]

Continuing this appeal to the "hearts of men," writers across the globe—from India to Ireland, Nigeria to Uganda, Haiti to South Africa, Sri Lanka to Sierra Leone—are reviving the slave narrative, a clearly bounded historical genre created for the single purpose of arguing for the abolition of slavery. What does it mean to view the life of a Sudanese refugee or "Lost Boy" through the black-white binary of Atlantic slavery? Or to narrate the experience of a child soldier in Sierra Leone or Liberia as the afterlife of slavery? Or to see the journey of a child sent to live with an urban family as a *restavec* in Haiti as a kind of Middle Passage? Why does Frederick Douglass's 1845 *Narrative of the Life of Frederick Douglass, an American Slave, Written by Himself* make an appearance not only in African American fiction by Charles Johnson, Alice Randall, and James McBride, but also in Colum McCann's *Transatlantic*, in Chimamanda Ngozi Adichie's novel about Nigeria's civil war, *Half of a Yellow Sun*, and in Helen Oyeyemi's uncanny *Boy, Snow, Bird*?[3]

To answer these questions, I locate the global proliferation of the slave narrative at the confluence of three forces: increasing large-scale migration, the ongoing appeal of sentimentalism to narrate trauma, and a historical tendency to see current events as repetitions of the past. The slave narrative, a story of escape from bondage, presented as a sentimental appeal to the reader's empathy, often vouched for by a sympathetic white editor, uncannily matches contemporary accounts of refugees, asylum seekers, survivors of trafficking and conscription in war. What W. E. B. Du Bois memorably called the "most magnificent drama in the last thousand years of human history"—the large-scale transportation of Africans to the Americas—seems replicated in the scale and trauma of contemporary migrations.[4] In an age when feeling, affect, and empathy appear as substitutes for social change, the sentimental idiom favored by abolitionists comes in handy to narrate stories of oppression from the Global South. The conditions of empathetic reader and traumatized survivor neatly mirror those of the slave narrative. Returning to the past—by replaying tropes of the slave narrative, including accounts of exile and natal alienation, the concept of social death, the quest for literacy, the journey north to freedom, and dreams of the Jubilee—contemporary literature chronicles the history of violence in a world that has not yet figured out a politics of reconciliation or reckoning.

Reading for the transformation of the slave narrative in contemporary fiction and nonfiction, I explicate as well as question the ways in which slavery remains at the heart of many models of transnational blackness. Because slavery has become a figure for contemporary inequality, an examination of the ghosts of past inequities not yet laid to rest, such returns to the past as much speak to a desire to understand history as they frame the possibilities of the present and the future. In exploring the contradictory uses of historical violence for contemporary politics, we need to not only return to the question of what slavery itself means but also account for how and when the slave narrative became malleable as a global form, available for adaptation across time and space.

Runaway Genres contributes to the analysis of slavery in African American studies by exploring its transformation as analog and metaphor, helping restage long-standing discussions of the peculiar institution's relation to empire, capital, and changing notions of race. It thus draws on and extends the conversation around the afterlife of slavery, asking what happens when the slave narrative goes global. The book further participates in the conversation around the morphing of postcolonial studies into global Anglophone, Global South, or world literature. By centering race and slavery to enable transhistorical connections, I propose new ways to think about American and global literature in relation. While the global is one of the most prominent rubrics in our lexicon, conceptions of the global are frequently murky and ill defined, invested in ideas of the new without adequately processing the remains and revenants of a violent history. This ambiguity is doubly true of the turn to global or world literature as a means of stepping beyond the stale Manichean frames of the postcolonial. By tracing how such seemingly new genres as the global novel are not only deeply haunted but fundamentally shaped by the slave narrative, my book places such new genres within history, reckoning with their geopolitical formation, as well as their aesthetic mutations as they circulate across the world.

Too often, contemporary literature is read without sufficient attention to history, as part of an endless present, or as world literature beyond race or nation. Searching for the imprint of historical genres like the slave narrative clears a path to return history to the conversation, enabling formalist and historicist approaches to work in tandem. Moreover, race has been a notable blind spot in postcolonial studies, as has the study of empire in many versions of American studies.[5] By offering a theory of form and how it travels, asking whether genres that come into being in specific times and places carry with them an ideology of form when transplanted elsewhere, *Runaway Genres* argues for the slave narrative as a new world literary genre, exploring the full complexity of the possibility of an ethical globalism. Taking form seriously in discussions of minority literature, I organize each chapter around a genre associated with the slave narrative: sentimentalism, the gothic, satire, surrogation, and revisionism.[6]

Refugees, detainees, child soldiers, and asylum seekers are some of the most vulnerable populations today, as forced migration is a central fact of contemporary life. These voices are the strongest possible validation of the humanities, for it is only there that we find the capacity to generate empathy, and create a social vision based on a shared conception of human rights. For a world connected like never before, my book answers some basic questions: who writes for whom, how and why do people in the First World react to tales of suffering from far away, how can literature make us ethical in a global era, and how do conceptions of race developed in the United States fare in an increasingly transnational context? At stake is the basic problem of how we see the relation between past and present, between historical violence and continuing forms of inequality, as well as how we conceive of resistance and agency, indeed our very definition of politics itself.

The Logic of Analogy

Considering one such analogy in some detail helps clarify the possibilities as well as the limits of such comparative efforts. The still-unfolding refugee crisis in the Mediterranean poignantly stages the concerns at the heart of this book as the fearsome crossings of African migrants across a hostile ocean strikingly recall the scene of Atlantic slavery. In April 2015, some seven hundred people traveling from Libya to Lampedusa drowned, amid nearly five boats sinking and twelve hundred people losing their lives. For many commentators, the only appropriate antecedent was to be found in the 1781 *Zong* atrocity, where a captain of a British slave ship chose to throw some 133 slaves overboard so that he could claim them as insurance losses. *Zong* immediately names questions of race, power, and terror, as its afterlife far exceeds its eighteenth-century abolitionist frame of moral outrage, legal maneuver, and humanitarian activism. Following in and amplifying J. M. W. Turner's footsteps (whose 1840 painting *Slave Ship* galvanized sentiment against slavery), numerous poets, novelists, artists, and historians have turned to the ongoing implications of this horrific event and the subsequent legal battle to make the very name *Zong* an iconic one for studies of slavery, race, and blackness, as well as for our conceptions of history and racial capitalism.[7] As Ian Baucom explains, the *Zong* atrocity does not name an isolated or exceptional incident—rather it emblematizes the very logic at the core of contemporary financial systems and human rights regimes, the heart of what we inhabit as Atlantic modernity.[8] Paul Gilroy's suggestion of a black Atlantic counterculture of modernity similarly refuses to see the past as settled, mining contemporary culture for coded and potentially transformative visions of justice derived from slavery, particularly from the chronotope of the ship.[9] Christina Sharpe connects such meditations on the slave ship to contemporary black life in "the wake" where African migrants to the Mediterranean and Europe "are imagined as insects, swarms, vectors of disease" and "the semiotics of the slave ship continue: from the forced movements of the enslaved to the forced movements of the migrant and refugee."[10]

The fact that the refugee camps of Calais, called the Jungle, serve as sites of repression, detention, and deportation for African refugees further echoes long histories of racialization and abuse of black bodies and their commodification as cargo. A young man from Ethiopia, for instance, compares the contemporary practice of biometric processing to the branding of enslaved people, arguing that "they are making us slaves, you know, slaves of (their) own country, by this fingerprint."[11] Other African migrants, refugees, and asylum seekers risking their lives at sea to arrive in Europe also make liberal use of the analogy to slavery in describing their experience of being processed, surveilled, and detained. Reports of people perishing in the holds of overcrowded ships, plans to house refugees in shipping containers, seemingly permanently, and repeated drownings at sea suggest the conversion of human beings into chattel associated with the Middle Passage. Accordingly, when the Forensic Architecture project charted the drift of the "left-to-die boat" where sixty-three migrants died while the boat drifted for fourteen days in 2011 within the NATO maritime surveillance area, the team explained their thematic use of the idea of "drift" by reference both to *Zong* and to the well-known 1789 drawing of the slave ship *Brookes*, which they term "a powerful antecedent of human rights forensics."[12] The "grim historical parallel" to slavery thus evokes familiar questions of race and power, terror and antiblackness.[13]

My book thinks through such evocations, asking what might it mean to view the contemporary refugee crisis through the lens of a historical event like slavery. How do such analogies galvanize public support or solicit historical memory? How do they testify to the enduring affective power of the language of slavery and abolition that continues to shape the scope of human rights discourse today? How does seeing the contemporary refugee as a specter of the Atlantic slave summon up the ethical claim of the past on us?

While the logic of analogy might suggest a simple and morally clear framing of the current plight of the refugees, it conjures up a far more complicated and potentially thorny set of dilemmas, requiring us to avoid conflating past and present, a hegemonic Global North and a perpetually marginalized Global South. As numerous activists and scholars have shown, the task at hand is to learn not to theorize the refugee as Agamben's bare life alone, or as a repetition of the paradigm of Auschwitz—"the pure, absolute and impassable biopolitical space"—but to move beyond abjection and recognize the refugee as a political subject, salvaged from the abstraction of victim or criminal.[14] To do so, the analogy to slavery may be enlisted to yield broader visions of justice and reparation, but only if we refuse to settle the meaning of either term being compared. That is to say, we should not assume that the place of slavery and the figure of the slave in US or European life has been reckoned with and can now be marshaled as a universally acknowledged truth. Slavery remains both "unspeakable" and "unspoken" in contemporary culture, and everywhere riled in debates about race and the human.[15] That Frederick Douglass can be thought of as a refugee and illegal immigrant in response to right-wing resurgence, as David Blight argues, helps counter ongoing amnesia about the nation's terrorist past and its unfinished project of emancipation, further underscoring the labile, unstable meaning of slavery in political culture today.[16] As Saidiya Hartman explains, "If the ghost of slavery still haunts our present, it is because we are still looking for an exit from the prison."[17]

Nor should we assume that the figure of the contemporary refugee can be defended with reference to the past alone and will not exact new frames, concepts, vocabularies, and imaginaries. Consider for instance the response of the African Union to President Trump's ban on immigration from Muslim-majority countries. Nokosazana Dlamini-Zuma, the president of the African Union Commission, charged that "the very country to which many of our people were taken as slaves during the transatlantic slave trade has now decided to ban refugees from some of our countries."[18] Such a statement requires the United States to connect its past actions to its present refusals, suggesting too a link between a history of racialization and the treatment of Muslims today. To make analogy work, we need a clear sense of both correspondence and difference. Rather than applying notions of race from the Atlantic to the Global South, a certain amount of flexibility and awareness of particularity will also ensure that such new concerns can be understood and combated in real time. This cognizance is especially urgent because the current refugee crisis has been a boon to human traffickers and has generated a massive increase in modern forms of captivity and exploitation. Moreover, as Hannah Arendt noted, refugees often distance themselves from the label, preferring "newcomers or immigrants."[19] The designation of refugee, migrant, or asylum seeker itself involves legal but also figurative and epistemological distinctions. While the Mediterranean refugee is denied the tag of immigrant even as the figure of the Atlantic slave is evoked to understand current trauma, human rights activists have called for a more radical imagining of a world beyond borders, not just focusing on frames of empathy or hospitality but asking for a deeper exploration of roots of the conflicts and inequalities that lead to large-scale movements. Such imperatives of global economic justice require a rethinking of the language of war, terror, security, and surveillance.[20]

Historical analogies of contemporary refugees to slavery thus work in several different ways: by invoking the familiarity of black bodies at sea, they attempt to interrogate the racism of existing disciplines and the power of resistive practices of viewing and representation; they re-read the past through slavery in terms of present categories in order to defamiliarize both past and present and make their juxtaposition yield better notions of human rights; they point to contemporary instances of slavery such as human trafficking and child abduction. All such efforts seek to connect different parts of the globe, emphasizing itineraries of belonging outside of nations and borders, as well as parallels across time, seeking to understand the present as an unfolding of a past not yet laid to rest. They thus demand a new comparative literacy across past and present, then and now, to comprehend the forms of power at play and to imagine paths of resistance.

To fully grasp the purchase of such analogies compels a deeper knowledge of the past—requiring us to see slavery as a still unsettled and unsettling figure, unspeakable despite being a twice-told tale. It also requires a more thorough knowledge of the present, asking us to discern what might be new about forms of power today, and whether the architecture of contemporary state terror (including drones and extrajudicial killings, maximum-security prisons and offshore detention sites, police killings at home and repression at the border) is best apprehended and resisted by referring to the past of slavery and abolition, or whether it entails newer configurations. Moreover, the power and prominence of slavery as a prism through which conceptions of black humanity, agency, and futurity refract and become visible should not obscure the contradictions race acquires as it travels across the globe. Rather than seeing the past of the United States as the present of the Global South, in a familiar move denying coevalness, what new relationships mapping space and time might be obtained?

My use of analogy as a heuristic throughout the book warrants some accounting of the term as a rhetorical figure as well as a sense of its historical and conceptual valence. In *The Order of Things*, Michel Foucault traces the history of forms of similitude, reminding us that analogy as a concept was ubiquitous in Greek science and medieval thought, structuring as well the Renaissance appraisal of the human sciences. Isolating four forms of similarity—convenience, emulation, analogy, and sympathy—Foucault shows how analogy "makes possible the marvelous confrontation of resemblances across space"; it also speaks of "adjacencies, of bonds and joints."[21] Because it is reversible and polyvalent, analogy has "a universal field of application": for Foucault, "through it, all the figures in the whole universe can be drawn together." In tracing the various uses of analogies to slavery in this book, my hope is that, as Foucault suggests, analogy can "extend, from a single given point, to an endless number of relationships."[22]

Thinking about analogy prompts the question of whether we privilege filiation, relation, and connection over essence or ontology. It is worth noting here a strong case against analogy proffered by the school of thought that has come to be known as Afro-pessimism. Frank B. Wilderson, for example, dispenses with the "ruse of analogy" altogether, insisting on the ontological difference between "the Black, a subject who is always already positioned as Slave" and everyone else, who then assumes the position of Master. Any analogy to blackness (for instance, to Native Americans or Palestinians) is thus a "mystification" and an "erasure" because "grammars of suffering are irreconcilable."[23] My exploration of the malleability of slavery in contemporary culture necessarily departs from such a stance, as I prioritize historicity over ontology. That slavery as an analytic invites claims to particularity *and* authorizes connections becomes an enabling contradiction for this study, as I foreground the underlying question of what makes analogy thinkable. Analogy, homology, resemblance, identity, relation, equivalence, commonality, familiarity, juxtaposition, proximity, linkage: such words appear time and again in the following pages. I hope to mine their common affordances but also emphasize the discrete work they do, believing that the critical labor of such distinctions matters. What work does analogy perform, what histories does it summon, what hidden relations between power and knowledge make visible? Do analogies to slavery prioritize associative connections to favor coalitional practice or allow metaphoric substitution to recenter the master's discourse? Are a reduction to the same or the glorification of alterity our only choices? In the end, I want to reserve the right to distinguish among generative and troubling analogies with an emphasis on the core logic animating our sense of how people across the world connect today, and how they make use of the past.[24]

The time of analogy thus emerges as a fundamental factor in such assessments as I explore whether the figure of the modern slave appears as coeval with us or as an anachronism or a specter haunting the certainties of the present with the residue of the undead past. Thinking in terms of neither seamless continuity nor sharp rupture, *Runaway Genres* focuses on the unpredictable entangled afterlives of slavery, colonialism, and racial dispossession. Ann Stoler's concept of duress helps assess the dynamics of obsolescence and revival I identify, as she emphasizes the durable impress of colonial history in the present. Stoler explains that "the hardened, tenacious qualities of colonial effects" generate "extended protracted temporalities," requiring us to read history as recursion, without clean temporal breaks of one age ending and another beginning.[25] Past and present articulate in uneven, uncertain, and sometimes intangible ways, calling for something other than totalizing explanations with origin and endpoint. Accordingly, drawing on a more layered sense of historical transition, I highlight messy beginnings, differential histories, and interrupted imaginaries. That people live in multiple temporalities, that the past is often present, that what we declare over regularly resurfaces is now generally accepted. So too is the notion that condemning postcolonial subjects to the past of the West denies them coevalness. Thinking the postcolony beyond the frame of leftover, facsimile, or anachronism, I probe the possibility of how renovations of past racial configurations may assist us in fathoming the possibility of alliance, solidarity, and coalition. At the same time, it is vital to realize that the history of racism itself must be reread, and involves both contact and contradiction, as Lisa Lowe reveals in *Intimacies of Four Continents*, unearthing the tangled threads of genocide, settler colonialism, indentured labor, and slavery that have shaped the world.[26] Historians of slavery have similarly underscored the distinction between writing a history of slavery and creating a memory of it, as Stephanie Smallwood argues.[27] Creative uses of metaphors of abolition, maroonage, and fugitivity abound in current parlance. But more literal usages are also harnessed for very different political purposes to export imperial terror across the world in the name of freedom. In 2003, for instance, George W. Bush called for an end to the sexual slavery of girls and women as an explicit goal of the War on Terror.[28] As I show in chapter 1, the discourse of modern slavery fully participates in the racial configurations of the War on Terror as well as intersecting with a carceral sensibility. Since the "paradox of comparison is that judgment of pertinence rests on the equation of unequal things," as Stoler puts it in *Duress*, my hope is that my tracking of the uses of analogy—the relations among objects, ideas, people but also the relations of those entities to their representations—functions as a "situated political act of discernment."[29] Focusing on formal revivals of the genre of the slave narrative enables comparison across history and the present, as well as across distinct national spaces.

Reinventing Form

Runaway Genres begins with the revival of the peculiar genre of the slave narrative in contemporary human rights literature, focusing on accounts of escape from modern slavery and the experiences of child soldiers in sentimental and gothic genres, respectively. Next, I turn to fiction commonly called a neo-slave narrative but deliberately eschewing any fidelity to historical realism. I then show how African American satirists trouble any notion of a seamless collapse of past and present forms of subjugation, as they navigate the charged conceptual realm of post-blackness. Exploring old and new genres in black diaspora writing, I next center on literature that writes back to the canon, revisiting historical figures that symbolize blackness with vivid intensity, such as Othello and Heathcliff. Finally, I reveal how celebrated writers from the new African diaspora in the twenty-first century create fresh itineraries of migration, insisting on unhooking conceptions of black mobility from the antecedent of slavery alone.

Runaway Genres begins with the most literal return to slavery—the phenomenon of modern slavery characterized by what I term sentimental globalism. Each chapter moves further away from this neo-abolitionist template, both in terms of insisting on a literal repetition of slavery as opposed to more oblique or metaphoric returns and in its distance from sentimentalism as the guiding force for generating understanding, activism, and a sense of relation across the world.

The first chapter, "Sentimental Globalism," shows how sentiment becomes a kind of enclosure in neo-abolitionist thinking, turning to the past to dehistoricize contemporary atrocities as revivals of a superseded Atlantic past. Modern slave narratives, explicitly written to abolish modern slavery across the globe (ranging across Sudan, Haiti, and Sierra Leone, promoted by various neo-abolitionist organizations), enshrine the language of sentimentalism as the most effective weapon in the human rights arsenal, defining a global relation between "us" and "them" solely as a matter of sentiment. Survivors outline an idyllic childhood, abduction and captivity, a life of servitude, until the moment of humanitarian rescue and a new life in America. Reading Francis Bok's memoir *Escape from Slavery* (2003) alongside Dave Eggers's novel *What Is the What* (2006), I trace how the formal exchanges among subject, author, and amanuensis generate a seemingly new way for Americans to imagine themselves as global citizens, constituting themselves as global via their humanitarian empathy for the African victim of atrocity. Showing how a modern slave transforms into an American immigrant in a slave narrative penned by a Sudanese refugee, I also propose a counteranalysis, one that draws on the methods outlined by scholars of slavery: reading against the grain of abolitionist control to uncover a narrative challenge to the project of making modern slaves speak their own cause. Drawing on foundational critiques of the affective aspects of abolition, I expose the perils of sentimentalism as the dominant mode of apprehending injustice.

Chapter 2, "The Gothic Child," focuses on the figure of the child as soldier. "Child soldiers are the most famous celebrities of the late twentieth century," as the narrator of Ahmadou Kourouma's *Allah Is Not Obliged* (2000) puts it.[30] Reading expansively across child soldier memoirs and novels, I show how the figure of the child shuttles between sentimental and gothic modes, the former universalizing, the latter calling attention to history, often repeating debates about American and Atlantic gothic. Best-selling narratives like Ishmael Beah's *A Long Way Gone: Memoirs of a Boy Soldier* (2007), Susan Minot's *Thirty Girls* (2014), and Uzodinma Iweala's *Beasts of No Nation* (2005) alongside recent humanitarian spectacles like Kony 2012 (condemning Ugandan warlord Joseph Kony) and the movement to #BringBackOurGirls (focusing on the Chibok girls kidnapped by Boko Haram in Nigeria) duplicate the conditions of production and circulation of slave narratives. Tracing how and why the African child soldier appears as the afterlife of the Atlantic slave, I unravel the assumptions about race in translation and travel at work. Lingering in gothic terror, refusing closure or redemption, Chris Abani's *Song for Night* (2007) and Kourouma's *Allah Is Not Obliged* compulsively unearth repressed histories in order to challenge the absolute innocence demanded by human rights advocates.

Chapter 3, "Post-Black Satire," stages the collision of post-blackness (an idiom increasingly used, albeit controversially, to define black identity in the post-civil-rights era) with the dominant genre of contemporary African American literature—the neo-slave narrative. A distinct body of work—what might be termed, awkwardly to be sure, post-black neo-slave narratives—mines the historical scene of slavery in the mode of satire. For Mat Johnson (*Pym*, 2011) and Paul Beatty (*The Sellout*, 2015), the neo-slave narrative requires neither solemnity nor historical reconstruction, while black masculinity itself emerges as a central problem. Johnson returns to the past of Edgar Allan Poe's *The Narrative of Arthur Gordon Pym of Nantucket* (1838) to reimagine the Middle Passage as a voyage into the heart of whiteness, while Beatty plumbs the racist past of blackface minstrelsy to eviscerate the aspiration of a postracial world, bringing back slavery and segregation to Los Angeles. Viewing satire as the lens through which debates about race and postracialism articulate, I explore how such satires combat the sentimental template of abolition and neo-abolition by refusing to collapse past and present. Through absurd juxtapositions, surreal analogies, and farcical adventures, post-black satirists expose the contradictions of the insistence on the unending history of slavery amid declarations of a break from previous racial regimes. The chapter concludes with a look at what might be termed a post-black post-satire, as Colson Whitehead's *The Underground Railroad* (2016) stretches time and space to transform the slave narrative into a flexible portal to practices of exploitation worldwide.

The trope of the "Talking Book" has framed the African American literary canon from its inception, as the slave picks up the master's book—the seeming source of authority—and wonders why the book remains silent. In chapter 4, "Talking Books (Talking Back)," I take up these questions of literary ventriloquism and surrogate authorship that long plagued the slave narrative but are now imaginatively reinvented by such writers as Morrison (*Desdemona*, 2012), Caryl Phillips (*The Nature of Blood*, 1997; *The Lost Child*, 2015), Robin Coste Lewis (*Voyage of the Sable Venus*, 2015), and M. NourbeSe Philip (*Zong!*, 2008). Often revisiting black historical figures who are allied to the history of slavery, but also removed from it in some clear fashion, such writers yoke together diverse histories (of the Holocaust, white feminism and colonialism), creating a series of openings to probe both past and present racial regimes. To do so, they return to the founding scene of the Talking Book of the Atlantic slave narrative, where the slave worries that the master's book will not speak to him or her. Staging a range of responses to analogy, these writers place slavery next to the histories of colonialism and the Holocaust, renovating but also complicating a classic postcolonial project of writing back to the empire in order to decolonize the mind. Their explorations return us to the meaning of slavery itself, its singularity, its relation to narrative, and to modern conceptions of race and racial formation. While earlier chapters pose a division between the United States and the Global South in their respective negotiation of the past, this chapter bridges Morrison and Phillips as black Atlantic interrogators of *Othello*. The still resonant text of modernity probing the relation between the black man and the white woman becomes a conduit to a black Atlantic circuit where boundaries of past and present, Talking Book and marginalized subject blur to open up possibilities for relational thinking. Such efforts renovate the classic project of writing back to the text of Western authority, evenly negotiating the pull of influence, intertextuality, and adaptation.

The study concludes with a discussion of recent celebrated fictions from the new African diaspora that remake American conceptions of race by placing them in relation to the history of the postcolonial state and its own itineraries of hope and despair, migration and return. In "We Need New Diasporas," I show how Chris Abani (*GraceLand*, 2004), Chimamanda Ngozi Adichie (*Americanah*, 2013), NoViolet Bulawayo (*We Need New Names*, 2013), Teju Cole (*Open City*, 2011), and Dinaw Mengestu (*The Beautiful Things That Heaven Bears*, 2007) appropriate various genres—the great American novel, the reverse imperial romance, the black Atlantic travel narrative, the ethnic bildungsroman—to delineate new conceptions of diaspora, beyond the assimilation mandated by the conventional immigrant plot or the melancholy sounded by critics nostalgic for simpler moments of opposition between Africa and the West. In moving away from the concerns of previous generations—anticolonial resistance, the clash of tradition and modernity, alienation and exile—these writers resist received notions of what constitutes African literature, even as they open up numerous critical possibilities for the study of diaspora, expanding previous geographies and weaving together race and class with location. Such writers demonstrate that no easy synthesis of the local and the global is possible, without reckoning with how the meaning of race has altered in the twenty-first century, even as it remains tied to a history it cannot disavow. By inviting the appreciation of varied histories and geographies of African migrations while rejecting a linear path toward immigrant assimilation in the United States, their emphasis on the diverse routes of migration that have generated the new diaspora helpfully counters the hegemony of any single genealogy of blackness.

The Peculiar Genre

It is now necessary to recall the peculiar features of the slave narrative, as well as its distinct conditions of production, since the rest of this book focuses on the repetition and transmutation of both aspects. A "nineteenth-century publication boom" (to use Morrison's words), slave narratives functioned at a charged intersection of celebrity humanitarianism, voyeurism, and advocacy.[31] Combining—and ultimately transforming—an array of existing genres (including autobiography and ethnography, captivity narratives and the picaresque tale, the domestic novel and the spiritual confession), slave narratives intimately linked literacy with freedom, constructing a speaking self as a kind of emancipation. As James Olney argues, "literacy, identity, and freedom" become intertwined and indistinguishable in such narratives, so much so that a figure like Frederick Douglass explains his privation as a slave by way of the instrument with which he finds his freedom: "My feet have been so cracked with the frost, that the pen with which I am writing might be laid in the gashes."[32]

The core of the genre is an account of the fugitive slave's journey from slavery to freedom. For antebellum audiences, editors, and publishers, this meant that the criterion for reading such narratives was veracity: they sought the truth of the matter, beyond propaganda or malice, demanding "a plain, unvarnished tale."[33] A realist or even documentary imperative thus structured all early African American writing, and most slave narratives before the war begin with a series of authenticating documents, testifying to the truth of the incidents described, praising the simplicity and restraint of the writing style that avoids exaggeration or melodrama, confirming the credibility of the writer with historical data, and swearing to the lack of editorial interference. All such attestations add up to the claim that the narrative describes "slavery *as it is.*"[34]

For some early critics, given that so many such narratives were manufactured or ghostwritten by white abolitionists, questions of whether slave narratives count as literature remain pressing.[35] Are they valuable as historical record or evidence of literary craft? The noble beginning of a glorious African American tradition of writing, as Henry Louis Gates Jr. would later influentially argue, or an always already compromised form, subject to white interference, marked by strategic omissions, and shaped by punitive audience expectations (both voyeuristic and sentimental)?[36]

Despite often lengthy prefaces, testimonials, appendices, engraved portraits, and claims on the title page—written by the author himself or herself—doubts about the veracity of the genre were not seriously dismantled in literary history until the 1980s. Even then, their literary merit was up for debate. For a critic like Olney, for instance, the narratives did not rise to the status of autobiography and were limited by their "overwhelming sameness."[37] Olney rightly identifies a "Master Plan for Slave Narratives," often beginning with the simple statement "I was born," and going on to describe scenes of childhood, often with an unacknowledged white father, the cruel induction into the horror of slavery (with scenes of whipping and torture), the exposure to the hypocrisy of Christian slaveholders, scenes of slave auctions, families torn apart, the assault of young girls, and a slow path to freedom with the acquisition of literacy, attempts to escape, and the taking on of new names to match a free self. Such constraints, along with the demands of the editors and the burden of sentimentalism, all combine to produce, in Olney's phrase, "something that is neither fish nor fowl."[38] Along similar lines, in his foundational account of black autobiography, William Andrews cautions especially against ghostwritten manuscripts, but even concedes that for all slave narrators "the reception of his narrative as truth depended on the degree to which his artfulness could hide his art."[39] Exemplifying this tendency to downplay artistic or rhetorical authority or intent, abolitionist editors often assured readers that they would see no craft on display. David Wilson, for instance, the white amanuensis of Solomon Northup's narrative *Twelve Years a Slave*, assures the reader that Northup "has invariably repeated the same story without deviating in the slightest particular."[40] Such a claim reinforces John Sekora's famous reading of slave narratives as "black messages" enclosed in "white envelopes."[41]

But slave narrators more often than not resisted or otherwise circumvented the demand for plainness and veracity, deploying rhetorical flourishes, startling imagery, and classical stylistic devices (like the apostrophe) to reveal their linguistic mastery. When William Lloyd Garrison asked Douglass to stick to "the facts" and leave the "philosophy" to experts, Douglass memorably refused this division of labor: it "did not entirely satisfy me to narrate wrongs; I felt like denouncing them."[42] Moreover, as Valerie Smith argues about Harriet Jacobs, even though the genre is "in general highly formulaic," Jacobs embeds a "subversive plot of empowerment beneath the more orthodox, public plot of weakness and vulnerability."[43] Proving that the journey to freedom cannot be narrated as the facts alone but requires art, slave narrators create the basis for a rich literary tradition that ties freedom to acts of reading and writing, thus inaugurating many of the conventions and achievements of later writers. For Henry Louis Gates Jr., for instance, the trope of the Talking Book found in numerous slave narratives serves as the perfect emblem for all subsequent African American writing, and the trope structures his canonization of the field in the *Norton Anthology*.[44] Houston Baker similarly calls slave narrators "craftsmen of a distinctive genre of literary works of art," while Robert Stepto influentially identifies how the quest for freedom and literacy derived from the slave narrative continued to structure classic African American literary achievements well into the twentieth century.[45]

Such a reading is already visible in the narratives themselves, which function, as Andrews notes, as "a running metadiscourse on the assumptions, conditions, and conventions necessary to discourse between black narrator and white reader."[46] The mixture of genres and the contradictory desires of the audience necessary for the slave narrative becomes a strength rather than a flaw. Douglass, for example, makes as deft use of the sentimental tradition (in descriptions of his grandmother in *Narrative* and *My Bondage and My Freedom*) as of the jeremiad (in the 1852 speech "What to the Slave Is the Fourth of July?"). Blending sarcasm and wit with lyricism and delicacy, Douglass shifts across modes with controlled economy, at the same time marshaling an enormous body of knowledge in his abolitionist efforts. As he notes in *Life and Times of Frederick Douglass* (1881), doing justice to the cause requires him to be "profoundly versed in psychology, anthropology, ethnology, sociology, theology, biology, and all the other ologies, philosophies and sciences."[47]

For Douglass, his encyclopedic knowledge and rhetorical artistry enable him to present himself as an exemplar of heroic masculinity, as his rise from humble origins through sheer force of will figures a similar epic destiny for the race. In his hands, therefore, the slave narrative transcends its status as propaganda and becomes art. At the same time, as representative leader of the race, he crafts himself as its founding father, at times authoring himself into being by canonizing his story and erasing a gendered experience of slavery. In contrast, an insistence on interiority, the demonstration of psychological depth, and the loving re-creation of community make the slave narrative novelistic in the hands of a figure like Jacobs. Jacobs blends the conventions of autobiography with sentimental fiction to expertly manipulate the confining binds of the "cult of true womanhood," as Hazel Carby shows, embedding love, piety, and virtue in the figure of her saintly and courageous grandmother. Between the bold opening claim of *Incidents in the Life of a Slave Girl*—"READER, be assured this narrative is no fiction"—and the concluding disclaimer—"Reader, my story ends with freedom, not in the usual way, with marriage"—Jacobs defies the limits of the sentimental tradition, remaking it to find "something akin to freedom" for herself and her children.[48]

To Rip That Veil

While it may seem that the resurgence of the neo-slave narrative in the late twentieth century affirms the ongoing rhetorical and political power of such strategies, much of this literature is in fact animated by a desire to turn to unspeakable figures—whether they are black slave owners, an African father guilty of selling his children, or a fugitive mother who would rather kill her children than have them returned to slavery.[49] If it is true, as Saidiya Hartman notes, that "every attempt to emplot the slave in a narrative ultimately resulted in his or her obliteration," then the task for contemporary artists becomes a struggle to "repeat the unrepeatable, to present the unpresentable."[50] It is thus not surprising that Morrison, not only the author of the most foundational neo-slave narrative but the inaugurator of an entire mode of historicism (what Stephen Best terms the *Beloved* moment), finds the slave narrative a problem to get through and beyond rather than an inspiration.[51] "Whatever popularity the slave narratives had," she claims, "the slave's own narrative, while freeing the narrator in many ways, did not destroy the master narrative."[52] Instead, "over and over, the writers pull the narrative up short with a phrase such as, 'but let us drop a veil over these proceedings too terrible to relate.'"

The task of the contemporary black writer, consequently, is "to rip that veil drawn over proceedings too terrible to relate" and to "fill in the blank slave narratives left."[53]

Despite common perceptions that the turn to slavery is about the recovery of the lost past, or an affirmation of an undifferentiated notion of a black community in an era that fractures such notions of unity, or even a kind of pathological melancholy, displaying an inability to get over "the psychic hold of slavery," neo-slave narratives constitute a far more diverse and challenging body of work, unsettling rather than reaffirming polemic or dogma.[54] At the center of many of the most acclaimed of these novels is moral ambiguity, or even the suggestion that no clear ethical choice avails, let alone a redemptive account of history. Although she based *Beloved* on the historical figure of Margaret Garner, a fugitive slave arrested for killing one of her children to save her from slavery, Morrison conceded that the example was "confining" rather than imaginatively enabling since the "repellent landscape" of slavery was "formidable and pathless." Accordingly, Morrison "would invent [Garner's] thoughts, plumb them for a subtext that was historically true in essence, but not strictly factual in order to relate her history to contemporary issues about freedom, responsibility, and women's 'place.'"[55] Hence her decision to feature the ghost of the murdered child, to refuse the reader certainty of time, place, or perspective, or indeed any moral certitude, in a landscape where neither remembering nor forgetting provides any solace.

That the neo-slave narrative became a major genre in African American literature since the 1960s (after a gap of almost a century, barring exceptions like Arna Bontemps's 1936 *Black Thunder*) is traceable in part to the social context of the civil rights and Black Power movements, which instigated a range of revisionist histories from below.[56] The pioneering writer Margaret Walker notes that she wrote *Jubilee* (1966) "to set the record straight where black people are concerned in terms of the Civil War, of slavery, segregation and Reconstruction."[57] Along similar lines, in the author's note to *Dessa Rose* (1986), Sherley Anne Williams admits to being "outraged" by William Styron's *The Confessions of Nat Turner* (1967) and inspired by Angela Davis's groundbreaking work on enslaved black women.[58] Such efforts to recuperate the absences and omissions of existing stories of slavery, to bear witness, and to identify the contours of lost ancestral traditions reverberate in Gayl Jones's *Corregidora* (1975),

Octavia Butler's *Kindred* (1979), and David Bradley's *The Chaneysville Incident* (1981).[59] Showing how descendants of slaves continue to be haunted by their ancestors, the exposure of buried family histories and secrets leads these writers to interrogate received accounts of genealogy.

A broader preoccupation with roots, origins, and memory in this era intersected with such genealogical excavations, as long-standing efforts to conserve memory in the African American tradition were bolstered by new developments in history and anthropology. Alex Haley's *Roots* (1976) galvanized the imagination of the entire nation, generating the archetypal tableaus of the neo-slave imagination: scenes of families separated on the auction block, widespread torture and whipping, and the resolute determination of the enslaved to maintain bonds of love and community.[60] Countering raging debates in sociology over the pathology of the black family instigated by the Moynihan Report, neo-slave narratives explicitly challenge the perception of slavery as the root of stereotypes of the Mammy, the Sambo, or the Uncle Tom. Stories about slavery, thus, helped reframe conflicts over race and gender, as writers like Butler and Williams seek to expand the frame of what is possible to be thought about the past and the future, creating a black feminist epistemology. Williams probes the possibilities of an alliance between black and white women in *Dessa Rose*, while in *Kindred* Butler forces a rethinking of notions of autonomy and resistance beyond black nationalist binaries of the house or field slave. *Kindred* explicitly refers back to Douglass to show how easily one is made a slave, as Butler sends her modern, independent protagonist back in time to slavery in Maryland only to have her assumptions about seemingly subservient figures of the Uncle Tom or the Mammy unravel. Forcing present-day readers to reckon with the complex inheritance of black and white kinship forged by the peculiar institution, many such fictions not only memorialize the past but find ways to tackle contemporary social divisions and fractures.

Gender, for instance, forms the center of such provocations. As Hortense Spillers influentially explains, under slavery, "the customary aspects of sexuality, including 'reproduction,' 'motherhood,' 'pleasure,' and 'desire,' are all thrown in crisis."[61] Drawing a distinction between "body" and "flesh," Spillers rethinks the gendering of the captive body, reading a "hieroglyphics of the flesh" in the cultural "vestibularity" of the black female slave, which enables the protection of the white woman and denies fatherhood to the black man.⁶² Where the slave narrative too often drew a veil over the scene of sexual violation, resorting to euphemism, neo-slave narratives repeatedly return to the sadistic sexual economies of slavery, centering questions of rape, consent under coercion, and the difficulty of articulating black desire under duress. Sensitive to the risk of repeating the violation, they also reckon with the challenges of such representations both then and now. As Hartman notes, a narrative like Douglass's begins with the "terrible spectacle" of Aunt Hester's whipping, a scene reproduced too often as a "horrible exhibition." Labeling the whipping a "blood-stained gate, the entrance to the hell of slavery," Douglass sees himself as both "witness and a participant," leading Hartman to wonder about our own relation to such scenes, as "witnesses who confirm the truth of what happened" or "voyeurs fascinated with and repelled by exhibitions of terror and suffering."⁶³ Such concerns structure the narrative choices and circumventions of neo-slave narratives, which have to perform what Hartman terms a "double gesture"—"straining against the limits of the archive to write a cultural history of the captive, and, at the same time, enacting the impossibility of representing the lives of the captives precisely through the process of narration."⁶⁴ The famed opacity of a novel like *Beloved*—with shifts in perspective, flashbacks, multiple temporal frames, elisions, and fragments resisting legibility—fulfills precisely this imperative. Morrison also refuses to follow the mandate of the slave narrative to represent spectacular scenes of violence and torture, choosing abstraction instead to illuminate the interior lives of the enslaved. As Hartman puts it, "What happens if we assume that the female subject serves as a general case for explicating social death, property relations, and the pained and punitive construction of blackness?"⁶⁵ Morrison's exploration of motherhood in *Beloved*, Butler's unraveling of the stereotype of the Mammy in *Kindred*, and Williams's probing of the possibility of interracial alliance between black and white women in *Dessa Rose* instantiate precisely this call.

The "unstoppable rate" of production of the neo-slave narrative may also be attributed to its convergence with late twentieth-century critical emphasis on postmodernism and appreciation of the blurring of the line between history and fiction.⁶⁶ Writers like Caryl Phillips conducted meticulous research into the accounts of plantations owners, colonization schemes in Liberia, and logs of slave captains to creatively fashion fiction that approaches the status of history even as it questions the possibility of ever being able to apprehend any historical truth. In a similar postmodern vein, Ishmael Reed's *Flight to Canada* (1976) hilariously savages *Uncle Tom's Cabin* (1852), while Alice Randall's *The Wind Done Gone* (2001) offers "an unauthorized parody" of *Gone with the Wind* (1936).[67] A comparable counterfactual impulse animates Bernardine Evaristo's *Blonde Roots* (2008), which reverses the black-white power dynamic of historical slavery to imagine "whyte Europanes" ruled by the great state of "blak Aphrikans."[68]

The *Zong* massacre forms the center of related revisionist efforts as Fred D'Aguiar's *Feeding the Ghosts* (1997) imagines that one woman thrown overboard survives and climbs back on the ship, while M. NourbeSe Philip's *Zong!* (2008, written using the actual words of the court case, *Gregson v. Gilbert*) channels an imaginary ancestor as cocreator. Such efforts dovetail with the attempt to preserve generational memory at "the moment that the last of those who had experienced New World slavery firsthand passed away," as Arlene Keizer observes.[69] In a foundational account, Ashraf Rushdy persuasively places contemporary versions of first-person accounts of escape from slavery to freedom as responses to the Black Power and Black Arts movements of the 1960s and early 1970s.[70] But as the category of the neo-slave narrative expands to include a larger variety of returns to slavery, fictions from the 1980s onward stage new issues of race and gender, with less clearly articulated political aims than protest. Subsequent scholarship of this emergent genre has reckoned with these more diffuse agendas through different critical approaches—including psychoanalytic theory and trauma, questions of citizenship, humor and stereotype, the politics of postmodernism, and the language of crisis around urban black culture and the figure of the book.[71]

In contrast to such explorations, some have questioned the obsessive return to the scene of slavery, wondering whether the sight of black bodies in pain serves rather than defies existing racial regimes.[72] It is also worth noting that many of these fictions have won major book prizes, thus ensuring visibility and acclaim—the Pulitzer for *Beloved*, *The Known World*, and *Underground Railroad*; the National Book Award for *Middle Passage*, *The Good Lord Bird*, and *Underground Railroad*; and of course the Nobel Prize for Literature for Morrison, and the Man Booker International Prize for Paul Beatty's *Sellout* (the first American writer to ever win that award). That the literary establishment chooses to reward past spectacles of suffering raises further questions about audience expectation and desire. Coupled with the fact that so many of these writers do not submit an empowering narrative of resistance, often highlighting the slave owner (for instance, Phillips's *Cambridge*), this causes suspicion about the subversive value of these fictions.[73] This is especially true in an era when the roots narrative is so firmly implanted that it has generated its own form of mobility—heritage tourism around the slave forts of West Africa, along with the manufacture of grief by nation-states and tour guides. Government-sponsored projects to memorialize the two hundredth anniversary of abolition in Britain and the management of memory by the UNESCO slave project further engender their own accounts of abolition memory. It is these concerns that motivate Mat Johnson to declare his fatigue with the subject: "I am bored with the topic of Atlantic slavery. I have come to be bored because so many boring people have talked about it. So many artists and writers and thinkers, mediocre and genius, have used it because it's a big, easy target. . . . They take the stink of the slave hold and make it a pungent cliché, take the blood-soaked chains of bondage and pervert them into Afrocentric bling."[74] In fact, even neo-slave narratives themselves question the possibility of representing slavery ethically or effectively. Novels like *Kindred* underline the limits of existing historical knowledge with scenes of burning books or maps, while *Beloved* and *Dessa Rose* align print culture with racial terror. Critics also emphasize the ineffable, the ghostly, the incomplete, and the impossible as their object of study as well as their practice, which must deform existing disciplines and methods.[75] As I show in the following chapters, the writers I study transcend fears about cliché and bling even as they evidence the need to break and deform critical frames of analysis. Confronting head-on the contradiction of speaking the unspeakable, the writers of *Runaway Genres* are sensitive to the dual imperative at the heart of the genre: that slavery cannot be represented and yet it must be.

From Atlantic to Global

While African American writers of neo-slave narratives distance themselves from the compromised conditions of production of the slave narrative, these conditions surprisingly return in a literal manner in a range of global situations, as the Atlantic frame goes global. Consider, for instance, Mohamedou Ould Slahi's memoir *Guantánamo Diary* (2015), outlining his fourteen-year unlawful detention and torture at Guantánamo Bay. Slahi explicitly likens his rendition from Mauritania to slavery: "I often compared myself with a slave. Slaves were taken forcibly from Africa, and so was I. Slaves were sold a couple of times on their way to their final destination, and so was I. Slaves were suddenly assigned to somebody they didn't choose, and so was I. And when I looked at the history of slaves, I noticed that slaves sometimes ended up an integral part of the master's house."[76] For Slahi, making sense of his current predicament involves an engagement with the US past, so that strategies of offshore detention, black sites, waterboarding, enhanced interrogation, kill lists, and extraordinary rendition that have characterized the War on Terror since 9/11 might be connected to the "scenes of subjection" that birthed the nation as well as the engineering of "social death."[77] Slahi's explicit analogy to slavery strikingly corroborates the need for such parallels, even as the racial optics of his shackled body or prohibitions against practicing his religion or using his language immediately recall narratives by such figures as Douglass, Jacobs, and Northup. Even more salient, however, is the fact that his manuscript was allowed to be published only after ten years of censorship and court appeal, and finally appeared with black bars redacting content on nearly every page. Moreover, we read not his words alone but those reframed by his editor, Larry Siems, who converted his 466-page document into 372 pages, correcting for grammar and narrative coherence along the way. Enclosed by the sympathetic editor's preface, marketed as an international human rights event by the publisher, and censored and reshaped by the CIA and the US government, *Guantánamo Diary* chillingly repeats the "black message" in a "white envelope" of the slave narrative.

To be sure, Slahi is not the only instance of such revenants. Similar efforts to transform a state of forced abjection into humanist triumph, precisely through the power of narrative, dominate contemporary human rights discourse, including experiences of trafficking, forced migration, and conscription into war. A clear example occurs in the prominence of novels about the African child soldier, often presented not as a new figure at the heart of the human rights story but as a repetition of a familiar one—the Atlantic slave. Ishmael Beah's *A Long Way Gone: Memoirs of a Boy Soldier* (2007) is one of many instances of this phenomenon, featuring an idyllic childhood, the corruption of innocence and loss of family, forced degradation, yet the struggle to maintain a pure soul throughout.[78] The chiasmus made famous by Douglass—"you have seen how a man was made a slave; you shall see how a slave was made a man"— recurs across several texts.[79] Scenes of whipping, the shaving of the head, and branding recur (signaling the production of what Orlando Patterson names social death).[80] A number of novels bring in the frame of slavery to universalize a specific experience, often refusing to give names or places to the conflicts depicted. Many of them are accompanied by paratextual materials (as well as websites or digital companions) attesting to the truth of the experience narrated, as well as a set of instructions for the reader to donate money or otherwise participate in the cause to abolish modern slavery, even as several authors have become modern-day abolitionists. Human rights legislation has also unequivocally likened the conscription of children in war as a crime akin to slavery.[81]

In these works, America's past becomes Africa's present, and rather than the hell on earth of antebellum slave narratives, the United States appears as the savior for fugitive slaves as asylum seekers, an example of a nation that has transcended its own horrific past, while Africa is narrated as a site of no political possibility or agency. While some novels like Emmanuel Dongala's *Johnny Mad Dog* (2002) and Ahmadou Kourouma's *Allah Is Not Obliged* (2000) explicitly attack humanitarianism, countless others converge to offer an undifferentiated picture of endless African conflicts, with cruel or absent adults, innocent children, and humanitarian saviors who come from outside. In Susan Minot's *Thirty Girls* (2014), a novel about the abduction and sexual slavery of Ugandan girl children by Joseph Kony's rebel army, a white woman's hackneyed search for love in Africa overshadows the ostensible subject of the girl's abduction and escape, as she is allowed a predictable frame of trauma and recovery only through therapy administered by the white savior.[82] The novel again stages a variation on the theme of the black message in a white envelope that characterized abolitionist control of the slave's own story. Such concerns about the manufacture of narrative have continually haunted Beah, whose famous account of his life as a child soldier in Sierra Leone has been questioned by many journalists and who has been charged with fraud, echoing the accusations of sensationalist exaggeration that also attended the historical slave narrative. In response, Beah has doubled down and insisted that he has "an excellent photographic memory that enables me to remember details of the day-to-day moments of my life, indelibly."[83] But inhibited by the genre of the memoir and its demands of truth, he has also turned to fiction. His 2014 *Radiance of Tomorrow* notably refuses the frame of rehabilitation through therapeutic storytelling of trauma, focusing on the ongoing violence of a transnational mining company in post-civil-war Sierra Leone, recalling the numerous efforts of slave narrators to gain control of their own stories.[84]

In contrast to many such best-selling narratives, Chimamanda Ngozi Adichie's *Half of a Yellow Sun* (2006) also calls on Douglass's narrative, but resignifies it unforgettably in Biafra, and in her sensitively imagined protagonist, Ugwu the houseboy. When Ugwu is conscripted into the Biafran army as a child soldier, and his battalion quarters in a former primary school, he comes across a copy of the *Narrative of the Life of Frederick Douglass*, which he reads carefully, memorizing the lines "Even if it cost me my life, I was determined to read. Keep the black man away from the books, keep us ignorant, and we would always be his slaves."[85] But Douglass's heroic journey of self-reclamation through violence and literacy isn't a fate available to Ugwu, as his teenage fellow soldiers tear out pages from the book to use as rolling paper. Goaded into a gang rape with a cruel and twisted echo of Douglass, "aren't you a man," Ugwu will not be able to navigate the divide of slave and man that Douglass set up the terms for so many decades ago. Adichie certainly enlists Douglass's *Narrative* to demonstrate the limits of the liberal intellectual culture exported to Nigeria, which proves unfit for the challenge of the civil war, and to underscore the tragedy of the loss of Ugwu's innocence, but also to ironically echo Douglass's trajectory of self-empowerment through writing as Ugwu himself becomes a writer, motivated by the memory of that rape, and guilt about his actions that he must hide from his former employers. His book, *The World Was Silent When We Died*, turns out to be excerpted throughout the novel, though the identity of the author isn't revealed to the reader till the end. Ugwu's book evenly echoes Chinua Achebe's District Commissioner of *Things Fall Apart* (who himself is an echo of Joseph Conrad's Kurtz of *Heart of Darkness*) and of Douglass. Adichie writes that Ugwu first wanted to call it "Narrative of the Life of a Country," as he wishes he still "had that Frederick Douglass book" but takes the title of Richard's book. The white Englishman Richard learns that "the war isn't my story to tell, really" as "Ugwu nodded. He had never thought that it was."[86] Again, this echoes the scene of writing and authority, and asks the still resonant questions—who can tell the story of atrocity, and who can edit it?

The shift from Atlantic to global also brings with it convoluted reworkings of gender. The global slave narrative often returns to the familiar formula of imperial culture where—as Gayatri Chakravorty Spivak memorably put it—"white men are saving brown women from brown men."[87] As we see in chapter 1, carceral feminists, for instance, read human trafficking solely as a problem of criminal justice and enforcement instead of trying to imagine a genuine abolition of the system that produces such suffering. Just as Slahi's recollections in *Guantánamo Diary*—where the CIA redacts female pronouns and words like "tears"—require that he place himself within a sentimental enclosure to prove his right to humanity, the variable uses of sentimental and gothic genres for the girl soldier and the boy soldier (as I show in chapter 2) index the ongoing hold of earlier forms of gendering and ungendering.

The global proliferation of the new slave narrative thus requires a closer look at the ethics and aesthetics of globalism, as the voices of the most exploited figures of our world—the child soldier, the victim of human trafficking, the refugee, and the detainee—come to us already filtered through a preexisting template. As the Congolese novelist Alain Mabanckou puts it, the prevalence of child soldier literature in this vein shows that we are not yet free of the vortex of *Uncle Tom's Cabin*.[88] The politics of analogy at work also beg the question of what it means to write an African experience in an American genre. The compression of past and present, here and there, causes further concerns.

That slavery now provides the occasion not just for revisiting the Atlantic past but for renarrating the global present requires a deeper consideration of this shift in geographic scale. As is well known, the black Atlantic paradigm forwarded by Gilroy insisted on seeing culture outside of essentialist notions of race, nation, or ethnicity, and for assessing the legacy of the Enlightenment tradition squarely in reference to slavery. Drawing on Morrison's reminder that "the concept of freedom did not emerge in a vacuum. Nothing highlighted freedom—if it did not in fact create it—like slavery," Gilroy's "black Atlantic counterculture to modernity" centrally derived from the thought of slaves and their descendants.[89] To think reason, secularism, humanism, ethics, and aesthetics, therefore, is to reckon with the legacy of Atlantic slavery.

Since at least the 1990s, such an emphasis on a black Atlantic or diasporic frame has led to important efforts to theorize race and black modernity in relation to submerged pasts of amnesiac nations (principally Britain and the United States) and multicultural futures. While the transformative impact of such rethinking has not receded, recent years have seen steady calls to move away from such core concerns about the interconnected histories of capital, empire, slavery, nationalism, and revolution, in favor of something termed—often quite nebulously—the global. In studies of diaspora, conversations about the cosmopolitan or the "Afropolitan" displace previous formations like the pan-African or the postcolonial, which often code a history of antiracist and anticolonial struggle. Similar shifts in the discipline of history from Atlantic to world history and in literature from postcolonial to global Anglophone or world literature mirror this development.[90] World literature as a term has been especially influential for comparative study, and the revival of Goethe's notion of *Weltliteratur* often focuses not on politicized histories of race and empire but on aesthetic forms of transnational contact. Defined as works that travel beyond their cultures of origin, that gain in translation, that are deemed classics that have stood the test of time, world literature as a frame has moved away from the restrictive model of national literatures largely by bypassing efforts such as the black Atlantic or the postcolonial, rather than building upon them.[91] It is thus no surprise that very few African American or black diaspora writers seem to make up the hypercanon of world literary texts, especially from the twentieth century.

Such a dissolution of the ethical and political charge named by the postcolonial is especially unfortunate in an age of rising extreme nationalism and xenophobia. Connecting the global movements of refugees, detainees, and survivors of trafficking and war helps restore focus to the core of the field—an attention to forms of power and possibilities of resistance. This involves a recognition of the semiotics and the geopolitics of US empire, including a consideration of how these relate to or depart from earlier European imperialisms. Any turn to the global thus necessarily entails connections across national histories. Focusing on slavery—as perhaps the most momentous global event the world has seen—demands a dialogue across the disciplines of postcolonial and African American studies, connecting US minority populations to those in the Global South. Conceptions of race in the twenty-first century must be able to conceive of it in a truly global context. To place the United States in relation to the postcolonial world, the circulation of a quintessential American genre—the slave narrative—helps generate new insights about how forms code social relationships and networks of power. Even though genres continue to be thought of as expressions of a national spirit, their transnational travel makes them transmogrify, such that they no longer remain modes of the core or periphery.[92] A genre like the slave narrative is at once compromised in its conditions of production, insurgent in its articulation of a racial self, and hegemonic in its circulation across the globe. Accordingly, when a Guantánamo detainee adopts the strategies of a Douglass, Jacobs, or Olaudah Equiano, he reshapes the experience of postcoloniality away from a historical experience to an ongoing spatial connection.[93] The postcolony thus appears as the site for the manufacture and revival of obsolete racial paradigms, as well as opening up avenues for imagining solidarity among subjugated peoples.

Formalist analysis often presumes a kind of universalism, leading to the suspicion that focusing on the taxonomy or circulation of genres may displace historicist modes of inquiry more clearly tied to political and ethical agendas. The common perception that studies of race and of form are mutually exclusive—the former the domain of cultural studies, the latter literary analysis proper—has its roots in a number of assumptions stemming from a presumed opposition between form and history, form and politics, form and identity. The debate may take the shape of advocating for universalism, or bringing back pleasure to reading, or a defense of the literary against the thematic paradigms or political imperatives of race, class, gender, sexuality, with the underlying notion that social and cultural analysis might be merely reflective, schematic, or axiomatic. Because form is often a proxy for a host of other terms (including style, genre, aesthetics, coherence, autonomy, and pleasure), it is crucial to recognize that calls for attention to form can mask a variety of ideological agendas. What such polemical understandings often conceal is that race has always been entangled with form. Not only are all aesthetic categories deeply racialized, identity itself has a form. Race, accordingly, is never a given, but must be read. As Mark Jerng explains, "Race has an organizing and shaping force that is often associated with genre," and genre and race "work to build, anticipate, and organize the world."[94] As a matter of rhetorical convention, cultural stereotype, and social pattern, race requires deciphering, interpreting, and critique to fathom its rules and norms (even when visible only in transgression). As Todorov puts it, "Genres, like any other institution, reveal the constitutive traits of the society to which they belong."[95] The study of the formal dimensions of race can thus help elucidate modes of power and hierarchy, hegemony and inequality.

Because both race and genre require social conventions and contracts, they generate taxonomies of their own, raising questions of individual relation to a larger collective. Form thus enables comparison across time and space—as John Frow glosses it, "the concept of form designates those aspects of a text which are recurrent as opposed to those which are singular."[96] If Todorov is right in noting that "a new genre is always the transformation of one or several old genres: by inversion, by displacement, by combination," then my analysis of the circulation of the slave narrative in contemporary culture should tell us something about how and why history repeats itself as form.[97] What counts as suffering and why? Whose life has value? These questions are determined by the choice of narrative form—hence the unceasing return to the slave narrative. As Charles Johnson explains, "No form *loses* its ancestry; rather, these meanings accumulate in layers of tissue as the form evolves."[98] Moreover, as Wai Chee Dimock notes, it is possible to conceive of genres as ever-expanding fields of knowledge since "the membership—of any genre—is an open rather than closed set, because there is always another instance, another empirical bit of evidence, to be added." Studying the "cumulative reuse, an alluvial process, sedimentary as well as migratory" can thus yield insights for literary studies as well as comparative histories.[99]

Extending Todorov's maxim about the origin of genres ("From where do genres come? Why, quite simply, from other genres"), we may say that contemporary racial formations also come from preexisting alignments and configurations, from other times and places.[100] Prompting recognition of the familiar, focusing on genres—the sentimental, the gothic, satire, surrogation, and revisionism—therefore sanctions new and exciting theorizations of temporality and futurity. In African American studies, debates over a melancholic relationship to time and history have been thriving.[101] Moreover, the postcolony has always been seen as the realm of the belated, rather than coeval. I explore how the two intersect in my study, as the time of the enslaved, the migrant, the detainee, or the refugee refigures notions of crisis, stretching and bending our conceptions of historicity and futurity alike. In the chapters that follow, I show how a sentimental mode relies on a progressive narrative of redemption, comfortable with seeing America's past (both of oppression and resistance) as the future of the world. The gothic refuses such narratives of progress or salvation, intent on raising the dead. Satire resorts to the absurd to disturb past and present, willing to discern their enmeshment, but refusing to collapse one into the other. Ventriloquism refuses the pastness of the past, insisting on seeing charged figures like Othello as surrogates for the here and now, showing that history is malleable and can be changed. Finally, new diasporas and new geographies of migration force innovative considerations of how travel through space rearranges time. The American story of immigration has to change, as do the boundaries of the African American experience, as new African migrants create a diaspora that intercuts here and there, with no final passage, no river to cross and never look back.

My account of African American and postcolonial returns to slavery necessitates a rethinking of empathy as the primary desirable response to stories of suffering. In recent years, diverse thinkers—including Martha Nussbaum, Lynn Hunt, David Palumbo-Liu, and Debjani Ganguly—have forwarded a robust case for narrative empathy.[102] However, an assumed universalism and an us-them dichotomy remain the center of even the most sensitive studies of empathy in world literature. As Suzanne Keen shows, common notions of literature promoting empathy and hence altruism and social justice require far more nuance and more circumspect claims about the moral technology of storytelling and reader response.¹⁰³ In focusing on contemporary mutations of the slave narrative, I hope to shift the conversation from such a binary and from a focus on the Western reader as the prototypical subject of empathy, with an assured distance from the spectacle of suffering she witnesses. In subsequent chapters, we move farther and farther away from empathy as the primary affective response demanded from the reader, as my writers evoke outrage, horror, humor, revulsion, and rumination, favoring aesthetic complication and historical entanglement over identification. Critique, therefore, of current inequities and amnesiac or distorted histories acquires force in repelling rather than soliciting empathy.

Runaway Genres opens with an epigraph from Octavia Butler's prophetic novel *Parable of the Sower* (1993), which imagines a dystopian future in California, where ecological and economic crises combine to produce vulnerable and fiercely guarded gated communities, circled by pyromaniacs and security forces armed with whips and pistols. This near-future novel represents a postapocalyptic landscape where former gated colonies are under constant threat from the "street poor" while pyromania—vaguely linked to a hatred of the rich—sweeps the nation.¹⁰⁴ As Butler explains in an interview, the novel is a cautionary tale about growing inequality, environmental catastrophe, increasing exploitation of labor by corporations, unregulated drugs, and the failure of government to build social institutions like schools or libraries but focus on prisons instead. Or, as Butler puts it, "I imagined the United States becoming, slowly, through the combined effects of lack of foresight and short-term unenlightened self-interest, a third world country."¹⁰⁵

As the young girl at the center of the novel loses her home and family, setting out into the apocalyptic landscape of survival of the fittest, the novel meditates on how this imagined future connects to or revives the "old and nasty" past. Lauren Olamina dreams of going north—"maybe as far as Canada"—echoing the flight of the fugitive slave to freedom, and gathering "the crew of a modern underground railroad."¹⁰⁶ Butler piercingly probes the question of whether the diverse forms of power and surveillance in this near-future world—including forced labor, debt bondage by corporations, polygamy, prostitution, domestic servitude, and an eerily prophetic president who wants to make America great again—involve a repetition of the logic that undergirded the control and exploitation of black people under slavery. The novel gestures to many different forms of slavery, without submitting a conceptual hierarchy either for distinguishing among these forms or for establishing one as the template for the other. Moreover, Olamina, the novel's figure for survival and community, is beset by a "biological conscience" in a world gone mad, afflicted with a hyperempathy syndrome that forces her to feel the pain of others. Confronted with unspeakable challenges, she wonders if her malady could also be a cure: "If hyperempathy syndrome were a more common complaint, people couldn't do such things . . . if everyone could feel everyone else's pain, who would torture? Who would cause anyone unnecessary pain?"[107]

These three concerns of the novel also encompass the project of *Runaway Genres*. The connection between the historical past of slavery in the United States and contemporary conditions of abuse, exploitation, and displacement forms the center of my concerns. What is the relation between a failing United States and the Third World, now commonly known as the Global South? (Might it be possible, as Jean and John Comaroff suggest, that the Global South embodies not the US past but its future?)[108] How might recalling Atlantic slavery help us not just exhume the past, but salvage the future by understanding contemporary forms of slavery, forced migration, and indentured labor? And might empathy extend a means to join the United States to the globe, a reader to an author, the connective tissue for a new kind of community, imagined by Butler as founded on the principle of change, adaptation, and flexibility? Finally, what is the role of reading and writing in all this? Butler's sequel, *Parable of the Talents* (2000), features a horrific return to slavery for Olamina's group. Undergoing conditions of extreme brutality, Olamina again turns to writing as a way of making sure that she can still imagine a future. Directly echoing the slave narrator's path to freedom, she insists, "My writing is a way for me to remind myself that I am human."[109]

The runaway of my title refers, of course, both to escaped slaves and to the condition of fugitivity that still attends black life and narrative. But it also calls attention to the fact that all the books I discuss in the following pages are runaway hits, best sellers, or award winners, extraordinarily influential in shaping public opinion and common sense on the subject of slavery, both past and prospect. In doing so, they testify to the truth enshrined during abolition—that the claim to the human rests in the power of narrative.

1

Sentimental Globalism

It doesn't take a revolution to set slaves free.
—Kevin Bales, Understanding Global Slavery

I deeply respect American sentimentality, the way one respects a wounded hippo. You must keep an eye on it, for you know it is deadly.
—Teju Cole, "Seven Thoughts on the Banality of Sentimentality"

In insisting that slavery still exists, modern abolitionists pose the question of the afterlife of slavery in stark, literal terms. To claim that there are more slaves in the world today than at any other time in history is to invoke both historical precedent and the urgency of now. Anti-Slavery International, for instance, unambiguously connects its efforts to combat bonded labor, forced marriage, and human trafficking across the world to historical efforts to end the transatlantic slave trade. Its Fight for Freedom 1807–2007 campaign "aims to revitalize the abolitionist spirit of two hundred years ago," joining "slavery past and present" by arguing that the "abolition of the slave trade in 1807 was achieved by a mass movement." Because "many people think that slavery no longer exists," a new mass movement is needed today.[1] Another such organization, Free the Slaves, describes its mission as "dedicated to alerting the world about slavery's global comeback and to catalyze a resurgence of the abolition movement." Explicitly linking its twenty-first-century work to Atlantic slavery, Free the Slaves claims that it "exists to help finish the work that earlier generations of abolitionists started."[2] From activism on college campuses to hearings before the US Senate, from consumer campaigns to sensational documentaries on television, from blockbuster films to a thriving body of crime fiction, modern slavery has become a fixture of the twenty-first-century public sphere. Whether child abuse in Haiti, debt bondage in India, wartime kidnapping in Uganda, or forced prostitution in Cambodia, modern abolitionists maintain that the appropriate touchstone for gauging the meaning, prevalence, and prevention of such practices remains Atlantic slavery. A vigorous twenty-first-century abolitionist movement clearly modeled on transatlantic slavery (led by such organizations as Free the Slaves, Anti-Slavery International, the Walk Free Foundation, Christian Solidarity International, End Slavery Now, Not For Sale, and the American Anti-Slavery Group) has thus generated a consensus about a range of contemporary hyperexploitative practices amounting to slavery.[3]

In this chapter, I situate the phenomenon of modern slavery at the charged intersection of the human and the global. As Pheng Cheah notes, the idea of human rights is one of the "primary ways of figuring the global as human."[4] Enshrining the language of sentimentalism as the most effective weapon in the human rights arsenal, the discourse of modern slavery defines a global relation between "us" and "them" solely as a matter of sentiment. To do so, best-selling memoirs, activist campaigns, and media spectacles converge to propose that the history of US slavery must be seen as the present and future of the rest of the world. Such a claim, I suggest, not only simplifies our understanding of the unresolved legacy of slavery in the United States, but also disorders our comprehension of the nature of exploitation and abuse in the present across the globe. Making slavery mobile like this—not just as metaphor but as the exemplary frame for thinking about oppression today—requires reckoning with what it might mean to insist on slavery as exception instead.

Modern slaves, according to the most recent estimates, are said to number some thirty million, across 160 countries.[5] Though these numbers are disputed, and many would quarrel even with the seeming oxymoron of modern slavery, neo-abolitionism is rapidly gaining increasing acceptance as the frame through which to view contemporary human rights violations.[6] Anybody who is forced to work, controlled by an employer with the threat of abuse or actual abuse, dehumanized, bought or sold as property and physically restrained is said to be in slavery. Such an understanding is ratified by law, as the Supplementary Convention on the Abolition of Slavery, the Slave Trade, and Institutions and Practices Similar to Slavery (1956) calls on the legal precedent of the Slavery Convention (1926) and the Universal Declaration of Human Rights (1948) to confirm that "debt bondage, serfdom, forced marriage and the delivery of a child for the exploitation of that child are all slavery like practices and require criminalization and abolishment."[7] The UK Modern Slavery Act of 2015 is one of many pieces of antitrafficking legislation ratifying the frame of slavery.

In order to claim that modern forms of oppression must be seen as reprising Atlantic slavery, neo-abolitionists revive the slave narrative for the present day. Modern slave narratives thus form a peculiar—and growing—genre of contemporary literature. Accounts of atrocities like human trafficking, capture in war, debt bondage, forced marriage, the use of the child soldier, and sex trafficking, such narratives are explicitly modeled on such Atlantic slave narratives as Frederick Douglass's *Narrative of the Life of Frederick Douglass* (1845), Harriet Jacobs's *Incidents in the Life of a Slave Girl* (1861), and Olaudah Equiano's *Interesting Narrative of the Life of Olaudah Equiano* (1789). Just as narratives by Douglass or Solomon Northup were sanctioned and promoted by white abolitionists, most modern slave narratives are ghostwritten by an amanuensis, and framed by a range of prefatory material guaranteeing the veracity of the story and the good character of the storyteller. For example, Damien Lewis, "a white English man in his thirties," tells the story of Mende Nazer, this "black Nuba woman in her early twenties" collaborating with the help of an English-Arabic dictionary in a "grand Georgian castle," and he credits the results with Nazer's oral tradition and her power of recall of memories of early childhood. He notes that "I keep trying to get her to write a daily diary," but she "hardly ever writes anything down." In the note after the text, he admits that there was a "creative process of selection and condensation" and some scenes were "deliberately fictionalized" to protect some people but also to "aid the narrative flow of the story" so that "it may be read in an accessible, compelling form."[8]

Both the primary literature of modern slavery and the scholarship that promotes it make explicit reference to US slavery to establish an equivalence with contemporary abuse and bondage, concluding that present-day slavery should be seen as a shameful anachronism. Rachel Lloyd's *Girls Like Us* (2011), for instance, links pimps to slave owners and argues that "our equivalent of slaves on the auction block is the ads on Craigslist, Backpage, and numerous other online sites, the street corners in certain neighborhoods, the stages of strip clubs."[9] Lloyd also invokes what she dubs Equiano's Stockholm syndrome toward his master to explain why the women subject to sex trafficking form attachments to their abusers. Zana Muhsen's *Sold: One Woman's True Account of Modern Slavery* (1991) connects her own bondage to the African American slave experience by drawing on her reading of Alex Haley's *Roots*, recalling Kunta Kinte's flight as she runs away from captivity.[10] Replaying familiar narrative tropes like exile and natal alienation, the idea of social death, the quest for literacy, sentimental appeals to readers, the journey north to freedom, and dreams of the Jubilee, modern slave narrators seek to arouse readers to action against modern slavery. Narrators emphasize an idyllic childhood, cruelly ended with their abduction and removal from a loving family, and chronicle a journey of servitude and exploitation as they forge a sense of self based on individual autonomy, the acquisition of literacy, and a life devoted to service.[11]

First-person accounts of horrific abuse and suffering, modern slave narratives may reprise the language and philosophy of the antebellum slave narrative, but they circulate in a changed geopolitical arena, where human rights advocacy must contend with ongoing disputes over war crimes and reparations, the so-called War on Terror and increased militarism in Africa and the Middle East, and the growing power of global evangelism. Given the changed landscape of the contemporary moment, why does the frame of slavery—and not even as a metaphoric antecedent but a literal one—continue to resound today? Kevin Bales, the foremost authority on modern slavery and founder of Free the Slaves, explains that "most Americans' idea of slavery comes right out of *Roots*—the chains, the whip in the overseer's hand, the crack of the auctioneer's gavel. That was one form of bondage. The slavery plaguing America today takes a different form, but make no mistake, it is real slavery."[12] Not just drawing on the rhetorical or affective power of Atlantic slavery to raise awareness for the cause, neo-abolitionists establish literal links to the past, emphatically refusing metaphor. What are the assumptions about the power of analogy and comparison at play here, as one form of exploitation is narrated through forms developed in another time and place? How does the choice of genre circumscribe the enunciative possibilities of the narrators? What is at stake in these claims to equivalence?

Just as nineteenth-century slave narrators were constrained by the limits of the white, northern US audience, modern slave discourse, in easily transposing an Atlantic genre to narrate stories from the Global South, offers a homogenizing story of African atrocity that affirms the primitivist and imperialist tropes that depict Africa and the postcolony more broadly. Since readers are already expected to be familiar with the story of American slavery, modern slave narrators are required not to prove their humanity but to insert themselves within the preexisting template. The politics of analogy at work reinscribe a global experience in a normative American genre to make their claims self-evident. Moreover, such narratives are also difficult to read in terms of concepts of race and racial formation, in relation to the status of slavery as an institution relative to other forms of labor exploitation. The valence of race in an era of neoliberal globalization remains unresolved, as race is variably rendered visible or invisible, anchored in history or unmoored from time and place, attached to certain bodies or continents or set free to float above and beyond them. For antislavery activists, modern slavery as a phenomenon is not racialized: as Bales claims in *Understanding Global Slavery*, anyone—of any race or ethnicity, nation or region, language or religion—can be enslaved. And yet, I want to suggest, the discourse of modern slavery is neither color-blind nor beyond race despite its protestations. This is so not just because the figure that is often invoked in visual representations of modern slavery is a black body, and Sudan, and Darfur in particular, have come to occupy increasing visibility and emblematic status in these discussions, but, more importantly, because constructions of race are the ghost in the machine (as Toni Morrison noted for an Africanist presence in American literature in *Playing in the Dark*), invisible but ever-present levers that lubricate concepts of the human in contemporary culture.[13] When a figure like Mende Nazer calls her North Sudanese captors racists, even though only a slight difference of skin color exists between north and south, claiming that "the Northerners define themselves as Arab and as white, and they call everyone else Black. They think that every Black person can be their slave," it is clear that differences of region and religion are as much at play as those of a black-white binary imported from the Atlantic context.[14] Such nuances deserve specificity of geopolitical context and demand a rethinking of concepts of racial formation for the contemporary world. As many modern ex-slaves migrate to the United States or Europe, their collision with various existing regimes of racialization—from antiblackness to the model-minority frame for immigrants—stretches and reshapes our understandings of the relations among race, migration, and conceptions of the human. Moreover, the entire project of modern abolition raises disturbing questions about the ways in which we understand slavery and its afterlife today, in terms of not just what slavery itself was as an American institution, the peculiarity of which has been much disputed, but also how and whether comparative transnational analysis may yield richer conceptions of race in migration.

Certain tableaus thus recur in the language and imagery of modern abolitionism, clearly derived from its transatlantic predecessor. First, modern abolitionists insist on literalism and simplification, with innocent victims and evil villains, favoring a sentimental and moral frame, often divorced of social and political structures of power. Accordingly, they claim that they are beyond partisan politics, geared toward a principled consensus among all political parties and communities against slavery.[15] Next, to combat modern slavery, such activists prioritize awareness, visibility, and exposure, claiming that revealing what is hidden and bringing such abuse out of dark corners will guarantee emancipation. Finally, they attach freedom to storytelling, editing, and publishing a vast body of modern slave narratives, which duplicate the connection between literacy and freedom established by the African American slave narrative.

For example, *To Plead Our Own Cause: Personal Stories by Today's Slaves* (2008), edited by Kevin Bales and Zoe Trodd, takes its title from the *Freedman's Journal*—the first newspaper set up by freed slaves, in 1827—which declared that "we wish to plead our own cause. Too long have others spoken for us."[16] Neo-abolitionist organizations circulate such edited collections of first-person narratives, often written with an amanuensis, thus echoing not only the form but also the conditions of production of antebellum slave narratives, leading to lingering questions of whose voice we hear behind the words.[17] Scenes of reading, instruction, and writing recur, repeating the antebellum slave narrative's emphasis on literacy and the trope of the Talking Book. Many narratives end with rescue in the United States through the aid of a humanitarian worker who appears as the modern-day abolitionist of the Underground Railroad in the Global North. But where the antebellum slave narrative condemned the United States as a hell on earth, modern accounts posit the nation as the savior for fugitive slaves, an example of a nation that has transcended its own horrific past while Africa emerges as a site of little political or human possibility. Both the norm and normative, the US experience of slavery becomes the locus of a universal experience of suffering and struggle.

In explaining their agenda, many of these narratives call into play the language of visibility and exposure to make their readers accept the designation of slavery. To do so, they insist on both transparency and tautology. Gloria Steinem, in a foreword to *Enslaved: True Stories of Modern Day Slavery*, hopes that "just as nineteenth-century slave narratives forced readers to recognize the humanity of slaves, these twenty-first-century slave narratives force us to recognize the reality of slavery."[18] If a figure like Douglass asserted over and again that he was a "man" and not a "slave," these texts emphasize the opposite, insisting that—to use the title of a film based on the Sudanese national Mende Nazer's experiences of captivity and abuse—*I Am Slave*. Nazer affirms that "there is slavery going on, right now, today. I am an example and I am the living proof and it happened to me, personally."[19] For the readers, victims like Nazer are "our contemporary Frederick Douglass, Harriet Jacobs and Lavinia Bell."[20]

Using the language of an exposé or scandal to bring to light the hidden existence of slavery, documenting and rendering visible become key abolitionist strategies, and anybody who attempts to parse the meaning of the terms used is suspect. Bales expresses this idea in *Disposable People* with some irritation: "When the public stops asking, 'What do you mean by slavery?' and 'You mean slavery still exists?,' then slaves will be on their way to freedom."[21] A neoliberal logic of surveillance similarly underpins Kony 2012, the viral video created by the aptly named Invisible Children Foundation, which foreshortens the distance between here and there, as the use of technology will illuminate the "dark continent" of Africa. By simply watching the video, and making the Ugandan overlord famous, the viewers are said to be launching a human rights revolution. The tagline of the campaign—"make him visible, make him famous"—encapsulates this notion perfectly: "Could an online video make an obscure war criminal famous?"[22] The discourse of modern slavery claims a certain obviousness, similar to what Joseph Slaughter terms the ubiquitous and commonsense claims of human rights, and attempts to dissuade us from geopolitical specificity favor of immediate (and universal) affective response.[23] Perhaps this is why it is tempting to simply repeat the titles of these books, since they give away the whole story: for instance, Jean-Robert Cadet's *Restavec: From Haitian Slave Child to Middle-Class American* (1998) and *My Stone of Hope: From Haitian Slave Child to Abolitionist* (2011) or Beatrice Fernando's *In Contempt of Fate: The Tale of a Sri Lankan Sold into Servitude Who Survived to Tell It: A Memoir* (2004) already divulge the journey that they will document, laying out the curiously flat temporality of the narrated lives, all of which are relentlessly moving toward rescue in the United States.

In several edited collections of first-person narratives, there is no systematic account of how the stories were selected, translated, or edited; the empirical claims are often unsourced, and there is little awareness of the political complexity of the experiences, or explanation of why and how child soldiers in the Philippines, debt bondage in Indian brick quarries, and prostitution in Cambodia or the former Soviet Bloc should all be seen as slavery, rather than as instances of labor exploitation. While the narratives often lack social specificity, they are invariably graphic in the depiction of suffering, and in the words of Elizabeth Bernstein, "nearly pornographic" when it comes to sexualized violation.[24] Such questions are especially apparent in the narratives focusing on sex trafficking. While neo-abolitionists view prostitution as a form of slavery that should be abolished, many of the stories of the women who are trafficked call for an understanding of the need for legal protections for sex workers, viewing prostitution as an issue of worker rights rather than a moral question. Separating sex trafficking from other forms of exploited labor serves only to decontextualize sexual violation and often to sensationalize it. Creating a moral crusade around the question divorced from the larger conditions that sustain it repeats earlier historical moments when notions of white slavery fomented panic. What Bernstein terms carceral feminism serves a repressive criminal justice agenda at home and an aggressive militarism abroad, packaged as a humanitarian cause.[25] The frame of nineteenth-century abolition further confuses the issue since the language of sentiment, contamination, and moral indignation forecloses contemporary feminist analyses of sex work.

Making Slavery Exemplary

To grasp the contours of the discourse of modern slavery, it is worth turning briefly to foundational accounts that developed its critical vocabulary. Bales elaborates the logic behind the term in *Disposable People: New Slavery in the Global Economy*, with case studies in five countries—the sex trade in Thailand, the water sale trade in Mauritania, the charcoal industry in Brazil, brick making in Pakistan, and bonded farm labor in India.[26] Bales argues that old forms of slavery were based on legal ownership and characterized by ideologies of racial difference. Slaves were expensive and often scarce, though the institution of slavery itself produced low profits and was often part of a rural and agricultural economy rather than a modern one. In contrast, new slavery is illegal everywhere, highly profitable, and often temporary. Slaves are not racialized, are abundant and dispensable, and are controlled through violence. New slavery derives from globalization, in tandem with government corruption, poverty, and population growth. Effective countermeasures, therefore, lie in liberal legal remedies like law enforcement and individual vigilance by good Samaritans. Appealing beyond partisan divides or ideological disputes, such cases are a way for people across the political spectrum to come together.

Such an account deploys a moral framework of good and evil rather than focusing on the larger political forces involved in trafficking and forced labor, with no discussion, for instance, of the weapons trade or the politics of oil and resource extraction. Numerous stories of forced abortions further intersect with a vigorous Christian agenda, and the attack on Islam is fairly consistent. When such scholars analyze root causes of modern slavery, they turn to culture and criminality.[27] Since there is little attention to how traditional forms of oppression have morphed into more modern forms, or to the history, politics, religion, or culture of the places discussed, the comparisons among various national sites and different forms of exploitation are assumed rather than demonstrated. Remarkably, there is little engagement with another body of work in the United States that also claims the moniker of modern abolition and likens incarceration—as a profoundly racialized practice—to slavery and segregation. Michelle Alexander's *The New Jim Crow*, Douglas Blackmon's *Slavery by Another Name*, which looks at debt peonage after Reconstruction, and indeed the burning political question of immigration justice in the United States become conspicuous by their absence.²⁸

Bales responds to many of these accusations of neo-imperialism in *The Slave Next Door: Human Trafficking and Slavery in America Today*, which brings the problem home by focusing on internal cases of human trafficking and modern slavery within the United States.²⁹ But again, the case studies of garment workers, domestic workers, farm workers, and sex slaves detach slavery from broader issues of work and labor practices, debates about immigration, and sex work.³⁰ Bales doesn't pause to consider whether different types of slavery have the same cause, use the same methods, or reinforce gender, ethnic, and class inequalities in the same way. In effect, he highlights criminality and policing rather than structural change or global inequality, as the language of moral outrage frames the experience of exploitation. In identifying consumption as the remedy, modern abolitionism empowers the Western consumer, focusing on personal ethical choices: "Slavery probably crept into your life several times today, some before you even got to work. Rolling off your bed, standing on that pretty hand-woven rug, maybe you threw on a cotton t-shirt. In the kitchen did you make a cup of coffee, spoon in a little sugar, and then kick back with a chocolate croissant and your laptop to check the headlines? All in all a normal day, but slavery was involved in almost every step."³¹ Accordingly, to end slavery we would need not more or better political solutions but better human beings, who would be vigilant good Samaritans and ethical consumers, eager to report any perceived abuse in their neighborhood to law enforcement. They would not have to think about broader issues of work and labor practices, debates about immigration, sex work, and the weapons trade, the politics of oil and resource extraction, or other gendered and class-based inequalities. They would just have to be outraged enough by the stories of suffering to sign off on a petition, thus choosing to stop "eating, wearing, walking, and talking slavery."³² They would not seek complex connections between practices of consumption in the First World and the ongoing production of systemic inequality in the Global South through coerced labor, involving hyper-exploitation along traditional hierarchies but also via reinvented social frameworks. Rather, the easy dyad of cruel slaveholder and innocent slave invites readers to imagine themselves as the humanitarian rescuer. Focusing on dramatic scenes of rescue, celebrity endorsements, and fund-raising, such activism often ignores key differences between past and present.[33]

Erasing such differences actively impedes the path of legal redress as well since, as Janie Chuang points out, the varied practices assembled under the umbrella term of modern-day slavery are each "separately defined under international law, subject to separate legal frameworks, and overseen by separate international institutions."[34] Moreover, focusing on the theft or kidnapping of children or young women (to mimic the innocent victim of the Middle Passage) makes it difficult to reckon with the fact that sex trafficking and labor migration today often involves voluntary transactions with a human smuggler. Simply attacking the smuggler as the new overseer of the plantation misses how many First World governments have responded by instating antimigrant policies and stricter border controls. Several abolitionist groups also reinforce the erroneous message of asking the migrants to simply stay home to be safe, regardless of whether their homes are able to afford them a livable life. The task, rather, as refugee rights activists show, is to attack trafficking not by controlling borders, but asserting a human right to movement and imagining a world beyond borders.[35] Along similar lines, assessing the work and life of "the underpaid, starved, and battered foreign maid" in the Asian metropolis may well involve, as Aihwa Ong shows, distinct moral economies, neoliberal labor markets, and various racialized nationalisms operating in the world today.[36]

More broadly speaking, most accounts of modern slavery jettison the larger legal and geopolitical framework driving migration and labor extraction today. Even the term "modern slavery" signals a deceptive temporality since the modernity of slavery is displaced onto the past, while the declared fact of contemporary slavery appears as anachronistic. When used for conflicts in such areas as Sudan, what Johannes Fabian has called the denial of coevalism is particularly apparent, as I explain below.[37] Another common tendency is to simplify the conflict into something easily understood and digested by the presumably Western reader or consumer, translating a faraway foreign experience to something more familiar and domestic. Anti-Slavery International, for instance, positions Darfur in Sudan as a global neighborhood watch program, which can be policed by vigilant netizens, who use satellite imagery without leaving their home to manage the violence in Darfur, at no personal risk. Reminiscent of the criminalization of minorities in the United States and the security-surveillance state as well as the war policy of recent governments that maximize collateral damage on civilians without any risk to their own army, using drones to create mass casualties, such an emphasis on policing reduces entire lives and histories to banalities. A larger discussion of work and wage labor (free and unfree), the consequences of extreme neoliberal deregulation around the world, and unfair terms of global trade would help situate these forms of exploitation alongside other kinds of structural and systemic forms of oppression, rather than appearing as the unspeakable horror of slavery.

But as Bales insists, modern abolitionists seek reform rather than revolution, since "it doesn't take a revolution to set slaves free."[38] Bales calculates the cost of freeing 27 million slaves at $945 million, arguing that markets can be made to serve the moral purpose of abolition. Abolition, in this instance, requires a critique of neither racial capitalism nor ongoing neocolonial domination. Rather, Bales advocates a fully neoliberal model of economic exchange among rational actors, hoping that ex-slaves will become consumers of the market. The logical culmination of such a belief emerges in the practice of slave redemption in Sudan, where Christian Slavery International buys slaves out of bondage for the cost of fifty dollars each, despite repeated revelations that the practice increases rather than curbs the abuse.[39] Remarkably, one of the most well-known activist modern slave narrators, Mende Nazer, refuses to support reparations for slavery since that means "putting a monetary value on human life."[40] In appealing to an obvious shared humanity, modern abolitionists disavow the production of racism as a central aspect of slavery and minimize ongoing legacies of colonialism even as they endorse a neoliberal reincorporation of the postcolony as the belated recipient of the philanthropy of the First World, and the site of unending and inexplicable atrocity.

Neo-abolitionist discourse further reinvents victims and survivors from the Global South as new American citizens who fit into a nation of immigrants, thus validating a liberal model of inclusion. President Barack Obama himself educes this logic in numerous speeches where he invokes the Lost Boys of Sudan as the latest entrants to the American dream, reaffirming that such a reinvention is possible only in the United

States, and so "America is exceptional."⁴¹ Two prominent texts that helped shape the terrain of modern slavery as a renegotiation of the relation between Africa and the United States—Francis Bok's memoir about his captivity and escape in Sudan during the Second Sudanese Civil War (1983–2005), *Escape from Slavery* (2003), and Dave Eggers's novel, *What Is the What* (2006), based on the experiences of a so-called Lost Boy from Sudan, Valentino Achak Deng—deserve further exegesis, as each dissolves the binary between the United States and Africa formally, by taking on the literary form of the other.⁴² Bok tells his story in the form of an antebellum slave narrative that then turns into an American immigrant story, while Eggers assumes the autobiographical persona of Deng, reprising the abolitionist formula in the name of globalism only to retrofit it for our neoliberal times. Both, I argue, shape their narratives as replicas of well-known slave narratives from the nineteenth century—a choice that goes to the heart of the ways in which these new discourses about Africa reshape existing politics of race, nation, and diaspora. Race haunts the construction of slavery and trauma in these works, as the circulation of genres and their reinvention across transnational sites also forces a reappraisal of the connection between human rights and narrative form.

Born Again in America

The best-selling memoir of Sudanese asylum-seeker Francis Bok, *Escape from Slavery: The True Story of My Ten Years in Captivity—And My Journey to Freedom in America* (2003), cowritten with an amanuensis, the American journalist Ed Tivnan, begins as an Atlantic slave narrative, and then becomes an immigrant tale of assimilation into the American dream. Captured in an Arab militia raid on a market in South Sudan at the age of seven, Bok was abused and held in bondage for ten years, before finding asylum in Egypt and the United States. At the time of publication, the twenty-three-year-old was well on his way to being a celebrity ex-slave, testifying before the Senate Committee on Foreign Relations in hearings on Sudan, writing an open letter to Britney Spears asking her to reconsider the language of the song "I'm a Slave for U," and speaking throughout the United States as an associate of the American Anti-Slavery group. The transition from the enslavement plot to the immigrant one takes place with a kind of bureaucratic baptism, as his name is misspelled on his passport, and since "I was my passport . . . I was born again—as Francis Bok. It cost eighty Sudanese pounds" (123). For Bok, the United States serves as a beacon of having overcome slavery in its past, and a model for countries like Sudan to aspire toward: "In Sudan and Egypt, opportunities were available only to a few. In America, the opportunities seemed limitless—for everyone, including us immigrants" (177). A curious construction of race powers the redemptive narrative. Bok gradually realizes that "there were black people in America" (138), who were once enslaved and are now free and his diasporic "American Journey" makes use of that existing narrative—as he inserts himself within the African American trajectory. In a church, an African American preacher responds to his tale saying "it was once this way with us" (190). With a laying-on of hands, the audiences marvel at seeing slavery come alive in a real person, as Bok becomes the past they have transcended: "Slavery had become a person they had seen, a young Sudanese whose hand they had actually shaken" (196). In a familiar denial of coevalism, Bok becomes a living embodiment of their own past.

In order to appear legible within preexisting codes of US readers, Bok presents the roots of the conflict in Sudan in Islamic fanaticism, which he interprets specifically as a form of antiblack racism. He links his story to that of the Taliban and al-Qaeda, noting that Osama bin Laden was in Sudan at the time of Bok's enslavement. The conflict thus appears not as a struggle over control of resources like oil and fertile land, or as a consequence of colonial British tribalization of Darfur (as political scientist Mahmood Mamdani shows), but as a clash of civilizations between the "Arab North" and the "Negroid South," a transposition of the black-white binary of Atlantic slavery, and an analysis particularly suited for the post-9/11 age of terror.[43] As the North-South dynamics of the American story transpose onto the Global South, the active processes of racialization in the postcolony appear as mere exports from the West. Reading Sudan as not another Rwanda (as the Save Darfur movement tends to do), or as part of a global struggle against a resurgent fundamentalist Islam reduces the geopolitical specificity of the political struggle in Sudan itself, a move that is not only intellectually threadbare but also politically risky. "Darfur" and "genocide" have become unhistorical watchwords in US foreign policy, as Mamdani argues, where humanitarianism is simply indistinguishable from neo-imperialism. It is thus perhaps not surprising that narratives like Bok's tend to assume a moralistic frame, where the Western humanitarian worker rescues the innocent victim from the evil slave owner. Resorting to the sensational language of nineteenth-century abolitionists allows minimal discussion of processes of racialization, local struggles over economic resources, causes of corruption or poverty, or the uneven impact of globalization. Adopting the form of an Atlantic slave narrative accumulates ideological baggage that assigns Africa to tragedy and the United States to promise, allowing US readers to read about a calamity that they themselves have transcended in their own history, rather than encouraging them to think more deeply about how events in the two nations have common politically entangled roots.

Making such a logic explicit, *Escape from Slavery* ends with a treatise offered by Charles Jacobs, the founder of the American Anti-Slavery Group and a second father to Bok, about the "human rights complex," a term Jacobs coins to explain the global neglect of Sudan. Jacobs argues that the human rights community, mostly made up of decent, compassionate white people, feels it has a duty to attack evil done by those are "like us." When Muslims in Bosnia were killed by white Christians, the West intervened. Since it was Arab Muslims rather than white Christians or Jews enslaving blacks in Sudan, nobody cared. Jacobs claims, "We Westerners, after all, had slaves. We napalmed Vietnam. We live on Native American land. Who are we to judge others?" (274). White culpability for past sins thus creates paralysis in the face of genocide in Rwanda or Sudan. Arguing for letting go of melancholic historical guilt, Jacobs presents military intervention in Africa as the only apt humanitarian choice.

While such moments in the text reaffirm the preconceptions of readers, I read Bok's narrative somewhat against its grain, drawing on techniques developed for the nineteenth-century slave narrative, at the same time recognizing that such a critical move can replicate US hegemony. Bok's narrative may be seen as a "black message in a white envelope" referring to the abolitionist editor and champion whose agenda often conflicts with the goal of self-representation of the former slave.[44] Recent scholarship on antebellum slave narrators has shifted away from a focus on what they couldn't say and do because of such control to stressing their creativity in finding what Harriet Jacobs termed "the loophole of retreat" and in transforming the alienating conditions of marginalization into modes of agency, theorizing the nature of freedom rather than simply baring their scarred bodies.[45] Scholars have also learned to read between the lines and against the grain of such narratives, which often had to draw a veil over proceedings too terrible to relate, what Morrison memorably termed "unspeakable thoughts, unspoken."[46]

Along these lines, I uncover two instances of Bok's narrative tussle with the neo-abolitionist agenda. In the first, Bok's voice breaks through editorial control. Alongside his high-mindedness, the desire to save other Sudanese, to fulfill his father's dream, another narrative about racial identification through consumer culture emerges. Watching basketball, buying sneakers and baseball caps, big T-shirts and jeans, and dressing like hip-hop stars on BET, Bok creates an identity for himself that is about expressing his freedom through consumption. Buying glasses "just for fun" and not for a corrective function, Bok confesses that "sometimes I would buy things because it made me happy" (176), noting the surprise of people around him at his choice of vanity frames. But the activists of the American Anti-Slavery Group who wish to enlist him as a celebrity ex-slave spokesman cannot understand those desires and have to buy him a suit and tie for public speaking. As Bok notes wryly in one of the rare moments of humor in the narrative, "I could not speak to the Baptists in Roxbury about my life in slavery looking like a refugee from a hip-hop video on MTV" (188).

The second moment is one that occurs time and again in several such narratives—a meditation on the nature of identity and storytelling. In Cairo, Bok has to tell and retell his story as part of the application for refugee status, and rather than signaling a therapeutic function, *Escape from Slavery* seems to allegorize the process of abolitionist editorial control over the raw matter of Bok's experiences. Bok tells his English-speaking social worker, Franco, the same story he has already narrated to the reader—we're roughly halfway through the book at this point—starting with the day his mother sent him to the marketplace, which was the happiest day of his life, which turned into the worst. The writing and reading of the book are thus both implicated in the process of deciding whether Bok is worthy of being a refugee. When Franco harangues him to get the story straight, Bok is puzzled since he knows that "this is my life, why should I worry about getting it straight?" Then follows an elaborate scene, which wouldn't be out of place in a metafictional postmodern novel, as Franco "listened and wrote down what I said. Then he read it to me, and we worked on it and got it all straight. . . . Franco looked at me, into my eyes. 'This is your true story, Francis. This was the way it all happened.' I stared back at this man I barely knew, this 'English teacher,' who was now testing me for truth, and told him that . . . it was not only all true, it was my life." Finally, Franco concludes that "mine was the worst story he had heard—and thus the best for getting chosen as a UN refugee" (134–136). Bok's life or death depend on the credibility of his storytelling: to narrate the story precisely, without error, every single time, in a mock reversal of the dynamic of trauma, and an embedded critique of the needs of the readers, who wish to check for fraud even as they insist on the sentimental frame of a universal humanity. As James Dawes notes, making sense out of incomprehensible atrocities requires storytelling because of the risks involved in representing and misreading traumatic testimony, as UN legal officers who follow the Convention on Refugees are constrained by the narrow definition of refugees and are cast in the position of the interrogator of people as they listen to stories of abuse and decide which are true and which are false, which deserve succor and which can be ignored.[47]

The schism between the needs of the neo-abolitionists and Bok's aspirations reveals how Bok is denied ownership of his own story even as ostensibly (as he notes at the end of the book) his amanuensis, Tivnan, "has transformed my thoughts onto the page and given me the words to tell my story" (282). Jesse Sage, the director of the American Anti-Slavery Group, recruits Bok precisely with the promise that "we want to help you tell your story" (182). In omitting the details of the literary collaboration, the text advances a realist claim—this is Bok's true story, told by himself. But the narrative doesn't sustain that claim elsewhere, undercutting referentiality, as the scenes of telling and retelling his story, getting it "straight" with the aid of the social worker allegorize the ways in which the author's control over his own narrative remains circumscribed. In this scene of a sentimental education, modern abolitionists insist that the stories they document are authentic, but also that it doesn't matter if they are not real.[48] Numerous narrators have faced accusations of fabrication, perhaps most famously Ishmael Beah, who at once claimed the truth of his experience of war and asked for the leeway of memory.[49] To advance this contradictory claim to a truthful experience at the same time that the demand for authenticity is undermined, modern slave narratives resort to a kind of formal tautology as they insist on the readability of the slave's body and story, situating the act of reading itself as a form of politics, indeed the very politics called for in the texts.

A Sentimental Education

That sentiment and abolition coincide is now a truism. Spectacles of suffering children separated from their loyal mothers, deathbed scenes of pathos, emotional and dramatic appeals to the reader, performances of pain and moral growth all emerge as archetypal sentimental tableaus, nowhere more effectively than in Harriet Beecher Stowe's *Uncle Tom's Cabin* (1852). Exalting feeling above reason, abolitionists sought to directly appeal to the hearts of white readers. The literature of slavery and abolition thus had a distinct didactic function—the moral education of the reader, in large part, the task of revealing to readers their own capacity for empathy. James McCune Smith's prescription for equality in 1846—"the heart of the whites must be changed, thoroughly, entirely, permanently changed"—implies, for John Stauffer, that whites had to "acquire, in effect, a black heart."[50] Such sympathy, more often than not, became a form of identification, or even substitution. Since the work of Jane Tompkins, claiming the cultural work performed by sentimental fiction of mid-nineteenth-century women writers (rather than simple escapist fantasy or guilty pleasure), arguments about the efficacy of sympathy and its limits have occupied American literary critics.[51] But even amid the acknowledgment of the valuable work performed by sentimentalism to manage race and gender, concerns about such imaginative substitution linger. As Lloyd Pratt forcefully observes, "When the white reader imagines him-or-herself to be feeling a fugitive's pain, he or she is actually imagining what it would feel like to be him-or-herself in the same position. In seeking to bridge an unbridgeable gulf of experience, the reader narcissistically substitutes him-or-herself for the enslaved, and the enslaved person undergoes a form of politically charged erasure."[52]

Sentimentality, as Lauren Berlant explains, "uses personal stories to tell of structural effects, but in so doing it risks thwarting its very attempt to perform rhetorically a scene of pain that must be soothed politically."[53] Replacing the possibility of radical transformation of existing social structures with the smaller talks of managing private feelings, sentimentality seeks to prove the humanity of the victim, to make her worthy of attention, sympathy, and (eventually) aid. It does not start from the assumption of humanity and equal human rights. In returning to the space of the home, it can also diminish the scope of the political. As Hortense Spillers elucidates, "The horror of slavery was its absolute domesticity that configured the 'peculiar institution' into the architectonics of the southern household." No separation of home or the marketplace existed for the enslaved, "because fathers could and did sell their sons and daughters, under the allowance of law and the flag of a new nation, 'conceived in liberty,' and all the rest of it."[54]

For slave narrators, the sentimental tradition presented both a trap and a possibility. As William Andrews explains, the slave narrative often distances a reader at first, and then draws her back in to actively encourage identification, even substitution, fashioning "a mode of autobiographical discourse that subtly reoriented a reader's response to his text away from a distanced perspective and toward one that authorized appropriation."[55] Moreover, feminist analysis by Hazel Carby and Claudia Tate reveals how slave narrators, despite unimaginable constraints, repeatedly manipulated sentimental conventions, creating loopholes of retreat amid restrictive notions of family, community, and womanhood.[56]

In the African American literary imagination, rejecting such sentimental origins has been a powerful current, perhaps expressed most cogently by Richard Wright, in his horror at the reception of his collection of short stories, *Uncle Tom's Children*: "I found that I had written a book which even bankers' daughters could read and weep over and feel good about. I swore to myself that if I ever wrote another book, no one would weep over it; that it would be so hard and deep that they would have to face it without the consolation of tears."[57] Such a resolve to deny the reader the consolation of tears resounds in the neo-slave narrative (as shaped by such writers as Morrison, Octavia Butler, Edward Jones, and Charles Johnson), which chooses to linger in horror and negation, refusing readers identification, edification, or healing.

The abolitionist sentimental template, however, revives itself almost verbatim in the discourse of modern slavery. In fact, as I show with my reading of Eggers, the managing of public and private spaces, interior and exterior lives so central to the sentimental tradition re-creates itself in his refiguring of Americans as sympathetic citizens of the world. It is his ability to empathize—to have, in effect, a black heart—that allows Eggers to write in the persona of a Lost Boy of Sudan, to great critical acclaim. Eggers calls the slave narrative into play precisely because it is an outdated form, a historic relic revived as an export to the Third World.[58]

Eggers's account of Valentino Achak Deng, a former "Lost Boy of Sudan," in fact makes sense only when read as a modern slave narrative. Even the title stages the indeterminacy between fact and fiction that is central to the project. The listed author of *What Is the What: The Autobiography of Valentino Achak Deng, A Novel* is Dave Eggers, who also appears as sole owner of the copyright. A brief preface by Deng calls the text "the soulful account of my life" (xiii) and explains that he met Eggers through Mary Williams, the founder of the Lost Boys Foundation of Atlanta, in response to a desire to expand the audience for his storytelling, by finding "an author to help me write my biography" (xiii). Author, character, subject are all roles in flux here. Deng continues, adding to the confusion of fact and fiction, claiming at once that the story should be read as fiction and that everything depicted actually happened to him: "It should be known to the readers that I was very young when some of the events in the book took place, and as a result we simply had to pronounce *What Is the What* a novel" (xiv). But, he insists, "all of the major events in the book are true" and "the book is historically accurate" (xiv). At the end of the book, a brief biographical note about Deng clarifies that all the proceeds from *What Is the What* will be directed to the Valentino Achak Deng Foundation, which seeks to provide education for those affected by the conflict in Sudan. It is never explained in *What Is the What* why the various "Lost Boys" converse in English. It is also significant that the book does not feature Eggers at all, and doesn't cover the encounter between the two that generates this text, even though the entire structure of the work is built upon scenes of storytelling, and the journey of Deng—his *Bildung*, if you will—rests primarily on wanting to tell his story to the world, and his often unsuccessful search for a listener. Even successful asylum depends on "the writing of our autobiographies" as the UN Refugee Agency requires all the "Lost Boys" to write about their lives and their desire to leave Kakuma for the United States. The narrator notes that "we knew our stories had to be well told . . . no deprivation was insignificant" (485). As a reviewer points out, it's further odd that for a story that is about dispossession in numerous forms, Deng doesn't legally own the story of his own life and has become a fictional character in someone else's novel.[59]

Unlike the narrative tussle between Bok and his neo-abolitionist friends, it is difficult to assess where Deng ends and Eggers takes over, or whose voice dominates the novel. Although *What Is the What* departs from Eggers's previous style (made famous by *A Heartbreaking Work of Staggering Genius*) and does not have (as a review pointed out) "a single grieving white male of high education and questionable maturity," Eggers's stamp can be seen all over it.[60] Eggers explains the origins of the association between author and subject in an essay posted on Deng's website. Although the two collaborated for over a year on an account written by Deng, Eggers was worried that it read too much like a Human Rights Watch report and decided to write it himself. But third-person narration seemed too remote to convey such a harrowing story, and hence he concluded it would have to be fiction, with Deng as first-person narrator. But this is fiction that claims the status of truth, as Eggers's fictionality comes cloaked with the authenticity of Deng's real life. As Sidonie Smith and Julia Watson note about witness narratives in an era when the demands for verification are rising in response to various hoaxes and scandals in the memoir industry, what such a narrative is supposed to do is to convince the reader of two things: "that the story is the 'real' story of a 'real survivor'—that a narrative is joined to an embodied person; and that the reading experience constitutes a cross-cultural encounter through which readers are positioned as ethical subjects within the global imaginary of human rights advocacy."[61] *What Is the What* offers what they call a "negotiable 'I'"—a double subject, Deng and Eggers, who together produce a sense of immediacy for the reader ("you were there") as well as a sense of parallel times (in the United States and in Sudan). The resulting words cannot be verified for accuracy but have to be trusted by the reader as an act of faith.

Perhaps this is why the book was greeted with almost no critical commentary and a showering of accolades, including a selection as finalist for the National Book Critics Circle Award for Fiction.[62] Many readers of the book have not objected to this confusion of fact and fiction, in large part because of the overdetermined place of Africa as a signifier in contemporary culture. Numerous reviews of *What Is the What* calmly conclude, as David Amsden does, that it shows "the primitive cruelty of African warfare." Literary critic Elizabeth Twitchell argues for the ethical and moral value of the novel, since it combats existing misrepresentations of Africa in American literary discourse and helps "bring light to the dark continent." Referring to questions about Ishmael Beah's lack of detail about his experience as a child soldier, Twitchell wonders, "Would the foreignness of the African voice to Western ears make any work of African auto-narration unmediated by a Western amanuensis ring false?"[63] Such a reading asks too little of the imagined American reader, not to mention bypassing the entire canon of modern African literature, which has been engaged in precisely the project of constructing the "African voice" called for by Twitchell. If the task of literature, as numerous thinkers (from Aristotle to Adam Smith, from George Eliot to Martha Nussbaum) have argued, is to produce empathy and enrich readers by bringing them into contact with otherness, it is surely too soon to start measuring and quantifying an acceptable measure of difference (what David Palumbo-Liu calls the threat of too much otherness) as Twitchell suggests in her reading of Eggers.[64]

What Is the What exposes the problems with such literary ventriloquism, or what we may call linguistic blackface, both structurally and thematically. Designed around numerous scenes of storytelling, the novel opens with Deng in his Atlanta apartment, being mugged by an African American couple, who leave a young boy to guard him while they make arrangements to transport his TV. Tied up and bleeding from his head, Deng narrates in first person the story of his life—his childhood in the village of Marial Bai, the attack on it by paramilitaries working for the government in Khartoum to suppress the Sudan People's Liberation Army, and his subsequent traumatic journey across Southern Sudan refugee camps in Ethiopia and Kenya over thirteen years, until he finds asylum in the United States and tries to make a new life in Atlanta. The novel concludes with Deng realizing that his role in life is to "tell these stories" since "to do anything else would be something less than human" (535). He resolves to fulfill this mission: "I will tell stories to people who will listen and to people who don't want to listen, to people who seek me out and to those who run. All the while I will know that you are there. How can I pretend that you do not exist? It would be almost as impossible as you pretending that I do not exist" (535). Deng thus understands the very purpose of his life to tell his story, and stripping his words of the status of testimony and turning them into fiction threatens to diminish the materiality of the experience itself. In debates about redress, reparation, or reconciliation, the physical body of the survivor and her words have always been sacrosanct, the only proper rebuttal to the perpetrators of genocide and torture. In fictionalizing an experience that has value as testimony, Eggers risks erasing that special status.

What Is the What assumes the template of the slave narrative by combining it with the immigrant plot. The arrival of horsemen interrupts Deng's idyllic childhood, and his subsequent captivity and escape are animated by his search for his family, presumed to be dead. He undergoes a process of renaming for each step of his journey. His crossing from Sudan to the United States echoes the flight from the US South to the North, where the North promises freedom but often turns to be another kind of hell. Deng's prefatory note promises the reader instruction that is not just exceptional but exemplary: "As you read this book, you will learn about me and my beloved people of Sudan" (xiii). The novel also outlines Deng's spiritual awakening—his path to understanding the meaning of the "What," his belief in himself as representative man, through the power of speech and storytelling, his resolve to make the world listen so that his people don't continue to suffer. The meaning his life accrues comes from helping others who haven't even found the modicum of freedom that he has in Atlanta. But even more than these persistent textual echoes, what links the novel to the slave narrative is the sentimental frame, the focus on producing feeling, empathy, horror, compassion, even pity to rouse the audience to some nonspecified action. It suggests that the sentimental mode has become the norm for processing stories such as Deng's.

However, despite the appropriation of the techniques of the slave narrative, the novel turns expected racial politics upside down. The story at the center of *What Is the What*—the traumatic wandering of the Lost Boys of Sudan—characterizes a textbook definition of diaspora as scattering and loss of home. But where dominant accounts of diaspora emphasize reconstructing lost identity through a search for community, Deng's experiences do not seem legible within such understandings. The novel never entertains the possibility of racial alliance across national boundaries, thus signaling a distinct shift in conceptions of race. Eggers begins not so much with misunderstanding or misrecognition among members of the black diaspora, but with active and vicious hostility. Deng's call is met with a brutal response, as his African American assailants mock him with the epithet "Africa" (5), "Fucking Nigerian motherfucker" (9), "Nigerian prince" (15), and "pimp" (15). As he's kicked and assumes a fetal position on the floor, his attacker clarifies that the animosity is personal and racial and has everything to do with Deng being an African: "No wonder you motherfuckers are in the Stone Age" (9). Deng recalls numerous instances of African American hostility toward the Lost Boys—teenagers who follow them and taunt them with accusations like "you're one of those Africans who sold us out" (18) and you should "go back to Africa" (19) and accept responsibility for the enslavement of their ancestors. Denying Africans coevalness by locating them in the Stone Age, mocking putative African royalty by bringing them into a racialized American stereotype ("pimp"), and exhibiting anti-immigrant xenophobia ("go back to Africa") as well as indicating a racial schism ("you . . . sold us out"), these taunts and threats establish hostility as the prime emotion between Africans and African Americans, in sharp contrast to the identification embraced by Bok. What we as readers are supposed to recognize is the grim irony that a figure like Deng, a Lost Boy who was a refugee, victim, and survivor of something very much like slavery, is being blamed for a historical event long past. The scene of assault the novel opens with immediately reminds Deng of one of the worst experiences of his trek, a primal moment of betrayal, where an Ethiopian soldier calls out to the Lost Boys—"Come to your mother"—only to shoot them down (6).

If Eggers undercuts the romance of diaspora, he doesn't quite replace it with a redemptive American dream that counters inevitable African tragedy. His America is made up of failing institutions, as neither hospitals nor police officers nor potential employers can ensure Deng health care, safety, education, or a living wage. What emerges as redemptive is privatized philanthropy—rich (white) liberals who punctuate Deng's narrative of uplift with financial and emotional interventions (making him part of their family life)—an allegory for a neoliberal sentimental humanism whose ultimate (unstated) champion is, of course, Eggers himself. Moved by his story, these benefactors (from Jane Fonda to Phil Mays to Bobby Newmyer to the Newtons) serve not just as heroes for the readers, but also as inheritors and saviors of the failed US state, the best kind of readers for Eggers's novel. Phil Mays, for instance, "an average white man of Atlanta," asks Deng to narrate his story time and again, not to check for fraud, but because it "affected him deeply" (171). After the first narration, Phil "put his hands in his lap and he cried. I watched his shoulders shake, watched him bring his hands to his face" (173). Once Phil becomes his mentor, Deng follows the weekly dinner at Phil's house with the "ritual" of "tell[ing] him the whole story" (177) in exchange for basic instructions about life in America. The "irrational, reckless" generosity of these families stands as a contrast to the erosion of institutions (as even the Lost Boys Foundation is disbanded in 2005), and the narrative repeatedly emphasizes that they don't just support Deng, but (in a move that parallels neoliberal economic theories of privatization, and the elevation of individual actions over social structures) make him part of their family—for instance, having him play with their children, including him on their Christmas card, and teaching him how to drive, cook, and do laundry.

One of the puzzling aspects of this literary collaboration is the seeming lack of fit between Deng's traumatic experiences and Eggers's signature style—half ironic, half sincere, emotionally manipulative but constantly showing the sleight of hand involved, as self-pitying as it is self-mocking.[65] The relation between author and subject involves a series of exchanges or substitutions—formal, racial, and sentimental—that render Deng's experiences not as testimony but as fiction. The very worldliness of the text, or its global feeling, itself comprises a neoliberal humanism that continues to package African atrocity as a form of self-constitution for the American reader. While America itself might be failing, Eggers as the silent specter, in effacing himself as author, becomes the true rescuer. In serving as the amanuensis for Deng, Eggers is able to play the metafictional postmodern games he is known for, but also to claim the title of truth for the narrative. Such a collaboration between author and subject speaks to the strange ironies of testimonial accounts of Third World subjects who serve as the raw matter of experience waiting for First World literary expertise, mapping onto the parasitical relation of the slave narrative's black message in a white envelope. Deng, constantly rebuffed, taunted, and beaten by a recurring cast of African American characters, finds his savior in Eggers, who is in turn saved from irrelevance by the moral clarity of Deng's suffering, thus becoming, as numerous reviewers point out, a kind of "Lost Boy" himself.

At the beginning of the novel, when the narrator recalls his arrival to the United States and his constant thought in response to every slight or annoyance—"*You would not add to my suffering if you knew what I have seen*"—his admonition is meant to refer back to the book the reader is reading, as an attempt to make us imagine, to feel the extent of his suffering. Given the succession of unwilling audiences Deng encounters throughout his voyage, the prime sin in his current life ends up being not being heard—his ethical demand is to be heard—and it is difficult not to see Eggers implicitly, though not acknowledged—as the answer to his prayers, the savior who listens, who translates his message, who promises redemption. In fact, as Deng, the protagonist of *What Is the What*, continually outlines various reading practices—explicitly telling the fictional characters he addresses (like the burglars, cops, neighbors, and hospital workers) how to listen to his story and how to think about it, the text approaches the feel of an instruction manual in developing sympathy for the victim of atrocity. But since Eggers is the stated author, an exchange of identities occurs: Deng's autobiographical experience and Eggers's writerly empathy become fungible. In usurping the place of Deng in the sympathies of the reader, Eggers revives the questions of representation that have always haunted the genre of the slave narrative, and bypasses the long history of critiques of white appropriations of faraway suffering by reanimating an uninterrogated sentimental reading practice. One could thus say that the novel, in the end, is the allegory not of the journey of a "Lost Boy" coming to America, but of Eggers's own salvation through his ventriloquism of Deng—his production as an empathetic, global human who can be moved by the story to action. The novel is the action required—it is the very politics it calls for. *What Is the What* not only muddles fact and fiction, subject and author, but also tells us, in the end, only that "what" is indeed "the what." Eggers dramatizes for the American reader how to relate to Deng—to assume the story as his own to tell means that Eggers is set apart from all those who refuse to respond to Deng's call. Each time Deng is rebuffed in his attempt to tell the story, the reader has the proof of successful storytelling in her hands, taking for granted if not guaranteeing the production of empathy, and of a worldly American reader, attuned to African atrocity.

This is why the first few pages of the novel are littered with the undermining of realist truth claims or the sanctity of experience, witness, and testimony, since the emphasis is on not Deng's experience but the reader's. The narrator notes that "at Kakuma, many of us lied on our application forms and in our interviews with officials" especially to deny an affiliation with the Sudan People's Liberation Army (SPLA). Since refuge in the United States was denied to anybody who had fought as a soldier, the applications had to excise any reference to such an experience: "The SPLA had been a part of our lives from early on, and over half of the young men who call themselves Lost Boys were child soldiers to some degree or another. But this is a part of our history that we have been told not to talk about" (17). He notes that stories of drinking urine, though apocryphal, impress people, and that there were "castes within castes" and other hierarchies among the walking boys. And yet "the tales of the Lost Boys have become remarkably similar over the years. Everyone's account includes attacks by lions, hyenas, crocodiles." Although the stories of the twenty thousand or so Lost Boys are all different, "sponsors and newspaper reporters and the like expect the stories to have certain elements, and the Lost Boys have been consistent in their willingness to oblige. Survivors tell the stories the sympathetic want, and that means making them as shocking as possible, my own story includes enough small embellishments that I cannot critique the accounts of others" (21). Early in the novel, the narrator describes staring "into the eyes of a lion" (8) in Ethiopia, but soon thereafter addresses the reader's expectations of stories about lions: "No doubt if you have heard of the Lost Boys of Sudan, you have heard of the lions" (30). He notes that if it were not for the stories about lions, the United States would not have been interested in them at all, but then goes on to counter the cynics by asserting that these stories "were in most cases true" (30), thus undercutting the testimonial value of the account.

Moreover, the narrator's voice remains ambiguous throughout. The novel's title comes from a Dinka creation myth that punctuates the entire narrative. Deng recalls his father telling the story of God offering the

Dinka a choice between a cow, which they could see and touch, and the What. The Dinka chose the cow, believing in the power of the tangible and the material over the unknown. They also believed that the Arabs chose the What, and as he flees militias and starvation, Deng wonders if the What refers to guns or horses. But at the end of the novel, as Deng makes a speech for the other Lost Boys scheduled to fly on September 11, 2011, to the United States and quarantined in Kenya, his reading of the What changes, and he chooses the unknown over the known: "The mistakes of the Dinka before us were errors of timidity, of choosing what was before us over what might be. Our people, I said, had been punished for centuries for our errors.... We had been thrown this way and that, like rain in the wind of a hysterical storm. But we're no longer rain, I said—we're no longer seeds. We're men.... This is our first chance to choose our own unknown" (531). Resolving to "keep walking" and hoping that after so much suffering "there will be grace" (532), Deng calms the fears of the other men, inspiring them to look forward to a better life.

How may we determine what's going on here? Is this Deng's realization, born of trauma, a form of what we may call retroactive rationalization? Or did Eggers imagine this, to provide cohesion to a literary narrative, with a recognizable metaphor of the What or the void (which has a long genealogy in Orientalism and Africanism) and to provide closure to the creation myth? That we cannot choose either side points to the complications of such a literary collaboration and the strategic silences about the conditions of its production. It is difficult to detect the tone here—hollow or sincere, self-mocking or resolute. Should Deng's words strike the reader as empty, since we already know that the boys found little grace in America? Or does the emphasis on keeping on walking function as a literary trope tying the novel together, signaling their ongoing struggle? Does Deng believe this himself, or does he just say it to calm the fears of his companions? Even after over five hundred pages of first-person narration, detailed, straightforward, and introspective, the gist remains unclear, and Deng emerges with no unambiguous voice of his own.

Scholars of Atlantic slavery have painstakingly and definitively shown that we cannot read slave narratives just for facts or content; we must read them for their complexity and literary artistry since the cultivation of a writing self was part and parcel of the process of gaining a self, of not just finding but crafting freedom.[66] In a similar manner, we may wonder why—when Deng's literacy and liberty are also connected, and he is well known as a public speaker and storyteller—his story needs an interpreter. As Didier Fassin points out, the "politics of life" of humanitarianism rests on the value of testimony, and creating a distinction between those who narrate their own story and those who become biographical subjects of someone else's narration fundamentally has to do with what counts as human.[67] Deng's humanity diminishes, to some extent, when he is denied authorship of his own life story.

Unthinking Human Rights

While new abolitionism may be criticized along the lines suggested above—as inadequate sociology, history, or economics—it is worth emphasizing in conclusion that what makes modern slave narratives work is the power we usually ascribe to imaginative literature: the capacity to generate empathy, sentiment, and an appeal to a shared conception of human rights. In such a scenario, literature can help develop ethical norms, plotting coordinates of hope, but refusing tidy cathartic conclusions. In recent years, many literary critics have shown how the work of human rights is remarkably akin to the work of narrative, as language, rhetoric, and textual representation matter equally urgently for both. In *Human Rights, Inc.*, Slaughter emphasizes the constitutive intimacy between the notion of human rights and the rise of the novel, particularly the bildungsroman, revealing how human rights are "as much matters of literature as of law," as both share a "conceptual vocabulary, deep narrative grammar, and humanist social vision."[68] This convergence demands greater attention to the ideologies of form called into play to narrate such stories since using a preexisting form of the US slave narrative necessarily circumscribes the kinds of questions that may be raised. To understand fully how texts of modern slavery circulate, we need to reckon with the different forces of genre and geopolitics, race and neocolonialism, humanitarianism and the War on Terror. It is also worth recalling that historians of slavery warn against reducing slavery to a generalized metaphor for exploitation, and insist on its specificity.[69] Moreover, the exclusion of numerous African literary texts that represent slavery, civil war, and genocide is also problematic, especially since historians argue that the civil war in Sudan has little in common with slavery (unlike Mauritania) and should be studied alongside Uganda, Sierra Leone, or Liberia. Tracking the circulation of the form of the slave narrative across widely divergent texts entails a deeper consideration of the transformation of race and form, opening up thorny questions of new paradigms of diasporic connection and fracture across the Global South. Stories of African tragedy and American triumph say more about how race works in a neoliberal age, as the end of politics declared in these universalizing narratives can proceed only by way of a disavowal of antiracist and anticolonial critique, as a resurrection of sentimental humanism that purports to be universal.

My critique of modern slavery is aimed not at reiterating the exceptionalism of slavery as an institution or refuting comparative approaches. The task isn't to define what is and isn't slavery, who is and isn't a slave. Rather, I am interested in exploring how the world slavery made may be likened to extreme forms of oppression today. To think slavery not as an exception but as part of a continuum of unfree labor and hyperexploitative practices must necessarily involve an analysis of race because how we understand race in the United States is centrally framed by the African American experience of slavery. An analogical approach across both time and space must thus find a way to connect racism, as a legacy of slavery, to colonialism as a rearticulation of the white man's burden. This may well mean not just a rethinking of blackness in the United States, as the African American story intersects with new geographies of migration, but the figuration of other bodies as raced in different ways. Given that according to Bales's estimates some fifteen to twenty million of the twenty-seven million modern slaves are in the Indian subcontinent, it's doubly odd that the transatlantic slave trade provides the forms for the telling of these stories, with little engagement with numerous NGOs and activist social movements in South Asia, which often use song and traveling street theater to raise consciousness. Moreover, given bonded labor's roots in feudal remnants, we may well need a local rather than transnational analysis, with caste at the center of the debate, not just understood as a proxy for race, in a form of "Atlantic exceptionalism."[70] Alternatively, it may be useful to think deeply about the possible intertwining of ideologies of race with caste, as Amitav Ghosh seeks to do in his recent Ibis Trilogy.[71] Along similar lines, in India both tribal and indigenous bodies appear as most vulnerable, and an analysis of the specificity of the situation may yield more productive scholarly accounts as well as more flexible political resolutions. Similar attention to gender and the state of being a child would likely return distinct epistemological and political challenges.

Fundamentally, what we need is a deeper excavation of the logic underpinning statements like "slavery still exists." Is slavery an anachronism? A sign of the past in the present, a symbol of unresolved inequities? A wound that is still unfolding? While some recent responses to the frame of modern slavery have questioned its claims, insisting on the particularity of slavery as productive of antiblackness, I am interested in an alternate path that neither subsumes a range of experiences under the banner of modern slavery nor disables potentially productive comparative conversations.[72] Because forms of blackness and models of human rights generated in the First World do continue to be hegemonic and shape the potential of what may be thought across the world, we need to find a way to seek difficult connections and comparisons. To do so, the first step is to recognize that enslaved Africans created visions of the world that launch a critique of the entire system of slavery, capitalism, democratic liberalism, indeed the entire edifice of the Enlightenment. And that it matters that every pillar of that world supported slavery— law, education, religion, and government. This is what Paul Gilroy means when he sees slavery as constitutive of what we understand as modernity, not an unfortunate aspect that might be reformed.[73] As a world-making, world-breaking institution, slavery must be understood beyond the language of reform or amendment. One of the most powerful provocations of *The Black Atlantic* was to insist that we place the slave at the center of modernity and produce our histories and philosophies from that vantage point, relocating the figure of the slave from silent victim to eloquent critic. Along similar lines, what requires further thought is how the vantage point of a Sudanese refugee like Francis Bok or Valentino Achak Deng may serve to interrogate the very foundations of a neoliberal philosophy of history, and help generate more politically complex notions of human rights. As David Harvey notes, the trajectories of modern human rights and neoliberalization are exactly parallel, coming into prominence after 1980, and the concern with the individual rather than with the creation of larger democratic and socially just institutions carries more risk than reward.[74] Human rights discourse has grappled with the seeming binary between an abstract universal notion of the human and the demands of cultural relativism. Critics of human rights point out that rights are often Western constructs that are foisted on to the rest of the world in an instance of cultural imperialism, while advocates counter that cultural relativism is often a mask for the exploitation of vulnerable populations.[75] But the universal-particular divide doesn't quite cover the exigencies of modern slavery, which calls for a deeper consideration of how we imagine relation across the globe.

In closing, I wish to turn to Chris Abani's 2005 novella *Becoming Abigail*, which also fuses an account of sex trafficking with an immigrant's journey, but to remarkably different effect from what we have seen above.[76] If there is by now, as I have been suggesting, a formulaic quality to such stories, this slim, elegant novel departs from that blueprint entirely. It refuses to narrate the tale of abuse in a straightforward fashion, where the idyllic childhood is interrupted by a moment of trauma, which brings with it a loss of family, language, and culture and ends with deliverance through Western nations with human rights organizations facilitating the journey. In *Becoming Abigail*, there is no deliverance, no claim on the reader's pity or even empathy, but a call for the imagination to dwell in the shadow of the incommunicable. The only time before the fall would be a return to the mother's womb.

Trafficked to London from Nigeria by an uncle, even as she escapes the unspoken desire of her own father, Abigail finds little peace in rescue. Feeling an "unassuming tenderness" (53) for her married social worker means only further reprisal, since the human rights workers tell her "that she didn't know what choice was" (119). Departing from the edifice of domination, rescue, and rehabilitation, Abani chooses an obliquely lyrical idiom for Abigail that rejects the possibility of agency, freedom, or redemption. Repossessing the colonial metaphor of discovering a woman's body ("she was a foreign country to them"; 29), Abigail chooses to become a "cartographer of dreams" by turning her body into a map of the world, with "the hook of Africa" her nose, "the Americas" her eyes, and "Australia her bottom lip" (74). She marks herself by cutting lines in her flesh to commemorate each experience of degradation and her transcendence of it through a corrosive notion of self. Return of any kind, wholeness, or home all seem impossible: "Sometimes there is no way to leave something behind. . . . To remember something that cannot be forgotten. Yet not left over" (61).

The novel's focus on Abigail's desire (for her father, the social worker, and, most intensely, for her dead mother) rethinks atrocity, making her wounded subjectivity part of the pain of a history too often rendered in anonymous or instrumental prose. Abani's choice of lyricism troubles the language of exposure or visibility, centering her interiority instead. Such a project is analogous to and reminiscent of recent work in African American neo-slave narratives that take up the hitherto proscribed subject of the desire of the enslaved woman for the slave master. Iconoclastic artists and writers like Kara Walker, Suzan-Lori Parks, John Edgar Wideman, Octavia Butler, and Charles Johnson stage the erotic and sexual relations between races as a way to think about history and its production of the present. Just like Morrison, Abani emphasizes memory: "How do you remember an event you were not there for?" Abigail wonders, recalling the circumstances of her mother's death during childbirth in an impossible effort of imagination (20).

Because *Becoming Abigail* resonates with the neo-slave narrative in its complication of notions of agency, choice, and selfhood, rather than repeating the slave narrative's journey from slavery to freedom in the manner of Bok or Eggers, Abani renders the two spaces—the Nigerian home Abigail leaves and the English present she inhabits (separated by alternating chapters titled "Now" and "Then" to indicate the troubling of temporal frames with shifts in space)—coeval. Abigail's preference for Chinese poetry over the poems of Dylan Thomas her social worker quotes, or even the novel by Armah he gifts her, further speaks to her refusal to be limited to expected narratives of cultural hierarchy. Neither asking the reader to identify or sympathize with Abigail in a straightforward manner nor fully closing off her subaltern subjectivity, Abani stages an ethical encounter with Abigail's traumatized mind and body that rejects sentiment in favor of confronting the full horror of her experience.

Abani's insistence on opacity counters the mandate for exposure and visibility of humanitarian liberation narratives. Desire re-creates Abigail beyond instrumental needs of human rights institutions, pinpointing the failure of states, relief agencies, and NGOs to acknowledge the humanity of the survivor of trafficking, or to accept the connection between border control and immigration quotas in the First World and how they enable smuggling and ongoing control of vulnerable migrants. Such more difficult encounters with representations of pain, both past and present, form the substance of the remaining chapters.

Each of the following chapters charts a departure from the terrain of analogical substitution and from the demand for empathy as an apt response to atrocity. The second chapter turns to the allied icon of the child soldier, an increasingly visible and mobile figure of Africa, blackness, and human violation. Here, I show how the rejection of the sentimental mode and the embrace of the gothic enables a different sense of relation between the audience and the figure of the victim, as well as a fuller appreciation of the itineraries of terror, rooted in colonial history, that have led us to this moment. Jettisoning the universalizing impulses of the sentimental tradition, gothic child soldiers raise ghosts and demons who claim a reckoning with the postcolonial histories that have birthed them.

2

The Gothic Child

The sensibility of slave owners is gothic.
—Toni Morrison, *The Origin of Others*

Why has the tale of terror so special an appeal to Americans?
—Leslie Fiedler, *Love and Death in the American Novel*

Around 2007, the African child soldier became "an American pop icon."[1] The year saw the publication of Ishmael Beah's *A Long Way Gone: Memoirs of a Boy Soldier*, an account of the author's capture by the rebel army in Sierra Leone at the age of twelve and his subsequent rehabilitation by UNICEF. Not only was the book a national best seller, it was selected for sale by Starbucks and sold over sixty-two thousand copies in the first three weeks.[2] Dave Eggers's claim therefore—that Beah is "arguably the most read African writer in contemporary literature"—is hardly an overstatement.[3] Along with other best sellers published in the first decade of the twenty-first century, Chris Abani's *Song for Night* (2007), Uzodinma Iweala's *Beasts of No Nation* (2005, adapted into a motion picture in 2015, directed by Cary Fukunaga), Delia Jarrett-Macauley's *Moses, Citizen and Me* (2005), Emmanuel Dongala's *Johnny Mad Dog* (2002, adapted for screen in 2009), Joshua Dysart's *Unknown Soldier* (2009), China Keitetsi's *Child Soldier: Fighting for My Life* (2005), Ahmadou Kourouma's *Allah Is Not Obliged* (2000; English translation, 2007), Grace Akallo and Faith McDonnell's *Girl Soldier* (2007), Emmanuel Jal's *War Child* (2009), and Susan Minot's *Thirty Girls* (2014), Beah's book helped create the African child soldier as a distinct emblem of the contemporary moment.[4] In the company of such Hollywood films as *Blood Diamond* (2006) and even children's books focusing on the subject—such as Jessica Dee Humphreys and Michel Chikwanine's account of Congo, *Child Soldier: When Boys and Girls Are Used in War* (2015)—the crystallization of the figure into a staple of modern life demands a perusal of the unstated politics of race and genre at work.[5]

Prompting recognition and estrangement at once, the child soldier genre navigates the distance of the far-off African landscape of war by bringing it into the intimacy of the neighborhood coffee shop. Beah delivers the prototype of the genre. The cover photograph features a young black boy wearing tattered slippers loaded with weapons—guns, ammunition, grenades—walking on a dust path. The boy looks down with a somber expression with his eyes hidden from us. In contrast, the author's photograph on the back of the book shows Beah smiling and gazing into the horizon—a classic portrait of his head and shoulders. The juxtaposition invites us to marvel at—as the title of the *New York Times* article published in tandem suggests—"The Making, and Unmaking, of a Child Soldier," as the small boy with the big gun transforms into the successful author and immigrant who helps raise awareness about children at war.[6]

I return to Beah at greater length below but will note here that the narrative plot—Beah's odyssey (as a blurb calls it)—approximates the frame of the slave narrative almost exactly. Trauma interrupts an initial happy childhood; the fall into sin and torture ends with rescue, redemption, and a life devoted to advocacy for all who have suffered like him. The tale of bloody terror thus comes enveloped in a familiar sentimental tradition, signifying not simply maudlin or pathos-filled prose but an emphasis on education, on the need for developing empathy through reading, and indeed the creation of the successful activist at the end of the story precisely by writing the narrative. Child soldier fictions mimic the form of the slave narrative in distinct fashion. They often replicate the structure of the narrative—an idyllic home, traumatic captivity, and descent into horror (often including rape), with ultimate rescue and a life devoted to advocacy. Their sentimental template may allow for the mention of the horrors of war, but these are largely subordinated to the overall narrative structure we saw in chapter 1: a peaceful childhood, a traumatic moment of captivity, abuse and violence, both inflicted and experienced, and often narrated as sin, followed by escape, rescue, redemption. The story concludes when the former child soldier becomes an abolitionist. The representative nature of the tale is never in doubt. As Emmanuel Jal puts it, "Everyone in my country has a story to tell, but I am telling mine to speak for all those who can't. I'm still a soldier, fighting with my pen and paper, for peace till the day I cease."[7] The child soldier genre thus reprises the link between writing and freedom enshrined in the slave narrative, cementing the unmaking of the man through torture and his making through culture.

Numerous other aspects duplicate the conventions associated with the slave narrative—the contradictory status of the author as both exemplary and exceptional, the figure of the editor or sponsor who arrives as the white savior, and an emphasis on the truth of the events described (along with frequent accusations of fraud or exaggeration that surface in the media for several of these works). The paratextual apparatus of the slave narrative—endorsements from abolitionist sponsors, dignified portraits of the ex-slave, letters affirming the truth of the events described—also appear in morphed form for the twenty-first century, including photographs of the author (and sometimes of the editors as well), digital accompaniments (websites that raise awareness and promote human right campaigns to end the use of children in war), reading group guides, Spotify playlists of music to accompany the text, and a series of acknowledgments or appendices from the author. Such fictions thus repeat the dynamics of abolitionism retrofitted for contemporary globalism.

The figure of the child represents the quintessential sentimental object—vulnerable, innocent, chaste, and, accordingly, ripe for redemption. As I noted in the introduction, much of contemporary African American literature has rejected the sentimental tradition derived from the slave narrative, seeking more unsettling engagements with historical violence and present dispossession. Meanwhile, as chapter 1 shows, current accounts of atrocity from the Global South seem to mirror the Atlantic past all too neatly, as white editors envelop the stories of survivors to promote feeling over reason, the moral education of the Western reader over the political agency of the victim. In what follows, I consider how the African child soldier novel redraws this humanitarian template, and how the figure of the child mediates the figuration of race and the human today. To do so, I draw a distinction between sentimental representations of the child soldier that affirm a therapeutic model and those that challenge such a model by drawing on the genre of the gothic. Tracing the unsettling figure of the child soldier in literature, media, and human rights discourse, I propose that the child emblematizes horror and terror in addition to sentiment. In shuttling between the sentimentalized object of sympathy, available for rescue through therapy for a new life in the United States, and the gothic disturbance of life and afterlife, home and abroad, at its best the child soldier novel redraws the humanitarian template outlined in the previous chapter.

That the use and abuse of children in war constitutes an extreme form of violence and degradation goes without saying. Raising questions about invisible norms in international law and criminal justice, the child in war poses additional challenges for narrative. Much of the scholarly conversation thus far has revolved around the ethics of life writing, the role of fiction in promoting empathy and social change, in raising awareness and countering the exclusions of law and the distortions of media.[8] Critical treatments of child soldier fictions have also posed the question of choice, agency, and moral culpability in contrast to legal definitions of the child (under the age of eighteen) as an emblem of absolute innocence and vulnerability.[9] Humanitarian work on the child soldier has rightly drawn attention to the mechanics of reintegration of a "lost generation" into a postwar society and highlighted the dilemma of rehabilitation. Without questioning the generative value of such approaches, my focus in this chapter is somewhat different. By exploring the sentimental and gothic exchanges visible in child soldier fictions in relation to similar dynamics in Atlantic slavery, I lay out the stakes that attend the production and consumption of such stories of violation, particularly as they construct the racialized figure of the black child. Doing so will allow me to emphasize the specificity of twenty-first-century geopolitical ambitions of the United States as the lone superpower, with an endless war machine, whose militarist arm is complemented by a philanthropic one (made up of humanitarian child rights advocates, global evangelical movements, anti-sex-trafficking activists, and viral campaigns in social media). By connecting the genre of the child soldier novel to the African American slave narrative, I explore what it means to revive the unprocessed past of slavery in order to translate the new degradation of the African child. If the American pop icon of the African child soldier appears as a familiar-but-surreal figure, I contend that the contiguity of the slave narrative and the repetition of abolitionist strategies create this trope. As comparisons and parallels between slavery and conscription in war proliferate, with human rights advocates insisting on erasing any of the differences between past and present, what are the uses of the gothic in such narratives? In what way does the child soldier novel as a genre trouble the assumptions of human rights conceptions?

If the sentimental mode of the slave narrative's structure of abduction, torture, and rescue linked the acquisition of self with the right to write, to own property, including the property of one's own name and narrative, it also allowed for substitution: the white reader for the traumatized slave, immigrant life in the United States as redemption for the slave past. The gothic, I argue, refuses to accept such exchanges, lingering in terror and monstrosity without relief, refusing the satisfaction of closure and recovery. The gothic fictions I explore in this chapter challenge the common perception of the child soldier figure in three distinct ways. First, they rewrite the innocent child insisted upon in human rights discourse as a compromised, complicit figure *as* able to inflict terror as to receive it. Second, they undercut the linear narrative of progress and redemption outlined in the first chapter because the former child soldier makes for an uneasy immigrant. Third, instead of promising the reader an education in sympathy and allowing for an imaginative substitution, these fictions create no such possibility of exchange, leaving the endings inconclusive and using various techniques of direct address to corrode any prospect of comfort, rightly insisting that a reckoning with the figure of the child soldier should not make for an easy reading experience. While the first half of the chapter tracks the persistent return to the sentimental, the latter half outlines more challenging approaches, ranging from lyrical opacity to scathing satire.

I begin with the media spectacle of #BringBackOurGirls, centering on the abduction of the Chibok girls in Nigeria by Boko Haram in 2014. Exploring two influential accounts based on similar incidents—Susan Minot's *Thirty Girls* and Grace Akallo and Faith McDonnell's *Girl Soldier*, I show how girl soldiers are available for recuperation in sharp contrast to boy soldiers, especially through presenting Western Christian education as the most effective counter to groups like Boko Haram or the Lord's Resistance Army. I then turn to Uzodinma Iweala's *Beasts of No Nation* and Ishmael Beah's *A Long Way Gone*, both of which deploy gothic tropes of monstrosity and failed narration, but ultimately affirm the power of therapy through storytelling. Following this, I describe more challenging attempts to represent the consciousness of the violated and violating child—Chris Abani's lyrical account of a child killed in war in *Song for Night*—to demonstrate how the promise of salvage is an uncertain one that must be complemented by a fuller reckoning with the destruction of childhood. Abani's novel also makes full use of the gothic, and in linking his ghostly protagonist with fiction's most famous gothic child, Toni Morrison's Beloved, I posit more complicated links across African and African American expressive cultures than the simple substitution outlined in the previous chapter. I conclude the chapter with Ahmadou Kourouma's firm rejection of the sentimental mode, and his turn to corrosive satire in *Allah Is Not Obliged*, which fully implicates liberal epistemologies in any attempt to see, hear, or believe the child soldier.

Reading in this way means abstracting the child soldier genre out of the African literary tradition, outside of debates over national allegories and postcolonial dystopias alone. In situating the child soldier novel—so often published and circulated in metropoles of the Global North—alongside questions of philanthropy and globalism, I expand its taxonomy to quintessentially American genres in order to bring into focus the unsettled past of slavery with respect to the differential status of US blackness in relation to histories of migration. The genre of the gothic has long been positioned as the exemplar of the original sin of slavery and genocide in American literary histories. Rather than revisiting the debate about the prominence of the child soldier as an effective or derogatory representation of Africa, in drawing on various conceptions of the Gothic—American, African, and Atlantic—I link the revival of past genres in contemporary literature to their travel across transnational space. This requires juxtaposing the notion of racial innocence formulated in the US context with that of Africa as a helpless child needing intervention—two long-standing formations that resuscitate in the twenty-first century with peculiar urgency. Placing the African gothic next to the American and Atlantic gothic (with slavery at their center) reframes the story of race and liberty in both spaces, enabling a distinctive account of the contemporary relation between Africa and the United States, as well as new conceptions of race, diaspora, and blackness in a global frame. Such a framing changes the African American narrative about slavery and its afterlife as well, as the circulation of the slave narrative engenders new contemporary genres—such as the child soldier novel that departs from the lineage of earlier war novels, national allegories, or bildungsromane, and emerges instead as a transnational genre.

Bring Back Our Girls

The 2014 abduction of 276 girls from the northeastern Nigerian town of Chibok by Islamist militant group Boko Haram presents a case study for the collision of humanitarianism with spectacle, underscoring the jagged suturing of past forms of abolitionism with present-day tales of horror. Prompting one of the biggest global social media campaigns, with tweeters using the hashtag #BringBackOurGirls (with contributions by Michelle Obama, Malala Yousafzai, and many more), the abduction has come to stand in for a familiar story of an attack on female education and the need for global action against militant Islam. The facts of the case, as they slowly emerge, tell a somewhat different story. Since 2014, the girls have appeared in Boko Haram propaganda videos, while rescued girls have been kept away from their families, and when some of them came to the United States, they described their anguish at being made to tell and retell their stories. Various deradicalization programs have been initiated for the rescued girls, who often face violence and stigma when they return. In 2016 and 2017, some of the girls escaped, while others were freed in a mass release after negotiations between the government and Boko Haram (including speculations of freeing political prisoners in exchange, possibly ransom payments as well). About a hundred girls remain unaccounted for.[10] Adaobi Tricia Nwaubani's ongoing reporting for Reuters has revealed that there seemed to be no plan to capture the girls, and the motivations may have been something other than an attack on Western education. Cautioning against turning Boko Haram into "superstar monsters," the journalist shows how the ensuing attention to the plight of the girls only strengthened the hand of the militants as they were able to derive concessions from the embarrassed government.[11]

At least two of the kidnapped girls, Naomi Adamu and Sarah Samuel, kept secret diaries, repurposing exercise books they were given for Koranic lessons into chronicles of their captivity and abuse. Sarah, still a captive (at the time of this writing), is said to have listed the names of her five siblings, ending with, "My father's name is Samuel and my mother's name is Rebecca."[12] Creating herself as a subject in this manner seems to repeat the strategy of the slave narrator's locating of the self in time and space. For many commenters in the West, this event reveals a polarized view of a confrontation between a liberal West that emblematizes freedom and Boko Haram. Much of the media coverage has focused on sexual slavery as well, helped by several militants who declare their plan to bring back slavery. Abukar Shekau, the leader of the group, boasted in 2014 in a propaganda video, "I took your girls. I will turn your girls into slaves."[13] But as Helon Habila points out, slavery in this context likely signifies something other than chattel slavery and works as a threat that is local to the Middle Belt of northern Nigeria, where the Sokoto Caliphate employed a workforce based on slave labor of so-called pagans.[14] It is these descendants of the pagans that Shekau threatens, tapping into decades of fault lines among Muslim, Christian, and "pagan" neighbors.

From all accounts, it seems clear that the Chibok abduction comprises a much more complex story, with various political actors with motivations that transcend an attack on education. The world's attention served to amplify the narrative about slavery and tied freedom to reading and writing. As the complexity of factors shrinks to fit the single story, the power of genre comes into view once again, as politicians, humanitarian organizations, concerned parents, and sympathetic global audiences rehearse the familiar story of freedom and slavery, rape and rehabilitation. The event also makes clear the contradictions of a media imaginary, particularly in the United States, which has been unwilling to show empathy to black children in visible pain (being shot, beaten, or kicked by police) but is able to empathize with black children in Uganda or Nigeria. Part of this, of course, is the ease of distance. Holding up a sign called "bring back our girls" in no way affects the safety or personal space of the First World inhabitant. But there seems to be more going on—as one traumatized black child is welcomed as a future model immigrant (a reprise of the former slave) while the humanity of the actual descendant of the slave is often diminished. Such a perverse logic is visible not only in the modern slave narratives I discussed in the previous chapter but in narratives of the child soldier as well. Reading a range of these fictions, I unravel this logic, further illuminating other efforts by a range of writers to imagine different kinds of relationships among African and African American populations. Certain tableaus and spaces recur in this landscape—the Chibok girls in Nigeria, Sudan and its Lost Boys, Uganda and its missing girls. Much of the literature, however, chooses to diminish specific conflicts or nations with an eye toward not bombarding the unfamiliar reader with too much information, already assuming the representative status of each experience.

While many omissions characterize the spectacular Chibok girls narrative, with much that we do not yet understand, an earlier abduction—that of the Aboke girls in Uganda—serves as a guide, given its similar notoriety and reductive political analysis in international media. The earlier incident also reprises the dynamics of abolition to recast humanitarian intervention as the only moral imperative in instructive ways. As one account of this incident affirms, the Aboke girls came to represent "thousands of children who have been kidnapped, dehumanized and forced into a nightmare existence as soldiers and concubine 'wives' for army commanders."[15] By reading two books that take up the same story of thirty girls abducted by Kony's rebel army, the Lord's Resistance Army, in 1996, from St. Mary's College, a boarding school in Aboke, Uganda, I show how these narratives fortify a humanitarian architecture of therapeutic healing from trauma by Western intervention—first through an explicitly evangelical frame and then through a fiction of white feminist self-consolidation.

The events themselves are straightforward. The LRA rebels captured 139 girls from the boarding school, but when an Italian nun followed them, negotiated the release of 109 girls. The remaining 30 girls came to be known as the Aboke girls, part of an international media spectacle, revealing the ways in which replicating the conventions of the slave narrative revives a sentimental substitution of a white female figure for the purported subject of the story—the female child soldier. While *Girl Soldier: A Story of Hope for Northern Uganda's Children* (2007) combines memoir with advocacy, Susan Minot's *Thirty Girls* (2014) transforms journalism to fiction, as both books seek to move their readers to action against the Ugandan warlord's actions. As one endorsement of *Girl Soldier* specifies, the goal of the book is to change the reader: "After reading this book, I will never be the same."[16]

Girl Soldier demonstrates the adaptation of the form and contours of the historical slave narrative with remarkable correspondence. Cowritten by Faith McDonnell, "an American activist and writer with a special concern for the future of the vulnerable Acholi people of northern Uganda," and Grace Akallo, a child soldier conscripted into the Lord's Resistance Army at the age of fifteen, *Girl Soldier* alternates their accounts, with Faith providing larger historical and political context and Grace writing in first person about her abduction and release. Several paratextual materials preface the book—a map of Uganda, a reference list of armies of Uganda, a foreword by one pastor and a preface by another, a long list of acknowledgments, and an introduction by Faith outlining the timeline of the events described. Henry Orombi, archbishop of the Anglican Church of Uganda, writes in the preface that "it is my hope and prayer that as you read *Girl Soldier*, you will see God walking with a young Acholi girl in her captivity" (16). The preface further emphasizes that this is "*a story of hope*" (15) despite the revelation of what the foreword called "the blackened heart of man" (13). When captured from their school, Grace Akallo writes, the girls were "led like slaves, . . . taken toward a life of torment" (105). Faith bolsters the connection, calling on anthropological studies and testimonies collected by Human Rights Watch to underscore that "practices of the nineteenth century slave trade are reinforced by the LRA" (131). The reader is given precise direction in how to read: "If a story about a man defending his family from brutal force does not make us think about our own families—how we would defend them and the cruel things that could happen to our own children—and if we are not able to put ourselves in the place of the story's characters, then it is not a story but merely the careless documentation of an event" (12–13). The book explicitly forwards empathic identification, substitution even, as its desired goal, where the horror of the tale serves the moral growth of the reader.

Grace's narrative provides a first-person account of her immense suffering, emphasizing both psychic and bodily injuries resulting from her abduction from St. Mary's school. Her primary concerns—finding her lost home and reversing the process whereby "seven months after my capture, I am no longer myself"—occupy center stage, while Faith's narrative ranges widely over Uganda's history, politics, and culture. In this way, the division of narrative labor recalls the famous conflict between abolitionists like Garrison (who claimed the right to frame the larger story) and ex-slaves like Douglass (who wanted to speak for himself, not simply retell the tale of woe). Faith occupies much more space, thus indicating how the "white envelope" of the slave narrative can overtake the "black message."[17]

The alternating accounts make for an unsettling reading experience as we shift between the personal and the historical, the wrenching account of Grace's abduction, abuse, hunger, torture, forced labor, and rape and Faith's dispassionate history of Uganda and the rise of Kony (which does not refer to the unfolding story it encloses). Faith addresses the reader directly at one point: "Imagine being abducted in the middle of the night. Imagine a friend or a sister or brother forced to march barefoot.... Imagine that is your daughter or son who must make a decision between killing another child, perhaps one of their own playmates, or being killed" (127). Thus inviting the reader to imagine her own kin in Grace's place, Faith seeks to draw the reader into the ambit of the story, foreshortening the distance through empathy. Grace herself seems to allude to the contradictions of this process when she wonders (echoing her captors) why the Aboke girls captured the imaginations of the world at large, indicating the selectiveness with which trauma registers, or which lives (as Judith Butler notes) are allowed to be grievable: "The commanders didn't understand why people around the world cared for this one group of girls. Some of them perhaps understood that the world looked at us and saw all the rest of the abducted children as well. People could not understand the thousands of missing children. It was too much to comprehend. But they could identify with thirty schoolgirls" (139).[18]

The question of scale and proximity in human rights fiction raises important questions about how and why we read, and how spectacularly violent events are rendered familiar or mundane in literary accounts. Habila, for instance, at the end of his short book on the Chibok girls, realizes the simple truth—the kidnapped victims were "ordinary girls," and many Boko Haram members were just "ordinary boys" not "two-headed monsters."[19] As Kamari Maxine Clarke has shown, the construction of the "African warlord" is a discursive act, involving the all-too-easy appeal to spectacles of the suffering victim.[20] The foreword of *Girl Soldier* juxtaposes the sentimental ("I stood outside and cried") to the gothic ("rows and rows of human skulls lined the back walls of the church)" (11). As the narrative unfolds, however, the sentimental frame prevails, not only universalizing the specific history, but establishing the necessity of an affective identification with a perfectly innocent victim as the template for social justice. The abolitionist emphasis on the moral character, purity, and vulnerability of the victim recurs, as the subject of the tale mirrors not complicity on the part of the reader but charity.

Such a formal emphasis reinforces the explicitly Christian message sounded throughout, as the names Grace and Faith take on clear symbolic weight. The foreword explains that "these are the stories that remind us why Jesus hung on a cross" (14). For Faith, an evangelical activist, the entire story of Uganda's history must be read through religious conflict—"a struggle between Christianity, Islam and spiritism" (37). Linking dictator Idi Amin and warlord Joseph Kony through their "shared ties to Islamic regimes" (54), Faith emphasizes the concerns of a militaristic Christianity, while Grace explains her escape solely as a product of God's mercy and his ability to beget miracles. Grace walks into a river: "I thought I would drown, but with gentle hands my God lifted my feet and put them on the growing grass in the water. I slowly crossed the river. It was a miracle, but there was no time to think about that. My friends with great surprise followed my way. One by one they crossed the river" (162). Such miraculous moments recur in the narrative of escape—as the girls throw away their guns and seek refuge, speaking in English to the people they meet since English was forbidden among the rebels, Grace repeats, "This is God, not me" (176).

Grace's final message in the United States echoes many of the strains of Faith's account—insisting that the Acholi "have a history of Christian faith, although it has gotten all mixed up with tribal religions" and lamenting the absent fathers who "go off and don't return" (195). She fully assumes her role as translator, intermediary of her people, speaking of "the Acholi" with ethnographic authority, as well as beyond that for all children in war: "I am speaking not just of the children in northern Uganda but all the little ones who are caught in the midst of war" (195). She also instructs the reader, "To those who read this book, I want you to pray for the children" (195). In contrast to many such works of advocacy that come with a list of humanitarian organizations to support, campaigns to publicize or donate to, or other forms of civil involvement, the primary task enjoined to the reader is to pray. But Faith is more specific—after praising the efforts of Invisible Children and various Christian activist groups and churches—she explains that "not all of the problems of northern Uganda are political" and declares that the "wounds of recent history" can be healed only by God (223). Readers are asked to donate money to Ugandan churches or World Vision International or to go to Uganda as a short-term missionary. Such efforts, the book promises, will "rewrite the history of northern Uganda" (225).

Where *Girl Soldier* marries sentiment to piety, Susan Minot's *Thirty Girls* scripts the same story of the Aboke girls in a decidedly feminist register. The novel also features alternating narration, juxtaposing the story of Esther Akello, one of the thirty abducted girls, with that of a blond American woman's travel to Uganda to pen a story about the girls. Jane, the journalist, offers an account similar to Minot's nonfictional account: both hear about the LRA and the abduction at a fancy dinner party and decide that "something must be done about this."[21] Although Jane has some anxieties about her abilities ("she had no real credentials as a journalist"; 57), the novel apportions far more space to her journey than to Esther's gruesome story of sexual slavery. Esther speaks from a rehabilitation center from the beginning of the novel, struggling to deal with what she did and what was done to her, unable to demobilize and resume civilian life. The novel's narrative choice of alternating first, second, and third person as well as its reliance on the hackneyed plot of the white savior helping the victim of trauma ensure that Esther's story is the sideshow to Jane's explorations of her own identity and longings.

Minot's curious choice to not only juxtapose these two voices but also apportion far more space and lyric intensity to Jane's account has two effects: it prompts the inevitable but difficult-to-answer question of how to value the two experiences together and, as I show below, ultimately displaces Esther's story in favor of a generalized notion of loss. *Thirty Girls* begins with a third-person account of the abduction of the girls from St. Mary's College, most of which is focalized through the experiences of the Italian nun. The novel subsequently alternates Esther's first-person account of her memories of abduction and cruelty by Kony and the LRA rebels to Jane's third-person sojourn in Africa. That the vast differences in station and experience between a young girl forced into sex slavery and war and the adventures of a privileged white woman offer an uneasy fit is not in question. Minot even underscores the differences by writing the sections in distinct narrative styles: Esther's narrative stance is spare, declarative, and blunt, while Jane's prose tends toward exploratory, lush, navel-gazing. Because Esther's trauma is narrated in linear, instrumental prose, no real interiority engages the reader. Her prose is straightforward—there is no "Rotten English" here, no traumatic repetition or hesitation. Given to extensive ruminations about her feelings, Jane fits the characters who people Minot's earlier works, mostly explorations of sexuality and desire among wealthy white women. Despite a couple of moments that recognize the absurdity of the juxtaposition—Jane realizes that "she was reading about hostages and terrorists while wondering like an idiot if a boy she liked liked her back" (100)—the novel takes every turn of her emotions so sincerely that an immanent critique does not emerge. In fact, the novel seems to suggest that Jane's earnest desire "to speak for the children" (168) is blocking her more important task—learning about herself. One of her companions even tells her "you just want to be free" (222) seemingly oblivious to the grotesque resonance of freedom in this context. Reviewers have followed this tack, seeing Jane as the real fugitive: "She is a fugitive from countless failed loves, a divorcee whose drugged-out ex-husband died of an overdose some years ago."[22] Another reviewer concludes that Minot shows her readers that "we are all at risk," while still another argues that "she too is a kind of victim in her brutal story."[23]

Thirty Girls therefore is best read as a manual for how a woman like Jane can process the trauma of the African girl child soldier and still go on with her life, without assuming that hers are trivial concerns alone. To do so, Minot has to negotiate some clever narrative exchanges, where the apparent subject of the story has to fade away and be placed into a standard plot of trauma and therapy while Jane can emerge in her full complex humanity as a character worth identifying with. Stealing the sympathy from the slave, so to speak, the humanitarian rescuer assumes the mantle of speaking for the victim and, in doing so, asserts her right to the space she occupies in the world.

When Jane and Esther meet (a scene narrated toward the novel's close), it becomes clear that Jane stands in for the reader of the novel. Esther has been reluctant to follow the script of telling her story on demand, thinking, "Why say these things when I want to forget them?"

(248). But Jane convinces her to speak: "The sisters at St. Mary's are also white-skinned, and seeing her made me think of them" (248). Esther concludes that Jane is no stranger and so begins, "They came for us in the night" (249). Just as Francis Bok in the previous chapter reflexively repeated the moment of storytelling, Esther clarifies that the words she has given us so far are exactly the same that Jane enables her to utter: "And I told her all these things I have told to you" (249), thus underscoring that Jane and the reader can substitute for one another. Even at this climactic moment, Minot alternates third and first person, showing us Esther through Jane's eyes to generate a distancing effect. The brief meeting proves to be a breakthrough for Esther: "The thought I was brave was a new thought. . . . She comforted me with her arm. I had never touched against a white person thus way. We remained there, soon we were talking to one another" (251). Jane's whiteness as currency proves key to Esther's rehabilitation. Jane reaches her own epiphany, crossing the line of the "journalistic code [barring] involvement": "She no longer was the neutral recorder. Listening to Esther had taken her past that" (251). Jane's real journey is her education in sympathy. She has to learn to jettison her journalistic pursuit of objectivity and allow herself to feel for the subject of her story.

This sentimental substitution is most clearly visible in a series of brief second-person interludes, each titled "The You File." This voice addresses the reader directly without any markers of who speaks. While it first seems that Esther is probing her experience—"You turn new in a new place. Where are you being taken?" (81)—it gradually becomes clear that these interludes fuse Esther and Jane's experiences into a single voice. But if this is a chorus, it speaks of a shared female consciousness that is impossible to find in the stark divides of the two lives, despite the novel's insistence on their commonality. How can an encounter with graphic abuse allow a privileged American journalist to claim the right to "feel in pieces" while "you are with strangers, in a foreign place, all far from home" (83, 81)? In an interview, Minot explains the thinking behind the choice: "I started to think of these sections in part as being the interior place where the characters of Jane and Esther perhaps overlap. Nearly all the text could be spoken from the point of view of either. Nearly all, for that matter, could be questions (though this recognition came after) that the reader might possibly ask of herself."[24] In this way, Minot displaces

Esther while locating Jane center stage as the true stranger to herself, never at home, troubled by memories of love, loss, and heartbreak, while the reader is invited in classic sentimental fashion to do the same. One reviewer responds right on cue: "It isn't often a novel brings me to tears, but this one did more than once."[25]

Perhaps this explains why *Thirty Girls* avoids any detailed historical contextualization or acknowledgment of political causes of the conflicts that bred the LRA. Kony himself emerges as a caricature, obsessed with women with "two vaginas" (173) who are "the portals of the devil" (175). The gothic aspects of the story—the rape of the abducted girls, their forcible killing of another child, ongoing hunger and physical pain— receive far less narrative space than Jane's trite story. Minot robs Esther of the ability to fashion a self, to find a way to live with the memory of trauma, to tell the whole story, written by herself. Minot has confessed that she herself is afflicted by "*mal d'afrique.*"[26] This is why Jane's story— one we have heard countless times—allows the reader to grant herself the sentimental satisfaction of tears, the assurance that her empathy is all that's needed to administer rescue, and to go on with her mundane life because loss is a shared human condition.

Africanizing the Child Soldier

While these narratives gesture to the horror but subordinate it within a frame of sentimental recovery, it is the fictions of the boy soldier that truly collide such approaches with the gothic aspects of the child at war. Boy soldier fictions are caught within two dominant frameworks—the human rights insistence on an innocent child and the pervasive Africanizing of the child soldier through recourse to a familiar gothic narrative about the heart of African darkness.[27] These two frames tangle in Beah's *A Long Way Gone* and Iweala's *Beasts of No Nation*, two best sellers that are short, accessible, and marketed by major publishing houses. Before turning to these celebrated works, it is worth recalling that even though the novel and the memoir brought the figure of the child soldier center stage as a distinct genre of modern life, developments in human rights legislations paved the way for such cultural representations. The International Labor Organization's Convention on the Worst Forms of Child Labor declared the recruitment of anyone under the age of eighteen a "form of slavery" or a practice "similar to slavery" in 1999. Similar legislations clarify that no movement across international borders is necessary for such classification. International treaties developed to protect children's rights—the Convention on the Rights of the Child and the Optional Protocol to the Convention on the Rights of the Child on the Involvement of Children in Armed Conflict—clearly define a child as anyone under the age of eighteen, prompting tricky questions in relation to criminal liability, a fact that has complicated the working of the International Criminal Court since its establishment in 2002.[28] Human rights groups emphasize coercion and abuse, frequently depicting child soldiers "as slaves or as commodities or even robots" (in David Rosen's words), refusing to admit nuance in questions of agency or choice.[29] The spectacular violence of rape, torture, and murder takes precedence over the daily labor of cooking, cleaning, or carrying provisions that often characterizes the work of the child in war. The slow violence of poverty and ecological disaster is often occluded as well, and the increasing militarization of Africa emerges as incidental rather than central to the accelerating use of children in various conflicts over the last thirty years. Reading across anthropological and historical accounts of child soldiers, Rosen finds that the categories of victims or sex slaves simply do not do justice to the complicated nature of children's participation in war—which varies in terms of identity, morality, resistance, agency, and mentorship, indicating a fluidity of roles rather than a flat narrative of persecution and rescue. Indeed, anthropologists caution against assuming the existence of a universal child.

Since genre categories frequently serve to universalize a particular experience, making it available to a diverse group of readers trained to recognize certain conventions and styles, charting the use of sentimental and gothic forms helps explain the prominence of child soldier fictions in the twenty-first century. But the inclusion of photographs of the authors (recalling the portrait of the slave narrator), along with maps of the countries, a timeline of events, and other details also underlines how readers are often encouraged to see these narratives as history. Meanwhile, their relationship to the histories they purportedly document remains vexed. Iweala, for instance, wrote *Beasts of No Nation* for his senior thesis in creative writing at Harvard. He explains the seed of the novel in a *Newsweek* article on child soldiers, highlighting the photograph of the unnamed child—"a small brown-skinned boy with skinny arms, a large head, and eyes that simultaneously accused the world of neglect and begged for forgiveness."[30] Rather than centering on Nigeria alone (the home of his immigrant parents), he relies on accounts of former child soldiers from Sierra Leone, Uganda, Cambodia, Colombia, and Yugoslavia to "tell a more universal story" (11). Reading about child soldiers allows him to differentiate bourgeois comforts in the West from spectacular suffering in the Third World, as he confesses how he regrets thinking he had suffered because of a tough workout from the track coach. Thus implementing a scaffolding of identification, forgiveness, and rehabilitation, he blurs the distance between fiction, memoir, advocacy, and journalism, part of a larger humanitarian reframing of the child as the archetypal subject of rescue and intervention.

Iweala insists that the "characters in *Beasts of No Nation* are not monsters. They are not psychopaths—at the very least not before war finds them" (9). In fact, he admits that his early efforts to write fiction were disastrous precisely because they were too gothic: "My young protagonist laughed maniacally; he showed no emotion except anger and bloodlust" (10). Concluding that his novel should be something other than "a Hollywood horror movie" (10), Iweala nevertheless calls on stock tropes of monstrosity and terror, referring to the fearsome Commandant as both demon and rapist.[31] The first-person narrator, Agu, a child captured and conscripted by a rebel army, describes his commander with a mixture of horror and fascination: "They are calling him the man who is driving the enemy to madness" and "he is seeing things that are making even the Devil fall to his knee and be begging for mercy. He is always saying that he eating people" (81). When raped by the Commandant, Agu also worries about his own feminization, noting both the Commandant's efforts at seduction ("He likes to be whispering to me as if I am woman"; 87) and the subsequent pain this occasions ("My tears begin to running down my face"; 89).

The choice of continuous present-tense narration limits any historical or political context for the conflict, making Agu a universal figure of violation. Such comic-book words as "KPAWA," "WHOOSH," "AYEEEIII," "PAH PAH PAH," and "GBWEM" punctuate the narration (134, 93, 50, 68, 66). Because the novel never interrupts the child's perspective, no larger analysis of the causes or major actors of the conflict emerges, as we hear sporadically about the enemy coming, people fleeing the war, a Commandant, a Luftenant, a Rambo, and finally Agu getting disgusted by the killing and laying his gun down. Such narrative choices construct the war experience as an ontological one, rather than as historical event: Agu notes, "Time is passing. Time is not passing. Day is changing to night. Night is changing to day" (52). The narrator's notion of time similarly alternates between the simplistic "before the war" (28) and the nightmarish present. Agu confesses his own inadequacy to comprehend the world around him: "How can I know what is happening? It is like one day everything is somehow okay even if we are fighting war, but the next day we are killing killing and looting from everybody. How can I know what is happening to me?" (52).

The happy childhood with loving parents, a traumatic abduction, a series of renamings, and several attempts to connect with his lost family relate the novel's structure to the slave narrative. Agu also explicitly references the state of being a slave when he likens himself to a "slave tree because I can never be doing what I want." He had earlier named a small tree with a vine that strangles it "the slave tree because they are slave to the vine that is using them to climb up to the sun" (41–42). But more than this explicit reference, it is the reference to reading and the novel's sentimental ending that sustains the connection to the earlier genre. To prove that he is not a "bad boy," Agu emphasizes his proficiency as a reader: "I am liking to read so much that my mother is calling me professor" (24). His schoolteacher father and scenes of his mother reading the Bible to him form a big part of his memories before the war. At the end of the novel, Agu enters a rehabilitation program, with a priest who talks of "Confession and Forgiveness and Resurrection" and Amy, "a white woman from America" (139–140), who ensure that his prewar reading can resume: "They are giving me all of the book I can be wanting to read because I am telling Amy that my father is schoolteacher and that before the war I am always reading whatever I can" (139). The novel thus ends with a classic sentimental tableau. Amy repeatedly asks Agu to speak, to feel, to consent to her help: "She is always looking at me like looking at me is going to be helping me. She is telling me to speak speak speak and thinking that my not speaking is because I am like baby. . . .

She is always saying to me, tell me what you are feeling" (140). Once Agu has presumably done so, the desired reaction ensues: "She is just looking at me and I am seeing water in her eye" (141).

That the same scene of rehabilitation through a friendly female social worker recurs almost exactly in Beah's *A Long Way Gone* indicates the hardening of the recovery narrative into a formula. In fact, the formulaic nature of *A Long Way Gone* has long aroused suspicion, as investigative journalists attempt to corroborate the details of the events described, but come across various inaccuracies and impossibilities. Not only have they imputed accusations of fraud or faulty memory, they point out the unlikeliness of all the events that befall Beah happening to a single child soldier.[32] Because Beah's account fits the model of capture, conscription, terror, escape, and rehabilitation so neatly, it indicates the composite nature of his narrative, functioning as exception and exemplar alike.

Signaling its goals of sentimental education, Beah opens with a scene in a New York City classroom, where his high school friends ask for the "full story of [his] life" (3). The memoir proper begins not with this full story but with an acknowledgment of how existing stories have already overwritten any attempt to represent: "There were all kinds of stories told about the war that made it sound as if it was happening in a faraway and different land" (5). People in his town even question the tales of the refugees fleeing the war because they didn't match prior accounts on the BBC news or in such films as *Rambo: First Blood* (1982). Just like Eggers in *What Is the What*, Beah thus offers a humanist tale of rescue and recovery structured by self-constitution through narrative encircled by metafictional comments on storytelling and self-fashioning. This self-reflexivity itself has become a trope in child soldier fictions, along with a sophisticated discourse on memory and trauma, and an insistence—almost an incantation—that the child is not to blame for his actions.[33]

Beah has to go through the memories of his days in war ("My squad was my family, my gun was my provider and protector, and my rule was to kill or be killed"; 126) and learn that "none of these things are your fault" (165). His inability to adjust to the rehabilitation program forms the bulk of the memoir, reading almost as a manual for stages of recovery. Beah writes, for instance, "I would try desperately to think about my childhood, but I couldn't. The war memories had formed a barrier that I had to break in order to think about any moment in my life before the war" (149). His breakthrough occurs through the intervention of a nurse named Esther, who succeeds in getting him to tell his story by gifting him a Walkman. Repeating the sentimental tropes visible in the narratives discussed above, Beah writes, "When I finished telling Esther the story, she had tears in her eyes and she couldn't decide whether to rub my head or hug me. In the end she did neither, but said, 'None of what happened was your fault. You were just a little boy, and anytime you want to tell me anything, I am here to listen'" (159–160). In this way, using his love of rap and reggae music as well as his dramatic facility for Shakespeare monologues, Beah's remaking through culture commences and he becomes an effective spokesman for the rehabilitation of child soldiers, pointing to himself as an example.[34]

Even the ending of his journey—finding a new family to replace his lost one, as he's adopted by a white American storyteller named Laura Simms—affirms the power of storytelling in an echo of abolitionism's emphasis on reading and education. Because Laura is familiar with the stories Beah heard in his childhood in Sierra Leone, she bridges the transition between the two worlds—New York and Sierra Leone, former child soldier and exemplary human rights activist. Beah notes his "awe of the fact that a white woman from across the Atlantic Ocean, who had never been to my country, knew stories so specific to my tribe and upbringing. When she became my mother years later, she and I would always talk about whether it was destined or coincidental that I came from a very storytelling-oriented culture to live in New York with a mother who is a storyteller" (197). The violation Beah experiences and the tortures he commits as a soldier hence emerge carefully packaged within a narrative of recovery and rehabilitation. Since reading and storytelling form such a crucial part of the means of Beah's survival, the book itself becomes a key resource in his search for freedom, not simply the evidence of his redemption, in other words, but its instrument.

In her thoughtful appraisal of the African war novel since the 1960s, Eleni Coundouriotis persuasively shows how child soldier fictions exhibit a form of "arrested dehistoricization" in contrast to war novels from the colonial and postcolonial era that were written in the context of movements for liberation rather than for a Western audience.[35] She argues that a generalized human rights frame often relies on "the self-help model of the recovery narrative" where the child soldier's autobiography becomes the proof of victimhood, abuse, or addiction, and the emphasis is largely on how the child was forced to join the army and commit actions for which he does not bear responsibility. She rightly notes that "an abstracted figure of the child soldier cast against a background of the 'dark continent' revisited has been commodified as the new authenticity out of Africa."[36]

In thinking of the gothic valence of the child soldier novel, accordingly, it is necessary to specify its relation to a long history of imperial gothic in representations of Africa. In the contemporary era, the afterlife of imperial gothic in film, fiction, and humanitarian discourse coalesces in the figure of the child as monster, directly challenging the human rights legal consensus about the fundamental innocence of the child soldier, likewise reviving a larger condemnation of African polity and sovereignty. "African Gothic," a 2007 essay by Christopher Hitchens, perfectly encapsulates this tendency. In a world full of "grim" events, African traumas are especially "weird and neolithic," Hitchens argues, reasoning that "General Idi Amin did keep human heads in his freezer. Samuel Doe of Liberia was videotaped having his ears cut off by the transition team of the incoming administration. Murders in Rwanda and Somalia were, perhaps, not morally different from or worse than murders in Bosnia or Ulster but seemed somehow more primitive, carried out as they were with clubs and axes, or with bare hands and by dancing, gibbering crowds." In other words, in Africa, Hitchens declares, "Human life is at its nastiest, most brutish, and shortest." He insists, moreover, on divorcing the squalor from colonialism or ongoing underdevelopment. He believes that in Zaire "it was worse than before colonialism began at all." While stock stereotypes punctuate the narrative—with regular reference to prior accounts by Joseph Conrad, Evelyn Waugh, and V. S. Naipaul—Hitchens also connects the misery he documents to slavery, but not as a cause of the problem. Rather, Hitchens argues that ongoing slavery in parts of Africa proves that European colonialism was not to blame. It should also serve as evidence of the failure of black nationalist languages of empowerment: "Yes, we know that colonialism was devastating and disruptive. Yes, we know that the political borders of Africa make no sense and were drawn without regard to human reality. Yes, no doubt the international-trade deck is stacked against African products. But does this explain why there is still slavery in Mauritania and southern Sudan (often but not always Islamic enslavement of Christians, and what do Mr. Farrakhan's Black Muslims have to say about that)?"[37] Connecting the new century's renewed anti-Muslim sentiment with the militarization of the African continent, the essay displays the poorly understood histories of slavery and colonialism, underlining how recourse to the racialized genre of the gothic can replicate colonial political lexicons of unending African failure.

American Gothic

Exploring the congruence of such stock frames of African gothic with long-standing discussions of the uses of gothic in American literature and culture, particularly in relation to representations of slavery, helps trace the ways in which the distinct histories conveyed by these traditions collide in the child soldier genre. Leslie Fiedler's landmark work of literary criticism, *Love and Death in the American Novel*, prioritizes the gothic form as the quintessence of the American literary imagination, claiming that "of all the fiction of the West, our own is most deeply influenced by the gothic, is almost essentially a gothic one."[38] Investigating the roots of the appeal of the tale of terror, he shows how "in our most enduring books, the cheapjack machinery of the gothic novel is called on to represent the hidden blackness of the human soul and human society."[39] Fiedler specifically links the prevalence of the gothic to a special guilt tied to the American experience of genocide and slavery: "the slaughter of the Indians, who would not yield their lands to the carriers of utopia, and the abominations of the slave trade, in which the black man, rum, and money were inextricably entwined in a knot of guilt."[40]

While traditional forms of gothic are associated with Horace Walpole, Mary Shelley, Ann Radcliffe, and Bram Stoker, scholars of American gothic have proven how central it was to notions of citizenship, race, and gender in the antebellum era.[41] That the genre entangles with racial politics is further complemented by the fact that childhood itself was also racialized. In *Racial Innocence*, Robin Bernstein shows how the idea of "childhood innocence" became "a crucial but naturalized element of contests over race and rights" as mid-nineteenth-century American sentimentalism transformed childhood not just into "a symbol of innocence but as its embodiment." Such innocent childhood was raced white, while the black child was transformed into the racist image of the "pickaninny"—effectively a redefinition as a "nonchild." In response, such African American activists as Douglass had to insist that "SLAVE-children *are* children," reclaiming basic norms of humanity.[42]

As Teresa Goddu explains, "The structural affinity between the discourse of slavery and the conventions of the Gothic" means that a fertile cross-connection and borrowing occurred across famous Gothic texts (including *Frankenstein*, *The Monk*, and *Jane Eyre*) and representations of slavery. The antislavery movement especially drew on the Gothic to present slavery as a "diabolical system of merciless horrors and the slaveholder as a relentless demon or a monster in human shape."[43] Words like "tyrant," "devil," "monster," and "demon," references to the Inquisition and to an earthly hell or a plunging abyss, and numerous scenes of whipping and other forms of torture punctuate nearly all slave narratives, but are especially resonant in those by women. Harriet Jacobs, for instance, makes extensive use of literary gothic for *Incidents in the Life of a Slave Girl*, while Hannah Crafts writes her narrative as a clearly identifiable gothic romance.[44] For some critics, this association continues well into the modern African American literary tradition, with Pauline Hopkins, Richard Wright, Gloria Naylor, and, above all, Toni Morrison transforming the rhetorical modes of the American gothic and the slave narrative alike.[45]

Such use of the gothic came with certain risk as well as possibility. As Goddu explains, while writing slavery as a gothic romance allowed white writers to dematerialize the specific history and politics of the institution, it also offered black writers a way to "haunt back" despite the fear that drawing on these conventions would make slavery's horrors seem like a story or fable. But the racialized nature of the Gothic tradition posed further challenges for slave narrators: as Goddu puts it, "How could they claim their humanity through a genre that played into their cultures' racial anxieties and fears?"[46] The trick then lies in getting the northern reader to identify with the suffering of the slave, and thus to reject the power of the racialized association of darkness with evil. Goddu explains that the gothic functions as a kind of white envelope that encases the slave narrative. Expanding the association, Laura Doyle persuasively argues for a long history of the African-Atlantic gothic in the race plot of Atlantic modernity, where slave narrators have to encounter the "paradox of writing an African-Atlantic gothic text: its already-framed arrival as its own story." For a writer like Harriet Jacobs, this means she has to "turn inside out the layers of Atlantic liberty narratives and take back the already-appropriated freedom story."[47]

The American gothic stages how sentiment and gothic played out in nineteenth-century US culture as exchanges. The question of sympathy or identification is central to these discussions of genre since sentimentalism was tied to the project of fashioning readers whose ability to empathize with suffering reaffirmed their exemplary humanity. Where the previous chapter of *Runaway Genres* showed how the modern slave narrative revives these conditions of the black subject and the white abolitionist savior, this chapter outlines a parallel trajectory where the horror of the child soldier narrative repels the reader and forgoes the simple call to action. A novel like *Thirty Girls* subordinates the gothic by persistent return to the sentimental. Reading the African child soldier novel within and against the history of the gothic genre reveals the cultural logic of slavery's revival across the globe, calling attention to the still-unfolding legacy of the original sin of slavery in dialogue with repressed postcolonial nightmares.

Gothic fictions are usually characterized by secrets from the past that haunt an uncertain present, as antiquated or alien spaces like abbeys, prisons, crypts, or decaying urban infrastructures like theaters and laboratories serve as the repository for repressed yearnings and fears. Child soldier fictions offer not so much ruined mansions or eerie castles but entire national or regional landscapes ravaged by war. The nation becomes the haunted house where the complete space of the postcolony is coded as gothic. Monstrous adults beget equally monstrous children, as family structures transform into the savage order of the rebel army. Such fictions also continue the genre's traditional disturbing of the order of things where the conjunction of that which is decreed to be separate—rational-supernatural, life-death, body-spirit, dream-reality—provides the occasion for the narrated crisis. Cannibalism, amputation of limbs, and recurring scenes of rape augment the unrelenting gloom of the dystopian postcolony. The dream of national liberation has become the postcolonial nightmare from which no one can awaken. The otherwise robust scholarly discourse on the subject has tended to elide the gothic contours of the child soldier genre.[48] That the child is also available for education and induction into societal norms, thus indexing larger national potential for rift and healing, traditionally makes the bildungsroman the classic genre for the experience of coming of age. Needless to say, the figure of the child in African literature and society follows its own distinct trajectory—often morphing from colonial accounts of Africa as a child needing saving to the self-governing child as the future of a new nation. When this promise of futurity is betrayed (as Lee Edelman and Elizabeth Stockton show in the US context), the child soldier appears as the emblem of the failure of the project of decolonization and postcolonial self-governance.[49]

Because gothic fictions so often reveal the present as structured by the relics of the past that refuse to die, their temporal structure immediately poses the question of the relation between history and the present. The child soldier gothic novel reroutes this temporal relation spatially—detouring through the US past of slavery and awakening the specter of the slave in order to imagine a global future for the present-day United States and Africa. Best-selling child soldier fictions turn to the conventions of the ghost or the demon, the frame of innocent victim being hunted by an evil monster and seeking to escape in order to detour a specific history and to universalize into a kind of global gothic. At its most effective, however, the child soldier genre registers the appeal of the sentimental frame, but infuses it with the gothic to refuse readerly satisfaction or catharsis. To do so, writers call on what Morrison has called the unspeakability of the past, to delve deeper into expunged, disremembered histories.

My goal in highlighting the gothic here is not to proliferate literary taxonomy but to understand how the exploration of form symbolized by the exchanges between sentimentalism and the gothic in child soldier fictions codes racial anxieties that are as much about African futurity as they are about US globalism. The question of genre criticism's relation to history can, of course, be vexed. Philip Holden, for instance, cautions that notions of the postcolonial gothic as analytical category can become hypostatized, embedding binaries of colonialism-nationalism or tradition-modernity that are no longer accurate, arguing for the need for historicized analyses of gothic fictions.[50] When child soldier fictions don't simply converge with conventional gothic elements but draw attention to their conditions of enunciation, circulation, and reception, they tap into the power of the genre to perturb dominant accounts of past, present, and future.

The gothic is generally thought of as a genre constituted by the interruption of linear narrative—gothic fictions frequently rely on letters, dreams, and other fragments—to interrupt sequence and genealogy. Eve Sedgwick has argued for the "structural significance" of "the difficulty the story has in getting itself told" in gothic fiction, as multiple narrators, stories within stories, notions of the unspeakable, mirror the "doubleness where singleness should be" of the individual self.[51] In their emphasis on the breaking of narrative—where the story cannot get out—child soldier fictions signal their clear departure from the connection between freedom and literacy established by the historical slave narrative and revived in the modern one. Ken Saro-Wiwa's *Sozaboy* (1985), the father of the African child soldier genre, is unthinkable without its subtitle—*A Novel in Rotten English*. This tendency of the gothic toward opacity and occlusion—where the story cannot get out, it cannot be told or heard—recalls canonical debates in postcolonial theory that emphasize opacity as a reading practice as well as a necessary concept for registering the consciousness of the subaltern. Iweala's invention of a language appropriate to the unspeakable nature of the boy soldier's experience signals such a quandary. As I discuss next, Abani's portrait of a child who cannot speak literalizes the subaltern's silence, but also insists that the story must be told, recalling Franco Moretti's words about the genre of the gothic: "The literature of terror is born precisely out of the terror of a split society, and out of the desire to heal it."[52] The gothic, therefore, is especially available for an engagement with the meaning of war in our own time, not just surfacing repressed histories of the postcolony, but triangulating through formal exchanges the history of American slavery as well.

What You Hear Is Not My Voice

Abani's 2007 novella *Song for Night* fully departs from the sentimental script, refusing to demand empathy from the reader or to prove the humanity of its child-soldier protagonist. Confounding rather than educating the reader, Abani provides no clear moral tutelage, lingering instead in the lyrically rendered interiority of a boy forced into war. In doing so, similar to what we saw in chapter 1 with *Becoming Abigail*, Abani suspends the questions of agency, choice, and blame that have long dominated the human rights conversation about child soldiers, imagining the boy's consciousness outside of such logic, emphasizing his inner monologue in place of questions of blame.

Saro-Wiwa's *Sozaboy* famously invented "Rotten English" as the appropriate idiom of his child soldier—"a mixture of Nigerian pidgin English, broken English and occasional flashes of good, even idiomatic English"—that "has the advantage of having no rules and no syntax."[53] Abani continues such a focus on the conditions of enunciation, but eschews pidgin or patois, choosing a densely metaphorical and poetic language. The question of the suitable speech of a child soldier comes up on the very first page of the novel, since My Luck is part of a platoon that uses children as mine sweepers, hence severing their vocal chords so that if one of them was being blown up by a mine, the children "wouldn't scare each other with [their] death screams."[54] My Luck explains that silence has led the children to invent a deeply metaphorical sign language, where "silence is a steady hand, palm flat, facing down" (19) and "truth is forefinger to tongue raised skyward" (79), while "mercy is a palm turning out from the heart" (83). Silence makes the children "better versed at the interior monologue that is really the measure of age, of the passage of time" (21). Departing from the seeming deficiency or immaturity of the language of *Sozaboy*, Abani's My Luck isn't a "genius" as he clarifies, but he certainly possesses a moral complexity gained from his experience. This is not to say that Abani isn't conscious of the questions of translation, access, or appropriation. The first-person narration of My Luck cannot exist in the form printed on the page, in neither language nor tenor nor craft. Abani highlights this at the beginning of the novel with a hailing of the reader: "Of course if you are hearing any of this at all it's because you have gained access to my head. You would also know that my inner-speech is not in English, because there is something atavistic about war that rejects all but the primal language of the genes to comprehend it, so you are in fact hearing my thoughts in Igbo" (21). That this is innately contradictory is likewise swept aside in the next sentence: "But we shan't waste time on trying to figure all that out because as I said before, time here is precious and not to be wasted on peculiarities, only on what is essential" (21).[55]

Abani thus sidesteps the relevance of any number of debates about language that have characterized African literary criticism (from Chinua Achebe's embrace to Ngugi wa Thiong'o's rejection, from Gayatri Chakravorty Spivak's insistence on questioning whether the subaltern can speak to J. M. Coetzee's rewriting of *Robinson Crusoe* with Friday having his tongue cut out).[56] Structured by My Luck's quest to recall the song his grandfather taught him as a way to find some peace and wholeness in the face of war, the novel emphasizes communication and artistic expression. In an interview, Abani dwells on the ethics of his representation:

> I chose to give him no voice because children, and particularly children like him, always have others speaking for them. I chose to take away his voice to force the reader into a visceral journey with him rather than the spectacle of watching his suffering. I chose to take away his voice to force myself to not be able to take credit for speaking for him, or others in such situations. I took away his voice because it has been a practice in certain wars. I took away his voice so the readers couldn't speak for him and thus distance themselves.[57]

In positioning the voicelessness of the protagonist as an ethical gesture of refusal to overtake the subaltern's subjectivity or to impose an easy catharsis, Abani firmly rejects the sentimental substitutions of so much of humanitarian discourse. In his own words, *Song for Night* "questions everything sentimental about war and boy soldiers and the kinds of ways in which we infantilize ourselves and our children so as not to confront our own pain and guilt."[58]

While he rejects sentimentalism, Abani draws on time-tested conventions of the gothic for his twenty-first-century rendition of the harrowing of the hell of war. In doing so, as I suggested in my reading of *Becoming Abigail* in the previous chapter, Abani usefully connects with Toni Morrison's comparable efforts to derive a political critique from an encounter with the spectral. Beloved and My Luck are both children who refuse to stay dead. Victims of the violence of slavery and postcolonial civil wars, they know this violence intimately, as domestic, familial, maternal, held close to the heart. Both apparitions indict the societies they haunt, refusing the satisfaction of easy blame, forgiveness, or healing. Staging ethical quandaries that really have no solution, *Beloved* and *Song for Night* require a less instrumental response from the reader, positing historical traumas as legible not through—as Abani puts it—"grand messianic and operatic gestures" but in a more unsettling, unceasing process.[59]

Song for Night contains the now-familiar scenes of cannibalism, rape, rampant killing, and an evil larger-than-life commander, both perverse and fearsome. But the unrelenting focus on the emotions of the child—lingering in guilt, shame, grief, loneliness, horror, boredom—ensures that questions of ethics are at the forefront rather than mere calls to action. Without foregrounding guilt or innocence, the novel explores the phenomenology of a child soldier outside of mechanistic or legalistic frames of agency, choice, and blame. Both allegorical and dreamlike, the book's lack of specificity is meant to universalize, but unlike *Beasts of No Nation*, it remains far closer to *Sozaboy* in its evocation of the local through the mythic.

The novel's use of gothic conventions comes through clearly in the central frame as My Luck is already dead at the beginning but the reader learns only slowly that he is a ghost who needs to learn of his own death. As the memories of his mother grow stronger, he meets a woman called Grace carrying a coffin. He slowly accepts his place in that coffin, ready to face death. It is at that moment that his mother appears to him, looking young and healthy, and tells him, "You are home." The novel ends with a restoration: "'Mother,' I say, and my voice has returned" (165). This closing of the complicated circuit between the textuality of the novel, the silence of the children, the symbolism of their sign language (which of course we don't see but read), seems in part to suggest two things at once: My Luck is home and his voice can return because he accepts his death and his existence in the afterlife, and My Luck has found his voice in the very novel we have just read (thus making Abani as the author the medium through which his subaltern presence registers).

While imperial gothic often resuscitates racialized tropes of an essential African heart of darkness, Abani's ghost, like Morrison's, reimagines gothic conventions to highlight the underside of the colonial and racial project and its ongoing legacy. The return of the repressed in Morrison's hands, famously, situates slavery at the heart of the American story.[60] The haunted house of gothic convention—the spiteful 124 of

Beloved—itself generates a kind of Rotten English.⁶¹ Stamp Paid listens to "a conflagration of hasty voices—loud, urgent, all speaking at once so he could not make out what they were talking about or to whom. The speech wasn't nonsensical, exactly, nor was it tongues. But something was wrong with the order of the words and he couldn't describe or cipher it to save his life."⁶² He realizes that the voices belong not just to Sethe, Denver, and Beloved but to "the people of the broken necks, of fire-cooked blood and black girls who had lost their ribbons."⁶³ Broadly allegorical of the losses of generations of enslaved Africans, Beloved's monologue—an evocation of the Middle Passage—unsettles time and space: "All of it is now it is always now there will never be a time when I am not crouching and watching others who are crouching too I am always crouching."⁶⁴ For Abani's child soldier, such a continuous present sense also prevails. My Luck notes that "time is standing still—literally" (*Song for Night* 53) seemingly because the watch he inherited from his father, his "most treasured possession," is broken (54). But time also has a hallucinatory quality, because the entire narrative takes place in the afterlife. My Luck notes his "curious experience"—"to be inside your dream and outside it, lucid and yet sleeping deeply"—which mirrors the surreal experience of reading the novel (59).

Gothic interruptions of progressive national narratives insist on ghosts that will not die, that refuse to be exorcised or forgotten, but also prove impossible to live with. Just as Morrison's *Beloved* would neither allow ex-slaves to heal nor forget, to mourn and move on or cling to the lost object in melancholy, child soldier fictions haunt without a clear referent. In doing so, they insist on the claim of ghosts that cannot be exorcised, that can hurt themselves and others, that release a flood of memories, that summon collective memory, that evoke anxieties that can't be contained, in a word, ghosts who can never become immigrants or citizens of a healed nation (unlike Bok, Beah, or Deng).

In contrast to the lyricism of Abani, Ahmadou Kourouma resorts to biting satire to extend his critique of the genre of the child soldier novel. *Allah Is Not Obliged* (2007), first published in France as *Allah n'est pas obligé* in 2000, refuses to subordinate the true horror of the child soldier figure. Birahima, the ten-year-old narrator, finds himself in the middle of Liberia's civil war when he leaves home (a village on the Ivory Coast and Guinea border) with an unscrupulous uncle after the death of his mother. His foul-mouthed and caustic narration provides no education or sentimental satisfaction to the reader, or even a chance to develop empathy, as he describes his life of AK-47s, drugs, frequent deaths and dismemberments. In fact, he constructs the reader as an outsider to the West African landscape he describes, and hence needing constant translation, tutoring, and tirade. The novel satirizes the possibility of understanding the experience of a child soldier by reading the story of his life, disallowing any sentiment to color the depiction of Birahima. The narrator harangues the reader relentlessly, refusing at times to continue with the story, frequently repeating definitions and descriptions of events without any seeming sequence, and withholding explanations, promising only that "it's not an edifying spectacle."[65]

Because Birahima carries with him four dictionaries—the *Larousse*, the *Petit Robert*, the *Glossary of French Lexical Particularities in Black Africa*, and the *Harrap's*—the reader can never ignore the scene of reading, translating, and explaining. Birahima clarifies that he has these dictionaries "so I don't get confused with big words" and because "I want all sorts of different people to read my bullshit: colonial *toubabs*, Black Nigger African Natives and anyone that can understand French" (3).[66] Birahima even introduces himself on the first page of the novel as a "little nigger" precisely because "I can't talk French for shit" and "if you talk bad French, it's called *parler petit nègre*" (1). Immediately linking the question of language to that of power and racialization, the novel continually draws attention to how meaning emerges through translation across languages—French, English, pidgin, and Malinké. But the need for such translation is especially vivid in a time of war, since nothing makes any sense anymore. Cleverly dismantling the pretensions of African leaders like Charles Taylor and Foday Sankoh (Sierra Leone's notorious founder of the Revolutionary United Front), peacekeeping forces like ECOMOG, and humanitarian agencies and NGOs alike, *Allah Is Not Obliged* condemns all ideologies of justice and liberal democracy. Birahima explains that "'humanitarian peacekeeping' is when one country is allowed to send soldiers into another country to kill innocent victims" (126); "'torture' is capital punishment that is enforced by justice" (133); and "women's rights" mean that "everywhere in the world a woman isn't supposed to leave her husband's bed even if that husband curses her and punches her and threatens her" (26).[67]

In a world where "child soldiers are the most famous celebrities of the late twentieth century" (83), such critique can still go unnoticed if the novel is dismissed as a mere horror story (as some reviewers have insisted). To fathom the power of Kourouma's corrosive satire, reckoning with the gothic contours of the fiction is necessary, as the horror is a central part of the novel's nihilistic political vision. For instance, the novel repeats a scene of human skulls mounted on stakes over and again, a clear call back to *Heart of Darkness*, but also a concession to the overdetermined quality of African gothic in contemporary media. Each camp or settlement Birahima arrives in, from Upper Guinea to Liberia to Sierra Leone, presents a similar spectacle. In Sanniquellie, a "border town where they mined gold and diamonds," the "military base had human skulls on stakes all around the boundary. In tribal wars that's really important" (104). A district in Zorzor run by Colonel Papa le Bon "was sort of a fortified camp, a compound with human skulls on stakes all around the border and battle stations protected by sandbags. Every station was manned by four child-soldiers" (63). A camp controlled by rebel warlord Prince Johnson had "human skulls on stakes all around the border of the camp, like all military barracks in the tribal wars" (126). In Sierra Leone, at a former girls boarding school made into a military camp, "the sentry posts were manned day and night by girl-soldiers. The camp was surrounded by human skulls on stakes all round the boundary" (180). Finally, at the Ivoirian border, "the compound there had human skulls on stakes all round the boundary like all the tribal war camps in Liberia and Sierra Leone" (206).

"Tribal wars" thus comes to mean very little, as Kourouma hollows out the phrase through repetition as a ready explanation of every atrocity that occurs. In contrast to the sanctimonious representation of schools in the works focusing on the Aboke girls discussed above, Kourouma allows no reverence or respite. Explaining that "a warlord is a big shot who's killed lots of people and has his own country with villages full of people that he's allowed to kill anytime he likes for no reason" (32), Kourouma represents all the powers fighting in West African wars as using the same irrational logic. Because the novel spends significant time giving sociopolitical details of various historical actors, colonial pasts, postcolonial failures, the interests of organizations like the IMF and American companies in Liberia, and dictators like Gaddafi and Samuel Doe, the picture that emerges is a stark contrast from the universalizing impulses of a writer like Iweala. The novel further refuses to widen the frame to an Atlantic or diasporic one, scrupulously locating the action in West Africa. However hallucinatory Birahima's narrative voice may seem—alternately channeling the racist accent of an apologist for colonialism or the paternalist tones of a human rights reporter for the history lessons—it enjoins upon the reader to learn the history of the places of conflict portrayed, underscoring at the same time the absurdity of wanting to know the truth about African history and current conflicts through a child's eyes. The novel's focus on dictionaries—as emblems of Western authority and knowledge—keeps colonial history in view. *Allah Is Not Obliged* thus highlights how deeply child soldier fictions have become a genre that serves up African gothic, deploying a self-reflexive tone to disallow the reader an escape route from the nightmare.

In foregrounding the conditions of enunciation and reception, Kourouma affirms the premise of Saro-Wiwa's *Sozaboy*—the need for "Rotten English" to tell the story of violated humanity. As Saro-Wiwa explains in a prefatory note, Rotten English "thrives on lawlessness, and is part of the dislocated and discordant society in which Sozaboy must live, move, and have not his being."[68] Language and form both have to stoop and curve to represent the horror of the experience of the child soldier. The sheer repetitiveness and circularity of the story further underscore the erosion of any stable narrative possibilities or social order, as Birahima loops back to ever-receding origins with the incantation: "let's start at the start" (157). The novel thus ends where it begins: the telling of the story with the help of the four dictionaries. Numerous initiation scenes of various children chronicle the breaking apart of ritualistic coming-of-age ceremonies that cannot compete with the brutal and accelerated coming of age in war. Birahima punctuates the novel with several funeral orations for each deceased child soldier, filling in the background of how each child came to become a soldier, embodying a profane mourning practice, that is as much mockery as tribute to the life lost. Exaggerating the chaos, meaningless violence, and collusion of foreign powers with homegrown dictators to overwhelming effect, the novel's grotesque sketches include genocidal peacekeeping forces and cannibal rebel leaders. No wonder that Aminatta Forna terms the novel "an African *Lord of the Flies*."[69] Repelling any effort to see the child as an object of pity or emblem of innocence, Kourouma voices the tragedy of war louder than any sentimental approach, refusing catharsis or redemption. Birahima tells us only at the novel's close: "The full, final, and completely complete title of my bullshit story is: *Allah is not obliged to be fair about all the things he does here on earth*" (215).

Such a nihilistic stance should not belie the achievement of the novel—a refusal to accept the compromised terms of much humanitarian discourse: to prove the claim of the victim to the status of human.[70] Rather than dismissing the novel as mere horror story, more challenging is reckoning with its suggestion that grotesquely sensationalized, spectacular, and hyperbolic violence might in fact be the appropriate mode of representation for children in war. Where a writer like Minot soothes, Kourouma corrodes. Where Abani insists on opacity, Kourouma favors excess. Abani's reconstruction of the interiority of violated innocence refuses to sensationalize. Kourouma takes the opposite approach, but achieves a similar effect in destabilizing hegemonic human rights frames that wish to tame the horror of the child-soldier, reverting to simpler, more digestible frames of rescue and therapy.

Similar jagged edges become visible in Beah's recent decision to turn away from memoir to fiction, as his 2014 novel *Radiance of Tomorrow* features a far less formulaic story of humanist reconstruction of a lost childhood.[71] *Radiance* focuses on the contradictory effects of transnational capital in Sierra Leone today, moving away from the abolitionist framework to feature different kinds of returns to the homeland. Eschewing linearity as well, *Radiance* upsets the corollary immigrant plot of the previous work, charting other itineraries of past, present, and future. Such works promise a more supple understanding of the landscape of war in the present moment, rather than reviving the starker outlines of past geopolitical divides. Several child soldier novels extend similar hints, asking for more varied interpretive itineraries, drawing more elliptical links across the United States, Europe, and Africa, without replicating the binaries of the triangular trade. In Bernard Ashley's *Little Soldier* (1999) for example, when the former child soldier, Kaninda, is being rehabilitated and introduced to his adoptive family, Ashley writes that "Kaninda stood as still as a slave being inspected for use in the home."[72] Similarly, Beah and his group of demobilized boy soldiers, when let go by their commanders and released to the NGOs for rehabilitation, wonder whether "the foreigners gave our commanders money in exchange for us" (*Long Way Gone*, 133). Such moments insinuate that the conversion of a human being into property appears not just in the moment of abduction or conscription into war by the nation's army or rebel forces, but in the moment of rescue, thus inviting a sharper look at the very logic of humanitarian assistance and the dynamics of empathy. The revival of imperial gothic in child soldier fictions recirculates common tropes of African savagery but, in the hands of such recent writers, can also signal something more resistant and impervious to the reader's sentimental education. In doing so, such works converge with the insights of cultural anthropologists of the child, who have long insisted that the child is a multidimensional being, not simply innocent and vulnerable, but an agent, capable of moral choice.[73] Kourouma's negation of now dominant frames of recuperation indexes the power of satire to repel sentiment. The next chapter takes up the mode of satire to explore how race is reconfigured in recent US returns to the scene of slavery, works that at once declare the end of the grip of history in favor of the newness of the "post-black," but insistently return to the unsettled past to mine it for their explorations of masculinity, impossible closures, and uncertain allegories. Showing how slavery exists as a kind of commoditized currency in the present, post-black satirists continue the shift away from the revival of the slave narrative as a contemporary global form.

3

Post-Black Satire

It's illegal to yell "Fire!" in a crowded theater, right?
It is.
Well, I've whispered "Racism" in a post-racial world.
—Paul Beatty, *The Sellout*

In 2012, the comedy duo Jordan Peele and Keegan-Michael Key debuted a sketch, "Auction Block," that seemingly achieved the impossible—a satirical treatment of slavery that did not cause offense.[1] Key and Peele play two of three slaves on the auction block, continually passed over for purchase as a crowd of clumsy white men selects an array of increasingly feeble men. The actors then begin to compete to be bought for absurdly low sums of money, flexing their muscles, with a nonstop verbal banter about their clear superiority to the purchased slaves, joking about what should be hallowed ground. The joke lands precisely because it refuses the iconic genre that represents such scenes of sale and separation—sentimentalism. Countering numerous instances of the slave auction as an emotional assault on human dignity, where families are estranged and the threat of rape is ever present, the actors prioritize neither historical accuracy nor indeed plausibility. Instead, Key and Peele focus on masculinity and its endless performance, as it plays out among and across black and white men. From first pledging to revolt as soon as they arrive on the plantation, the actors go on to showcase their own attributes of strength, docility, and magic, until their dismissal of a short black man prompts the auctioneer to call off the event on account of *their* bigotry. Because the actors playing slaves seem to be in control of the incongruity of their actions, as they strive to be sold with bravado and self-assurance, Key and Peele manage to say something about contemporary masculinity even as they trace it to the fraught origins of American slavery.

Such efforts are rare—not just in their dexterity as comedy or knack for sidestepping outrage, but as a form of effective political critique.

The subject of slavery understandably does not lend itself to satire easily. And yet, a distinct impulse in contemporary African American literature is one that almost immediately seems incongruous—neo-slave narratives penned by authors who otherwise abjure all strictures of politically committed art. Such celebrated iconoclastic writers as Paul Beatty, Percival Everett, Mat Johnson, and Colson Whitehead are more commonly discussed in relation to postmodernism, post-soul aesthetics, or post-blackness rather than neo-slavery, and yet all have recently taken up the creative transformation of the slave narrative I identify in this study as a substantial development in contemporary culture.

These writers are known precisely for rejecting sentimentalized portraits of blackness, for resorting to irreverence and farce, and for refusing the seriousness ascribed to dialogues about race. For instance, a character in Beatty's 2015 novel *The Sellout* notes that "the only certainties I had about the African American condition were that we had no concept of the phrases 'too sweet' and 'too salty.'"[2] Whitehead offered an ode to the first thin president when Barack Obama was elected, undercutting the euphoria of that moment.[3] He also mocked liberal delusions about affirmative action in "Visible Man" mapping the distance from Ralph Ellison's potent metaphor in contemporary political landscapes, where "The Guy Who Got Where He Is Only Because He's Black" is repeatedly accused of elitism.[4] Whitehead had joked about writing a "Southern Novel of Black Misery," while Everett devoted an entire stinging novel to his critique of expectations surrounding authentic black literature.[5] In *Erasure*, Everett eviscerates the publishing industry, scholars, and readers alike for their fetishization of "offensive, poorly written, racist and mindless" fiction as "true, gritty real stories of black life," chafing against the aesthetic limits binding black writers.[6]

In his introduction to *Hokum: An Anthology of African-American Humor*, Beatty complains about precisely such restrictive definitions of African American culture. Recalling his introduction to black literature in eighth grade in the form of a copy of Maya Angelou's *I Know Why the Caged Bird Sings*, Beatty felt that he was "growing ever more oppressed with each maudlin passage."[7] His subsequent exploration of the black canon still felt like it was "missing the black bon mot, the snap, the bag, the whimsy upon which 'fuck you' and freedom sail. It was as if the black writers I'd read didn't have any friends." He thus identifies a second canon existing next to the more formal one, anthologized in his volume and not characterized by "sobriety—moral, corporeal and prosaic." Suggesting that the conventional notion of African American writing derives from "a tradition of abolitionist 'And ain't I an intellect?' activism aimed, then as now at whites," Beatty prefers art that validates "our humanity through our madness."[8]

In this vein, while one dominant tendency in African American literature over the last four decades has been the return to slavery, another seemingly contradictory trend has been toward declarations of the end of blackness itself, or at least a significant shift in how blackness may be defined in the post-civil-rights era.[9] While several terms characterize this taxonomical quest for a new language (including post-soul, the new black, postmodernism, and post-postmodernism), the rubric that best encapsulates this shift is that of the "post-black." Emerging from the art world, in Thelma Golden's description, post-black best describes a generation of black artists born after the civil rights era struggles were over, who refuse to be contained within the category of black artist, yet continue to return to debates about black aesthetics to structure their practice.[10] Bertram Ashe defines post-soul as those artists and writers who came of age after the civil rights movement, and favors the idea of a post-soul matrix, web, or sensibility, characterized by a "cultural mulatto archetype," an "exploration of blackness" or "blaxporation," and "allusion-disruption gestures," usually centered on the Black Power movement.[11] Ashe concedes that there are parallels with what came before, but suggests that the fundamental distinguishing feature is that the "quest for black freedom" that was a "constant" in earlier literature could no longer be assumed to be so.[12] Often described as a "troubling" or "queering" of blackness, post-black artists disregard calls for racial unity by offering both intragroup satire as well as externally directed critique.[13] Various manifestos by such thinkers as Trey Ellis, Mark Anthony Neal, and Touré emphasize that post-black artists defy all prescriptions for appropriate subject or method, highlighting improvisation, subversion, parody, comedy, and satire as their dominant aesthetic modes.[14] While Neal identifies a shift from essentialist notions of blackness to "metanarratives on blackness," Ellis, in a much maligned though influential declaration, "The New Black Aesthetic," proposes an art that disregards both black and white expectations of authenticity, advocating the efforts of "cultural mulattoes" like himself with "complicated and sometimes contradictory cultural baggage."[15]

While it may seem that such a stance either smacks of elitism, apathy, or a disavowal both of history and of continuing racism, defenders of the idiom deny any collusion with more mainstream notions of postracialism and color blindness, as well as with an "apolitical, art-for-art's-sake fantasy," to use Ellis's words.[16] To adopt the term "post-black" in an era of unchecked antiblack violence and rising white supremacy immediately seems perverse. Yet, as a description of an allied set of aesthetic strategies—which is where the term originated—it continues to resonate, and part of my goal here is to deploy it as a heuristic, more to expose its contradictory genealogies than to align it with any manner of postracial assumptions. In a recent volume on *Post-Soul Satire*, Derek Conrad Murray identifies a "broad rejection of the generational passing down of racial trauma" as the core of the elusive term "post-blackness."[17] Because its idiom is explicitly defined against a focus on slavery or a constitution through trauma, it is clearly contradictory, an oxymoron even, to suggest the existence of post-black neo-slave narratives. And yet this volatile conjunction is exactly my claim in this chapter. I trace an unstable, often incoherent relationship between the post-black and the neo-slave imaginaries in contemporary culture, an awkward conjunction that yields some insight about both formations, revealing what they may share as well as where they depart. Doing so illuminates both what we know about the impulse to "posterize," as Paul Taylor puts it, and the desire to look back.[18]

Although I emphasize contemporary writers and artists, it is worth noting at the outset that an absurdist impulse attends representations of slavery from its very inception—whether in the euphemism of the despotic lusts Harriet Jacobs will not describe, the restraint of Frederick Douglass over the possible benefits of a shadowy root, the trickster tales, the cakewalk, or various performances of black abjection from Joice Heth to the Hottentot Venus. Writers as varied as Charles Chesnutt, Sutton Griggs, and George Schuyler step outside of realist modes to explore the power of folklore, fantasy, extravagance, and humor. But it is only in the last three decades that a self-conscious school of black art coalesces, pivoting on satire, giving credence to such polemical nomenclatures as the post-black. In the hands of such writers as Beatty, Everett, Johnson, and

Whitehead, the refusal to be limited by racial categories of aesthetics or politics goes hand in hand with a relentless exploration of what may be presumed to be the blind spot in such thinking—slavery and its afterlife.

The distinct body of work of post-black neo-slave narratives immediately stages the contradictions and schisms attending both impulses (the excavation of the unending history of slavery and the declaration of a break from previous racial regimes). That the intense exploration of the freedom enabled by post-civil-rights identity since the 1990s coexists with a similarly inexorable impulse to plumb the slave past must be thought of as something more than a temporal coincidence. The volatile clash of the two imaginaries remains necessarily unstable, impossible even, because the core of the neo-slave imaginary is to insist that slavery never really ended, and we are living "in the wake," with black life ontologically linked to the figure of the slave.[19] On the other hand, the very definition of post-blackness leaves behind the history of slavery and the constitution of the contemporary subject through that historical trauma.[20]

Perhaps most provocatively self-contradictory is novelist Charles Johnson, who, after writing two acclaimed novels about slavery—*Middle Passage* and *Oxherding Tale*—as well as a collection of short stories—*The Soulcatcher*—declared in 2008 his fatigue with (indeed his contempt for) the subject of slavery. For Johnson, the dawn of the twenty-first century demands new narratives for black America: "new and better stories, new concepts, and new vocabularies and grammar based not on the past but on the dangerous, exciting, and unexplored present." This involves "leaving behind the painful history of slavery and its consequences," since it enables only a hackneyed narrative of victimization.[21]

Belying such qualms, however, the sheer range of engagements with the subject of slavery over the last four decades testifies to the limits of such assumptions about a single story of slavery. In addition to the writers named above, such writers as Bernardine Evaristo, James McBride, Suzan-Lori Parks, and Alice Randall join the efforts of comics like Key and Peele to turn to farce, satire, and the ridiculous in their retellings of slavery. As we saw in the introduction to this study, the most powerful ethical presence in the neo-slave imaginary of our times has been Toni Morrison's wrenching and challenging exploration of the weight of the past in *Beloved*. Morrison was committed not only to an evocation of historical truths (as her research on Margaret Garner shaped her story of Sethe and her children), but also to an unsettling of historiographical assumptions themselves.[22] Her novel, thus, writes a history that does not accept historicism as a valid frame, prioritizing instead the interiority and psychological trauma of the enslaved. Morrison insists on deepening our apprehension of what slavery entailed (the horrors of the Middle Passage, the brutality of rape, and the exigencies of motherhood and sacrifice) even as she obscures our easy access to the narrative itself (via narrative techniques of circling around the main event, shifts in perspective, breaks in syntax, and a clear departure from realism in favor of the ghostly). In doing so, she helped implement such frameworks as trauma and the impossibility of healing, the double edge of memory, and the ghostly presence of the unresolved past as influential models for processing the legacy of slavery.

Recent debates in African American studies have probed the possibilities generated by a melancholic attachment to the past as well as the prevalence of narratives of healing or "getting over" the trauma of slavery. Saidiya Hartman influentially called attention to the "time of slavery"—that is, "the relation between the past and the present, the horizon of loss, the extant legacy of slavery, the antinomies of redemption (a salvational principle that will help us overcome the injury of slavery and the long history of defeat) and irreparability." She refuses redemptive and romantic plots, both personal and state sponsored, that urge a return to the origin, as well as narratives of progress that promise a better future by forgetting the slave past. Instead she recommends, like Morrison, living with the unlivable, becoming "coeval with the dead," refusing to abjure grief or rage.[23]

Such accounts are now the dominant lens through which the most innovative examinations of slavery and its afterlife are beheld, signaling, in some ways, the ascendance of psychoanalytic frameworks to understand the resonance of slavery today. Whether as affective uses of misery in the slave hold, an insistence on melancholy over memorial and mourning practices, a search for alternative forms of wake work, or a focus on psychic afterlives, much of this conversation has developed with reference to the work of Morrison, Dionne Brand, and M. NourbeSe Philip.

In this chapter, I turn to a body of literature that departs quite clearly from such a paradigm, examining satire as the mode through which the history and afterlife of slavery takes shape. My goal is to probe the ways in which satire enables an expansion of the conversation around the afterlife of slavery, and whether it makes visible a different relation to the past, present, and future. Does satire yield a new understanding of the past and present beyond a melancholic attachment or the narrative of healing or getting over? Or does it leave the past behind, focusing instead on its commodification in the present, so that we may say that despite the ostensible subject matter, post-black neo-slave fictions have little to say about slavery itself, choosing to focus their contempt and ridicule on present-day racial legacies and inconsistencies? Centering on genre, for me, offers a different approach to the familiar question of the material and symbolic legacy of slavery in the contemporary era. Viewing satire as the lens through which debates about race and postracialism become visible or refract, I am interested in exploring whether such satires effectively combat the sentimental template of abolition and neo-abolition, whether they produce new knowledge about the past or open up generative ways of imagining the present and future.

Satire and the African American Tradition

The long-standing link between African American cultural production and the tradition of protest has not always allowed for an accounting of the many uses of humor and the absurd. No matter how nonsensical or surreal the plots of some African American writers, that is to say, scholars find in them little challenge to established forms of critique. Darryl Dickson-Carr explains the relative obscurity of African American satirists in discussions of literature and culture precisely this way, noting the critical tendency to highlight social protest as the primary function of black writing. He seeks to understand how African American literary satire works to entertain without instruction, to subvert and parody without acceding to either American liberalism or black nationalism. For Dickson-Carr, the body of work he explores across the twentieth century forms a "sacredly profane" tradition—where the shifts conventionally understood to mark African American history (slavery, the Harlem Renaissance, interwar realism and modernism, civil rights and black nationalism, and the advent of multiculturalism) accompany the work of such well-known writers as Zora Neale Hurston, Langston Hughes, George Schuyler, Ralph Ellison, Ishmael Reed, Toni Morrison,

Darius James, and Trey Ellis. The primary context for understanding these works remains the political terrain of racism, beginning with the impulse to "lampoon the (il)logic of chattel slavery and racism itself."[24] Such rhetorical elements as irony, reductio ad absurdum, and signifying, along with the archetypal figures of the trickster or the picaro, can thus be traced to African American folk culture rooted in slavery.

Similarly locating its origin in slavery, Glenda Carpio shows how African American humor begins "as a wrested freedom, the freedom to laugh at that which was unjust and cruel in order to create distance from what would otherwise obliterate a sense of self and community." Viewing it as a "coping mechanism" and a means of "redress," Carpio nevertheless insists on seeing African American humor as "an energetic mode of social and political critique."[25] In reading post-black satire, which explicitly rejects the burden of such critique, Steven Weisenburger's influential differentiation of generative from degenerative satire in American literature helps stratify the varied uses of irreverence and parody. Contesting Northrop Frye's claim that satire goes "stale and mouldy" in the twentieth century, Weisenburger argues for a degenerative mode of postmodern satire that "functions to subvert hierarchies of value and to reflect suspiciously on all ways of making meaning, including its own." Rather than building consensus, rectifying norms, or endorsing hierarchies, degenerative satires are excessive, grotesque, and carnivalesque, enacting "the return of a repressed horror or violence, an unbridled outrage spreading irrevocably through signification in general." Undermining the rationalist norms underpinning influential accounts of satire, which must inevitably "scourge" and "purge," helps expand our understanding of the many uses of satire, beyond an almost automatic subversion of dominant ideology.[26]

Because most histories of the African American literary tradition trace a linear narrative of a progressive emergence from the slave plantation to Jim Crow segregation to incarceration and police brutality today, it may make perfect sense to view Beatty and Everett as part of the line that begins with William Wells Brown or Charles Chesnutt, carried on by Richard Pryor or Dave Chappelle (as Carpio shows). But disassociating contemporary forms of satire from those that originated during slavery may finally yield a richer understanding of the contradiction of a post-black neo-slave imaginary. The age-old debate in studies of satire about whether the goal of the satirist is to denounce and correct with an implicit norm in view or if the ridicule of society serves as an end in itself remains relevant here. Much of the humor in post-black satires comes precisely from refusing the linear conception of time and the premise of racial progress (the long arc of history that bends toward justice) that accompanies it. Their satire, in fact, rests on exploding out of such forms of historicism and the suggestion that one cultural form logically and sequentially derives from or comes after another. An alternative, then, to liberal progressive accounts of history, as well as melancholic forms of an arrested historicism that allows neither movement nor stasis (in the Morrison vein), post-black satirists pose a weightier challenge to the status quo than one advocating a better social order.

Post-black satire, in fact, unsettles the very assumptions that underwrite the effort to define or apprehend blackness as a fixed entity—whether as a consciousness, a community, a people, an ontology, or a standpoint. Challenging the assumption that collectivity can be assumed, post-black satirists point out divisions within black communities, refusing to accept the white gaze as the permanent object of address. Explicitly embracing stereotype—the cover of Beatty's anthology *Hokum* features a watermelon slice in lieu of a smile—they also indict previous black thinkers for seeking racial justice through the politics of respectability. The writer at the center of *Erasure*—a figure much like Everett himself—author of "widely unread experimental stories and novels, considered dense and often inaccessible," is constantly told "you're not black enough" as the reason publishers reject his novels.[27] But there is no room for a writer of his kind in a world that demands authentic portraits of black life, more often than not fulfilling voyeuristic desires for a window into the tangle of pathology so memorably described in the Moynihan report. Everett's author, Thelonious "Monk" Ellison, explains himself clearly to no avail: "I never tried to set anybody free, never tried to paint the next real and true picture of the life of *my* people, never had any people whose picture I knew well enough to paint."[28]

Such satires refuse to grant legitimacy to conventional forms of heroism or resistance. This often means that they mock black resistance at the same time that they unmask white racism, skewering icons of black heroism from Frederick Douglass to Rosa Parks to W. E. B. Du Bois. In a caustic vignette in *Erasure*, for instance, Everett imagines D. W. Griffith meeting Richard Wright and telling him "I like your book very much."[29]

In McBride's *The Good Lord Bird*, the tragic heroism of John Brown becomes farcical adventure, the sublimity of revolution idiosyncrasy and superstition.[30] As Baz Dreisinger writes in a review, "It is officially o.k. to be boldly irreverent about not just the sacrosanct but also the catastrophic." But for her, such "irreverence becomes not a lampooning of champions and calamities but a new kind of homage," thus making Brown "more a hero than ever before."[31] For Héctor Tobar, in contrast, McBride's "broad and bawdy comedy" is "downright sacrilegious," especially his portrayal of Douglass as a lecherous old man.[32]

Sacrilege, however, is the goal. Beatty's narrator (schooled by his father in "elaborate schemes to educate me on the plight of the black race and to inspire me to make something of myself") firmly rejects the role of race representative—"I couldn't care less about being black," he says, going so far as to fill out "Californian" on the census form (*Sellout*, 43–44). Black nationalists come in for special contempt across a range of texts, as Beatty mocks Amiri Baraka's "Sacred Chant for the Return of Black Spirit and Power" as "unintentional comedy."[33] Focusing on complicity, objectification, and voyeurism, post-black satirists undermine any notion of agency or resistance. At the same time, a novel like *The Sellout* cannot be read as a manifesto for postracialism or as a critique of Obama (as many interviewers wish to establish, to Beatty's visible discomfort), but demands a closer look at the difficult stance it takes—somewhere between critique and skepticism, euphoria and nihilism.

Rather than trying to illuminate some truth about slavery or even about contemporary racial oppression, post-black satires operate in a deliberately antihistorical vein, with ludicrous juxtapositions of past and present and rampant use of anachronism and reductio ad absurdum. Such experimentation with time and history means that satire refuses both the substitution imagined by sentimentalism and the possession feared in gothic returns. It even challenges the theorization of blackness as an ontology derived from the natally dead status of the slave, influentially theorized by Afro-pessimist scholars, Frank B. Wilderson and Jared Sexton.[34] In contrast to common assumptions that returning to slavery coheres a community, shores up a narrative of progress (signaling the distance from a difficult past), or fixes black figures in positions of victimage, these satires break open the meaning of blackness, futurity, and history alike.

Doing so means that post-black satires do not aim to produce new knowledge about the past in a vein of recovery or revision. Unlike a novel like Octavia Butler's *Kindred*, for example, which sends a modern character back into the time of slavery to have her learn firsthand the complexity of notions of agency, resistance, and community under slavery, post-black neo-slave narratives eschew such a historicist project as well as the tendency to collapse past misery with present subjugation.[35] *Kindred* challenges binary accounts of slavery that oppose militant resistance to treacherous complicity. Refusing the narrative of progress that the nation has come a long way, as well as any notion of a utopian future, *Kindred* may underscore the conflicting needs of past and present (for Dana to live, her ancestor must suffer), the inadequacy of historical knowledge, and the inability of fiction to capture lived experience with any accuracy. It may also insist on the loss of the past—at the novel's conclusion Dana travels to the site of the former plantation but finds no historical records or markers that have survived. Her lost arm remains the only tangible symbol of her journey. But in the end, *Kindred* reaffirms the ongoing and inexorable tangle of present-day black lives with slavery, even as it expands our sense of possibilities in the present and the future. In contrast, the writers I explore next revisit the past (whether of Edgar Allan Poe's racist novel, blackface minstrelsy, or runaway slave advertisements) to adapt it, oscillating between assertions of transcending trauma and demonstrations of the enduring power of slavery's legacy. Taking up the risky task of telling the story of the afterlife of slavery in a political climate resistant to it without trying to recover the slave's agency and humanity, post-black satirists stage the question of whether the link between politics and aesthetics established by the slave narrative, written to prove the slave's humanity, can indeed be broken in the twenty-first century.

By focusing on exposing hypocrisy in the present, such satires show how unevenly the past is understood and how often it is commercialized and made to serve strange purposes. Centering the question of the commodification of slavery rather than slavery itself, they return repeatedly to the black text as fetish. In this way, even though they declare their distance from a conventional black literary tradition or black aesthetic, they remain locked in an uncertain dialogue with it. Though the conditions that structured the production and reception of the slave narrative and had shaped its many compromises of form (including the need for veracity or authentication, the manipulating presence of an editor, the presumption of a hostile audience) are long gone, post-black writers remain caught within such debates, grappling with the link between freedom and literacy established by the slave narrative.

The two dominant conceptions of temporality in contemporary African American literature—avowing the post-black and insisting on the ever unfolding afterlife of slavery—thus collide in the works I examine. Johnson returns to the past of Edgar Allan Poe's *The Narrative of Arthur Gordon Pym of Nantucket* in *Pym* (2011) to reimagine the Middle Passage as a voyage into the heart of whiteness. Beatty plumbs the racist past of blackface minstrelsy to eviscerate the aspiration of a postracial world, bringing back slavery and segregation to Los Angeles in *The Sellout*. Whitehead's homecoming to the African American slave narrative in *The Underground Railroad* (2016) resolutely plays with both realism and fantasy, offering a fable that reads like history. Drawing on analogy to stretch time and space, to comment on past and future, these writers elucidate contemporary rituals of race: deformations, contradictions, and grotesque and generative appropriations alike.

Despite the presence of such formidable iconoclasts as Kara Walker and Suzan-Lori Parks, post-black satire tends to be dominated by male artists and writers. And masculinity remains an explicit focus (as we see with Johnson's *Pym* and Beatty's *Sellout* below). Whitehead's choice of a female protagonist, Cora, and his overt homage to Harriet Jacobs in *The Underground Railroad* deliberately depart from such an emphasis on masculinity. Johnson and Beatty expose the ways in which anxieties about racial authenticity emerge through efforts to claim access to a reconstituted manhood, which remains laughably elusive for their protagonists, whose inadequate sexual prowess forms key elements of both plots.

Into the Heart of Whiteness

Johnson's *Pym*, "a comic journey into the ultimate land of whiteness by an unlikely band of African American adventurers," begins with a preface by the protagonist, Chris Jaynes, a professor of African American literature whose denial of tenure triggers this expedition to "the last continent," Antarctica.[36] Jaynes's first-person preface explains the genesis of the book as the insistence of "gentlemen in Richmond, VA" to make his story public (3). Worried about his own abilities as a writer, the accuracy of his memory, the lack of photographs or recordings of the event, and also charges of paranoia or invention, Jaynes shares his initial hesitation with the reader. He overcomes these, he tells us with a metafictional wink, on meeting "Mr. Johnson, at the time an assistant professor of language and literature at Bard College, a historically white institution."[37] Johnson recommends writing it as fiction, not just to prevent being sued but because "doing so provides a level of synchronicity with the seminal text that began my journey" (4). Jaynes continues, "In this age when reality is built on big lies, what better place for truth than fiction?" Both claiming and disavowing truth at once, Jaynes insists that what we are about to read is real.

It will be clear to any reader of Poe that Johnson hews very closely to Edgar Allan Poe's introductory note to *The Narrative of Arthur Gordon Pym*, which appeared in the *Southern Literary Messenger* in 1838. Gordon Pym's concern that he kept no journal during the journeys becomes Jaynes's worry that he took no pictures or recordings and barely cracked open his laptop. Pym's sense of religious duty transforms into "sociological and historical purposes" that entail the telling of the story. Pym's worry that his story will be dismissed because the only evidence lies in a single individual, "and he a half-breed Indian," becomes in Johnson, "a single corpse who was in life a drunken, two-hundred-year-old pickle"—in other words Gordon Pym himself. "Distrust" of one's ability becomes insecurity; and accusations of "an impudent and ingenious fiction" morph into "the rant of a paranoid" (3).

Poe's Pym saw the decision to present the story as fiction rather than fact a "ruse" that did not fool readers, since they were able to see that it was not "fable"—"I thence concluded that the facts of my narrative would prove of such a nature as to carry with them sufficient evidence of their own authenticity, and that I had consequently little to fear on the score of popular incredulity."[38] In contrast, Johnson's narrator lays claim to ownership of the story, insinuating that the author, Johnson himself, is neither in control nor in charge: "This exposé being made, it will be obvious to those who would compare the few works of Mr. Johnson where his brief assistance in this narrative begins and ends. Regardless, it should be emphasized that I have approved the following manuscript and in thought, intent, and theory I claim it as my own" (4).

Echoing the peculiar conditions of the slave narrative as a form—with its many prefaces, claims to veracity, and testimonies to the good character of the narrator—at the same time that it rewrites Poe, Johnson's narrator assumes the role of both amanuensis and subject for himself. This dual inheritance—the authenticating gestures of the slave narrative and the oscillating movement between fiction and fact of nineteenth-century novels—structures the riotous journey of the novel, as it eviscerates myths of origin of blackness and whiteness alike.

Jaynes is fired because he declines to fulfill the role of "Professional Negro" on his all-white campus, which meant that he refused to sit on the Diversity Committee and insisted on teaching American literature rather than just African American literature, especially Edgar Allan Poe in a course called "Dancing with the Darkies: Whiteness in the Literary Mind" (7). He insists that the path to a truly postracial society will be through the "source"—which is why he studies Poe rather than Baldwin or Ellison: "If we can identify how the pathology of Whiteness was constructed, then we can learn how to dismantle it" (14). Replaced by another black man, the not too subtly named Mosaic Johnson, who calls himself a "Hip-Hop Theorist" (17) and "deal[s] with the ghetto" (18), Jaynes tells him that by playing the role of "the angry black guy," he is "not fighting Whiteness [but] feeding its perversion" (20).

To return to the source of whiteness, Johnson's novel takes as truth the fantastical journey depicted in Poe's *Narrative*—where Gordon Pym sails to the South Pole to the island of Tsalal with Dirk Peters and finds a group of "savages" so black that even their teeth were black, whose only access to language seems to be shrieks of "Tekeli-li." Just as the slave narrative's primary claim was to veracity, Johnson insists that Poe's fantastical tale is real. "The most wicked, hypocritical, vindictive, bloodthirsty, and altogether fiendish race of men upon the face of the globe," in Poe's words, become, in Johnson's comic reversal, the very object of fantasy for his protagonist, signaling the dream of a black homeland untouched by whiteness. "Horrors from the pit of the antebellum subconscious" thus morph into the dream "that there was a group of our people who did achieve victory over slavery" and created "Tsalal, the great undiscovered African Diasporan homeland" (29, 39).

This quest doubles itself as a parody of the academic discovery of a lost manuscript. Finding *The True and Interesting Narrative of Dirk Pe-*

ters, Coloured Man, as Written by Himself (1837), Jaynes is convinced that "this was the greatest discovery in the brief history of American letters" (39). Dirk Peters—"the half-breed Indian" of Poe's coinage—turns out to be the true author of the tale, and Poe the thief who filches his story, in an echo of contemporary debates about white appropriation of black culture. Poe's unfinished ending that has perplexed many a reader and critic thus turns out to be baffling because it is stolen—a copy of a black narrative, whose unacknowledged theft situates the black text as the original, and whiteness as counterfeit. Claiming that Peters was really black (a forerunner of the Indiana residents who claim to be Native American), Johnson finds—in an ever-receding movement in the search for lost origins—that Peters himself was an "Uncle Tom," albeit one before the book was written (63). Harriet Beecher Stowe, whose *Uncle Tom's Cabin* "changed the dialogue of African American literature dramatically" (43), is held responsible for elevating fiction over autobiography.

But if it seems that *Pym* sets out to correct this hierarchy by giving us the real story of Dirk Peters, the novel does something else entirely, by centering the figure of the black professor of literature who is obsessed with Poe and the heart of whiteness. *Pym* imagines Peters in the nineteenth century as having to authenticate himself as a free man through his story: when he meets Poe to get him to ghostwrite his tale, Poe keeps asking him, who is your master? Only the proof of the handwritten document can keep Peters safe. As a parallel in the contemporary moment, Jaynes has to authenticate his identity as a black man, a scholar of African American studies, through his presence on the diversity committee, which he considers a "slave hold" (17). He shapes his own identity through reading slave narratives. Bullied as a child for his light skin, he seeks refuge in the library, where Olaudah Equiano's narrative reads like "the diary of the first black nerd" (137). "Diving into the pantheon of slave narratives, through Mary Prince and Harriet Jacobs and Solomon Northup and the others," Jaynes announces, "I found my people" (138). It is, in fact, Jaynes's collection of rare African American books (inadvertently ruined by his university) that finances the trip to Antarctica.

A revision of Poe as well as a rewriting of the slave narrative, *Pym* begins with the firing of a black professor and the destruction of rare black books as the enabling violation that finances the journey to the lost black homeland. The only path to utopia is through the racist imagination of Poe, as *Pym* reimagines the slave narrative as a journey to freedom from academia to Tsalal. For Jaynes, all imitations of the slave narrative risk both "pungent cliché" and "Afrocentric bling" (159). The narratives themselves, in contrast, "are by their very nature original, even when they draw on the forms of earlier literary sources. They are never duplicitous, because they all have one motivation: to document the atrocity of chattel slavery and thereby assist in ending it. Their artistry is surprising, considerable, devoid of pretension and with passion in its place" (159–160). Here he sets up the slave narrative as an original, the real thing, which its always already compromised present-day incarnation could never match. While *Pym* dethrones one original—Poe and by extension the literary canon of whiteness—it elevates another.

Morrison had influentially claimed in *Playing in the Dark* that "no early American writer is more important to the concept of American Africanism than Poe." The unfinished ending of the novel, with an image of impenetrable whiteness, also seems to her deeply resonant, making whiteness "mute, meaningless, unfathomable, pointless, frozen, veiled, curtained, dreaded, senseless, implacable."[39] *Pym* literalizes these observations, as the African American adventurers searching for a "hidden tropical utopia" (67), find a race of "prehistoric snow honkies" (160), "albino monsters," with "colorless lips," "alabaster tongues," and "porcelain" gums (123). Just as grotesque, brutal, and gluttonous as Poe imagined the black Tsalalians, these "snow monkeys" (153) soon enslave Jaynes and his crew, helped by Gordon Pym himself, resurrected not as a ghost but a slowly decaying body that refuses to die. Worshipping whiteness, Pym sees the creatures as "perfection incarnate . . . the end of being . . . *Gods*" (140). Meanwhile, the novel plays with the possibility that they are just "crackers . . . plain old, backward-ass white people" (141).

As the Middle Passage from Africa to the New World across the Atlantic becomes an adventure trek to Antarctica, the ostensible search for a black nation entails an encounter with whiteness. The two, in fact, cannot be separated. In other words, *Pym* claims that to get to the dream of black autonomy, you first have to reach the source of whiteness itself. Linking the contemporary racial order to the uses and abuses of the slave past, the novel's commentary on the absurdity of race rituals in the present frames its exploration of the past. Revisiting slavery stages a satire about the present, as everything from DNA testing to right-wing survivalism, conspiracy theories to tenure review, saccharine art to eating Debbie cakes turns out to center on the unstable power of race. Refusing to conflate past and present in any way, *Pym* parodies both black resistance and white control to comment on how the past of slavery is appropriated now.

Like Dana of *Kindred*, Jaynes notes that his "thorough and exhaustive scholarship" of slave narratives "in no way prepared [him] to actually become a fucking slave" (160). But *Pym* veers away from the description of atrocities suffered under slavery fairly quickly, and even the scenes that repeat recognizable tropes of the slave narrative—the separation of families, violence to quell resistance or escape (an attack on Jeffree's eye recalls the act of branding), near starvation—insist on their difference from their antecedents. Jaynes never loses his wry, ironic tone, filtering these events through his own irreverent thoughts—about boredom for example, or his hope that his ex-wife will leave her second husband and come back to him, as he dreams of something heroic that will win her back. His cousin's reaction is most telling, as the man who once sat "Malcolm X-style" in a juice bar seems to find a kind of peace in compliance and subjugation, as if his "worst fears in life had been realized and justified all in the same moment" (173).

Another way to put this is to say that since the novel is so preposterous, no illusion of realism emerges for the reader at the level of empathy, as an ironic distance even from the experience of slavery persists. Even Jaynes's friend's betrayal—bartering his own freedom for a box of Debbie cakes and eating the rest overnight instead of saving the others—prompts ridicule rather than anger. Jaynes's own concern—muscling his way into Angela's affection by manipulating her misery—balances her desire to somehow convert the experience to some kind of profit. No lofty dreams of liberation nor any glimmer of racial solidarity or a sense of historic mission materialize. Angela dreams of buying "a mansion in Oak Bluffs, with a maid for every floor" when this is all over, and even as Jaynes recognizes the absurdity of the dream, he admits that his own obsession with an all-black homeland or Garth's with a commercial Eurocentric painter were no different. In fact, he realizes that "we were in this moment because of the futures we imagined for ourselves. That even without the snow beasts, we were enslaved. By our greed, our lusts, our dreams" (188).

This strange moment—perhaps a parody of an epiphany—is difficult to take at face value not only because it seems to assign blame to the enslaved, but also because it risks expanding slavery as a metaphor so far that it loses all historical specificity. But it also points to the necessary distance between past and present, insisting that contemporary accounts of slavery—even when imagined as actual enslavement by fictional snow beasts—can never pause to simply sink into the empirical description of suffering, but must always maintain a self-reflexive distance, perhaps even a self-mocking stance that this novel never loses. The novel thus achieves something that much of contemporary culture seems to be reaching toward—an exploration of slavery whose irony protects it from charges of banalization or offense.

At the same time, the novel layers its exploration of slavery with other historical forms of oppression, including genocide, indenture, and colonialism. The meeting with Arthur Gordon Pym, for instance, replicates the colonial encounter of "Mr. Livingston, I presume," a moment that stands for white civility and manners, the persistence of western civilization among the barbarians, at the same time that Gordon Pym assumes that Jaynes, the "octoroon," has brought black slaves for him to trade.[40] While the crew debates how they could market Pym's "fountain of youth"—a discovery potentially more marketable and lucrative than "a village of albino monkey people" (142), Pym treats them like chattel, and Jaynes their master, even trying to check their gums to ascertain their health and referring to them as beasts. The irony of contemporary subjects inhabiting a neoliberal capitalist logic (when they see something they want to patent and market it) hits up against the antebellum logic of owning black people as property.

When the African American crew first meets the shrouded white figures, their chief impulse is to patent the rights to marketing them as spectacles. "Think of the *movie rights*" becomes the refrain that enables survival, a talisman that almost makes up for present degradation, as the hope for fame and money in the future allows them to endure. In fact their first sighting of the mysterious creatures prompts nothing other than a contest over ownership and naming, in short over property rights. As they prepare to enter into the cave where the glimpsed monster disappeared, they spar over whether Jeffree can name the cave "the Jeffree Tube" (111). "Since I found it, I should be able to name it," he reasons. Angela, Jaynes's ex, concurs that naming rights are "real intellectual property," and asks, "If there is something down there, something huge, something with major social or scientific implications, whose ownership claim is that going to be?" (113). When Jeffree encounters the creatures, he wants to call them "Carlton's Carrions" using his "finders keepers" logic again (128).

All these different explorations of race in the present—the thinly sketched upwardly mobile black woman, the light-skinned professor worried about not being black enough, the laid-off Detroit childhood friend with a love of Debbie cakes and Eurocentric paintings, the conspiracy theorist deep-sea diver cousin, the gay couple invested in adventure precisely because it's unexpected—remain relevant even once conscripted into slavery. Jaynes's cousin, Booker, collects slave memorabilia as "evidence" (100), names his dog White Folks with a slave collar around his neck, and believes that "life is too short to be reading more books by white people" (99–100). But when enslaved, he falls in love with his Tekelian mistress, Hunka, and learns to disdain separatism, coming to believe that "you can't run from Whiteness" (209). Like his namesake, Booker T. Washington, he argues that they have to engage the whites on their own terms, and teach them how to respect blacks, since salvation only lies in being loved by the whites (209). Although Jaynes mocks him for Stockholm syndrome, he too empathizes with his own master, whom he names Augustus, after Poe. No agency, community, or heroism surfaces under slavery. To save his friends, Jaynes commits genocide on the Tekelians (with the help of a right-wing survivalist couple hilariously modeled after the "painter of light" Thomas Kinkade), serving them rat poison in a massive feast. The scene of hospitality that turns into carnage reverses the encounter and mass extermination of indigenous peoples with invaders. It also reveals both whiteness and blackness as pathologies alike. Poe (already the site of radical perversity), the racist predecessor who explicitly dehumanizes blacks, and the post-civil-rights descendants (who inhabit an equally precarious present in racialized capitalism) meet in *Pym* to render the neo-slave narrative unrecognizable. Rather, other genres—the colonial quest narrative, imperial romance, the contemporary satire of race, the rewriting of the master's text, the campus novel—usurp the place of the familiar story. In his refusal to venerate black resistance, identity, or community, as well as his pursuit of the origin of the ideology of whiteness, Johnson inverts all conventions of the slave narrative, in its both historical and contemporary incarnations. Leaving the meaning of race and slavery unsettled, the novel ends not with a discovery of the promised land but with an ordinary recognition—reaching a tropical island, the sight of which finally kills Pym, Jaynes and his friend are welcomed by a group of natives: "On the shore all I could discern was a collection of brown people, and this, of course, is a planet on which such are the majority" (322).

Bringing Slavery Back

Beatty collides the two tendencies—post-black and neo-slave—in volatile fashion in *The Sellout*, as a black character enslaves another and brings back segregation. Taking up the idea of the sellout to satirize contemporary racial politics, Beatty shows a Compton-like inner city—suggestively named Dickens—reinstating slavery and segregation to rejuvenate itself. The object of his satire is not simply a racist white audience or the black bourgeoisie, or even a desire to expose a pernicious history of neglect and abuse. As an exposé of the absurdities of the twenty-first-century discourse of postracialism, *The Sellout* casts its caustic eye on subjects as wide-ranging as the unbearable sweetness of Satsuma oranges, the distinctions among "Regular Whiteness," "Deluxe Whiteness," and "Super Deluxe Whiteness" (227), the racially inflected seating preferences of passengers riding a bus in Los Angeles, the ongoing appeal of blackface minstrelsy, and BDSM clubs catering to those aroused by racial insults.

Dickens, the "invisible city," has been wiped off the map of California as "part of a blatant conspiracy by the surrounding, increasingly affluent, two-car-garage communities to keep their property values up and blood pressures down" (148, 57). It can reappear on the map of the United States only if re-segregated, this time for the notoriety it will gain for barring white students in a public school, assigning priority seats for whites in a bus, or, most provocatively, bringing slavery back. In actuality, the city and all public spaces are already segregated. What might it then mean to re-segregate an all-black school or the city that could be called the "Last Bastion of Blackness" (150)?

Part of what Beatty does with reference to Dickens is of course to suggest that two cities overlay one another—Los Angeles and Compton—

much in the manner of two distinct nations, undergoing a time of rupture and crisis. He also shows the construct of an inner city or an "agrarian ghetto" to be full of odd, eccentric, expressive personalities, each of whom have their Dickensian traits. His father, for instance, an eccentric if not deranged sociologist of "blackology," performed psychological experiments on him as his homeschooling, making the narrator (known only by his last name "Me") his very own "Anna Freud" (28). The loss of his father in an unprovoked police shooting sets in motion the plot of the novel, a quest for Me's identity: "Like the entire town of Dickens, I was my father's child, a product of my environment, and nothing more. Dickens was me. And I was my father. Problem is, they both disappeared from my life, first my dad, and then my hometown, and suddenly I had no idea who I was, and no clue how to become myself" (40).

Becoming himself requires reckoning with the past—albeit in distorted form. The past of blackface minstrelsy is ever present yet elusive in the novel in the form of the purported existence of videotapes of "really racist *Little Rascals* movies" (241). It also appears as a canon of books that Foy Cheshire (a parody of a black public intellectual) bowdlerizes and, of course, as the narrator's dead father. Beatty comments on how easily past struggles for justice are commodified—establishing their lack of meaning in the present: "We like to think [history] is a book—that we can turn the page and move the fuck on. But history isn't the paper it's printed on. It's memory, and memory is time, emotions, and song. History is the things that stay with you" (115).

Even these "things that stay with you" aren't easy to access, however, in the face of rampant official memorializations of a selective past. For Me, culling through his "vast repository of daydream blackness" readily dredges up "the scratchy archival footage of the civil rights struggle . . . that incessant Black History Month loop of barking dogs, gushing fire hoses, and carbuncles oozing blood through two-dollar haircuts, colorless blood spilling down faces shiny with sweat and the light of the evening news, these are the pictures that form our collective 16mm superego" (18). Rather than restore some sense of dignity or purpose, Me finds that "the film inside my head begins to skip and sputter. The sound cuts out, and protestors falling like dominoes in Selma, Alabama, begin to look like Keystone Negroes slipping en masse on an affirmative-action banana peel and tumbling to the street, a tangled mess of legs and dreams akimbo. The marchers on Washington become civil rights zombies" and the "head zombie" is "exhausted from being raised from the dead every time someone wants to make a point about what black people should and shouldn't do, can and cannot have" (19).

Militating against such prescriptions for appropriate blackness, Beatty castigates postracial advocates and "dum dum donut intellectuals" alike who seek to sanitize the past by renaming *Huckleberry Finn* "*The Pejorative-Free Adventures and Intellectual and Spiritual Journeys of African-American Jim and His Young Protégé, White Brother Huckleberry Finn, as They Go in Search of the Lost Black Family Unit*" (95). Insisting that "black literature sucks" (143) and that being offended "is not even an emotion," Me embraces being "a fucking race pervert" who has "set black people back five hundred years" (130). Current accusations of being a sellout—dragging all of black America back with him—derive from the sanctity of the civil rights struggle and the sobriety of abolition, which do not allow for the more profane imaginings the novel explores.

Most corrosive perhaps is the tirade against the figure of the black intellectual, lampooned in the person of Cheshire, responsible for labeling the narrator "the sellout" and for stealing his father's ideas. Cheshire produces an entire curriculum called "Fire the Canon" made up of such rewritten classics as *The Point Guard in the Rye*, *The Great Blacksby*, and *The Dopeman Cometh* (165–166). Cheshire even generates a "politically respectful edition" of *Huckleberry Finn*: "Where the repugnant 'n-word' occurs," he says, "I replaced it with 'warrior' and the word 'slave' with 'dark-skinned volunteer'" (95–96). The Dum Dum Donut intellectuals led by Cheshire after the passing of Me's father use "EmpowerPoint" with fonts like "Timbuktu, Harlem Renaissance, and Pittsburgh Courier" (99).

Such instances of naming, renaming, and misnaming end up as the very sites on which contemporary racial norms are negotiated and fought over. Just as past fiction and history is available for such bowdlerization and selective memory (on the part of both black and white Americans), space itself is similarly subject to such partitions and distributions. Dickens, the invisible city, is rendered so not just by decades of neglect but simply by erasing the name of the place off the map. When the narrator sees that the sign announcing "DICKENS—NEXT EXIT" is gone, he has no way of knowing that he was home anymore (87). Believing that "what are cities really, besides signs and arbitrary boundaries," he decides to bring Dickens back simply by replacing the missing sign himself. After all the town disappeared in a similar fashion: "Dickens didn't go out with a bang like Nagasaki, Sodom and Gomorrah, and my dad. It was quietly removed" to aid gentrification (57).

Beatty makes it impossible (or at least challenging) for the reader to approach the subjects of urban crisis, inner-city deprivation, segregation, and slavery as spectacles from the past that can affirm a narrative of progress. Segregation and slavery can be revived easily—and farcically—because the social divisions and inequality they generated have not been dealt with in any meaningful way. For Hominy Jenkins, an octogenarian member of the former *Little Rascals*, "freedom can kiss my postbellum black ass" (83). A virtuoso at genuflecting, Hominy is never happier than when giving up his seat to a white woman in the newly resegregated LA bus (played by an actress hired by the narrator). But Hominy doesn't exist just as a symbol of the past that will not die—he is necessary for the nation ("Anything that, like baseball, keeps a country that's constantly preening in the mirror from actually looking in the mirror and remembering where the bodies are buried"; 87), and as a mirror for the other inhabitants of Dickens: "We recognized the face he was wearing as a mask from our own collections" (131).

When the narrator agrees to enslave Hominy, to make him happy, the county sheriff and deputies debate what crime to charge him with—hoping to settle on "vandalism of state property" even though the narrator notes that what he did was a clear "violation of the First Amendment, the Civil Rights Code, and, unless there's been an armistice in the War on Poverty, at least four articles of the Geneva Convention" (263). But the Geneva Convention, of course, doesn't apply to individual citizens, nor is enforceable for any violators. The California attorney general (presumably Kamala Harris) argues that the defendant has violated "the Civil Rights Acts of 1866, 1871, 1957, 1964, and 1968, the Equal Rights Act of 1963, the Thirteenth and Fourteenth Amendments, and at least six of the Ten Commandments." If it were in her power, she claims, she'd try him for "crimes against humanity" (265). The novel renders her righteous rage risible by asking the judge to gauge the proof of his humanity in the sweetness of the nectarines he grows, and the judge sets bail at "a cantaloupe and two kumquats" (266)—an absurd proposition that reveals the equal and unspoken incongruity of the fact that slavery and segregation cannot be seen as a crime under the law with any ease. Beatty's sketch not only parodies the assumption of the due process of law, but also emphasizes the ironies of "a female state's attorney general of black and Asian lineage, a black defendant, a black defense counselor, a Latina bailiff, and . . . a Vietnamese-American district judge" trying to determine the "very existence of white supremacy as expressed through our system of law" (265).

When the case goes to the Supreme Court in *Me v. the United States of America*, the justices also struggle with trying to ascertain what charge to lay at his door. If charged for exploitation of labor, corporations would have to be charged for unpaid interns. If indicted for human trafficking, they would have to reckon with the fact that "he's never been bought or sold" (264). If they take him to the International Criminal Court and accuse him of apartheid, he can argue that not a single South African was prosecuted for it. Clearly underlining that the world still has not understood how to see slavery as a crime, the narrator claims that his only offense is that he has "whispered 'Racism' in a post-racial world"—akin to yelling "'Fire' in a crowded theater" (262).

While the plot of the novel never quite resolves (and how could it?), these moments of raging against prescriptions for blackness and post-racialism alike constitute the most cogent missive of the novel. The sole resolution of the several interwoven strands is that the lost *Little Rascals* tapes are found in the possession of Cheshire, who turns out to be harboring the dirty secret that he himself was a Little Rascal, alias "Black Folk" (281). In response, Jenkins quits being a slave and Dickens reappears on the weather forecast on the news, "back on the map" as a result of the notoriety the court case garners (284).

The Sellout, however, doesn't believe in closure, echoing Me's father, who called it a "false psychological concept" meant to "assuage white Western guilt" (261). The novel's last brief chapter—"Closure"—offers nothing of the sort, explicitly challenging the postracial triumphalism that accompanied Obama's presidency. Me recalls asking Cheshire waving an American flag "after the black dude was inaugurated"—"What about the Native Americans? What about the Chinese, the Japanese, the Mexicans, the poor, the forests, the water, the air, the fucking California condor?" (289). That the story of contemporary racial formations requires expanding the black-white binary not only emerges as an imperative but also entails eschewing linear narratives of overcoming.

A closing scene gets to the heart of the novel's provocation. An open-mic comic kicks out a white couple who laugh just a little too loud at his jokes about black people. Not only reminiscent of Dave Chappelle's similar experience, the moment also suggestively comments on the voyeuristic desires of the audience for the novel itself. Me tells us that while he understands the conditions that lead the comic to exclude the whites, saying, "Get out. This is our thing," he still doesn't know "what exactly is *our thing*?" (287–288). While the novel does not and cannot answer this question, it does offer various substitutions, analogies, and hilarious juxtapositions, where the meaning of anything in comparison slips and slides, but also expands. Enlisting an array of unexpected juxtapositions, farcical comparisons, and endless lists of items, Beatty challenges the assumption that anything can be demarcated as a single object, fixed in meaning or space. If slavery is like apartheid, the Nazi Holocaust, caste discrimination, and corporate abuse all at once, what kind of ontology or historicity can it claim? And what kind of special status can blackness accrue—either in terms of discrimination or redemption?

Using the logic of analogy for comedy and mockery, Beatty neatly reverses the sentimental uses of analogies across then and now, here and there. He emphasizes instead the fissures and fractures that make equivalence of anything impossible—institutions, places, people. Is slaveholding the same as "pimping," for instance, because "like children, dogs, dice, and overpromising politicians, and apparently prostitutes, slaves don't do what you tell them to do" (81)? Or is the United States "the latent high school homosexual," "the mulatto passing for white," or "the Neanderthal incessantly plucking its unibrow" (87)? What kind of logic is at work in the statement conflating current postracialism with genocide, when Me claims that "the popularity of the spicy tuna roll and a black American president were to white male domination what the smallpox blankets were to Native American existence" (149)? Or when planning citywide discrimination, Me and Hominy cycle through various options from a global history shop of discrimination—concentration camps, apartheid, the Indian caste system only to decide that "farmers are natural segregationists" (214), and agriculture offers the best precedent? Skewering all in his critique of historical and current forms of racism, Beatty offers neither a consistent manifesto or even a coherent or plausible plot, but rather his own form of "Unmitigated Blackness": "essays passing for fiction" (277). Each of these surreal tableaus works as an invitation to linger in the shock, comedy, and tragedy of contemporary narratives of race. As Kiese Laymon writes in a review, "It's fairly obvious that the United States is a Kara Walker exhibit and a Paul Beatty novel unknowingly masquerading as a crinkled Gettysburg Address."[41]

Pondering the question of how past forms of exploitation are similar to or different from the present, Beatty also takes up analogy and relation spatially, in an extended refrain on what might work as a sister city to Dickens. Trying to restore the city that's been wiped off the map, the narrator finds that Chernobyl, Juarez, and Kinshasa refuse to be sister cities, claiming that Dickens is, respectively, too polluted, too violent, and too black. Rather than turning to places known for contemporary blight or symbols of present disrepair, he has to resort to the mythical or the fabricated. The three sister cities the narrator is able to eventually secure are the studio set of Thebes constructed for the silent movie *The Ten Commandments* (buried under sand dunes in California), Döllersheim in Austria (the site of Hitler's putative Jewish ancestry, evacuated during World War II), and the "Lost City of White Male Privilege" (148). All three "disappeared under dubious circumstances," like Dickens (148), and are sites of repression, simulacra, and confusion. In suggesting a relation between such places and Dickens, Beatty reveals the constructed, nay overdetermined nature of a city like Dickens. Real-life Compton that Dickens signifies is indeed the site of all kinds of phantasmatic projections in the American psyche.

One Supreme Court justice, noting the perverse paradox that the resegregation of Dickens has in fact promoted racial equality, verbalizes the central question of the novel: "*Me v. the United States of America* demands a more fundamental examination of what we mean by 'separate,' by 'equal,' by 'black.' So let's get down to the nitty-gritty—what do we mean by 'black'?" (274). The novel refuses any simple codification of black identity, essence, or community in response to this question. Me's sociologist father had believed in the possibility of taxonomy, identifying three stages of Quintessential Blackness—the self-hate of the "Neophyte Negro," the racial pride of the "Capital *B* Black," and "Race Transcendentalism," or the need to fight oppression (275–276). Me, in contrast, wants a "Stage IV of black identity—Unmitigated Blackness" (277). Embracing a range of personas who embody it—including Marcus Garvey, Richard Pryor, Frida Kahlo, Godard, and Björk—unmitigated blackness "doesn't sell" (277). In the only conclusion proposed by the novel, Me proclaims with a flourish—"Unmitigated Blackness is coming to the realization that as fucked up and meaningless as it all is, sometimes it's the nihilism that makes life worth living" (277).

States of Possibility

Neither post-black in any definition nor satirical at first glance, Whitehead's celebrated 2016 novel, *The Underground Railroad*, does not fit the work of the authors discussed above nor the rubric of post-black satire in any simple way. And yet it serves as the fitting conclusion to this discussion, as well as a conduit to the project of historical revisionism, the focus of my next chapter, "Talking Books." In moving past his usual mode of post-black satire, Whitehead's novel may be read as either a deliberate shift into the earnest race-based critique he formerly eschewed or something still slightly askew from such a project despite the difficult subject matter. While reviewers have signaled both approaches, I suggest that aspects of the two seemingly contradictory stances coexist in the novel, making its import at once overly literal and elusive. Beginning with the illusion of straightforward history, the novel embeds a much more complex allegory in a seemingly matter-of-fact narrative. Its speculative aspects stretch time and space, without resorting to melancholic notions of living with the lost object, or offering narratives of overcoming or redemption, or compressing present concerns with historical ones. Readers may view the novel as evocative of current racial injustice, but the novel itself never makes that analogy explicit. Instead it uses analogy to open outward, to uncertain comparisons and subtle evocations that do not rely on equivalence, or may even be apprehended rationally. As a racial allegory, the literal train of *Underground Railroad* does function like a time machine, but reveals the movement of the runaway slave to be neither progress nor escape.

In drawing on existing slave narratives, especially those by Douglass and Jacobs, as well as the interviews conducted by the Federal Writers' Project, *The Underground Railroad* establishes clear claims to the authenticity of the history it represents. Many readers have noted the ring of truth the narrative possesses, seeming to echo the voices of the slaves in the interviews from the 1930s. Such an illusion further gains ground from the actual advertisements for runaway slaves placed strategically in the novel, gathered from the North Carolina Runaway Slave Advertisements project.

But after the realist imperative is fulfilled (quite rapidly in the first sixty pages or so), the novel shifts into a speculative register and imagines alternate histories instead. The deliberately fantastical strategy challenges the conceit of the rational apprehension of slavery today as well as a visceral identification with the slave ancestor. As a narrative prop, speculation enables Whitehead an expansive scope and span as he dips in and out of various racial regimes of the nineteenth, twentieth, and twenty-first centuries. By departing from realism, Whitehead situates US chattel slavery in its most iconic form—a cotton plantation in Georgia—in clear relation to a range of other forms of racial expropriation, some of which call forward to African American experiences of abuse yet to happen—such as the Tuskegee experiment—while others spiral outward to such farther flung experiences as Nazism. For instance, when Cora hides in an attic in a genocidal North Carolina, which has, in an echo of the Final Solution, "abolished niggers" instead of abolishing slavery, Whitehead evenly draws on Harriet Jacobs's account of concealment for seven years and on Anne Frank's memoir of captivity under the Nazis, encouraging readers to ponder transracial and transhistorical connections.[42]

If Whitehead was once the poster child for a postracial aesthetic, whose fictions prioritized indirection, metaphor, and irony over social critique, *The Underground Railroad* seems to announce his return to the canon. Certainly, this is how Oprah Winfrey introduces his book as her pick for her book club—the return of the prodigal son to a welcoming community of readers, who no longer have to figure out what elevators may or not signify, but can have their hearts thrill to Cora's escapades, imagining their own families wrenched apart in sentimental tableaus, or align the police killings of today to the slave patrollers of years past.[43] Whitehead himself presents the novel as the fruit of his own maturation, as he reveals his sixteen-year-long gestation period for the novel, only to be put aside because he wasn't ready.

Even Whitehead's first novel, *The Intuitionist* (1999), however, was structured by the link between reading and freedom. Deforming the plot of the passing novel almost beyond recognition in his parallel universe of empiricist versus intuitionist elevator inspectors, Whitehead nevertheless locates the central character's epiphany in the truth sanctified in the slave narrative. On discovering that James Fulton, author of *Theoretical Elevators*, is passing for white, Lila Mae finds "a new literacy: In the last few days she has learned how to read, like a slave does, one forbidden word at a time."[44] Recalling such connections helps situate *The Underground Railroad* in relation to Whitehead's other fictions, not simply an embrace of what he once abjured. It also helps frame the story of trauma that he writes as something other than realist or redemptive, but an alternate history of slavery, satirical rather than sentimental, cerebral rather than visceral.

In claiming both realism (the events described really happened and we learn something meaningful about slavery) and allegory (gesturing to parallels with Jonathan Swift's *Gulliver's Travels* or Gabriel García Márquez's *One Hundred Years of Solitude*), Whitehead reshapes the genre of the slave narrative in curious fashion. Jettisoning plausibility (the slave narrative's historical commitment to truth, to represent slavery as it really was), Whitehead takes the form of a slave narrative with its central structuring journey—from South to North, slavery to freedom—and cross-hatches it with a range of other practices. Some of these practices can be construed as the afterlife of slavery (the terrors of lynching, the massacre of black towns, medical experiments on black inmates, the paternalism of uplift programs, the sanitized and deformed memorial practices of museums runs by the victors of history). Others are more varied—with genocide of indigenous populations, mass sterilization, eugenics and selective breeding, the refusal of sanctuary, the purchase of escaped slaves and other labor by governments for biopolitical ends, mass extermination, selective immigration of the Irish to pick cotton—all of which seem to be plucked from a global history shop of atrocities. All of these racist regimes thus acquire some of the ring of truth granted by the scaffold of the historical slave narrative, even as they are tugged out of their own time, or harnessed from some future dystopia. Even though technically each chapter is set in 1850—the year of the Fugitive Slave Act—the events seem to be out of time, as 1850 becomes the endless present of America.[45]

Two distinct conceptions of time propel the novel. First, time is relentlessly linear, as the slave's quest for freedom and the slave catcher's pursuit structure each section. There is little suspense because both are foregone conclusions. Cora will run, and Ridgeway will hunt and capture. Her escape is not possible, not real, and yet running gives her life meaning and the book hope. Within this larger temporal structure, Whitehead inserts a second logic—where time is endlessly flexible and endlessly manipulated, such that a future experiment in Tuskegee from 1932 to 1972 bisects the experience of the Fugitive Slave Law of 1850, or the Nazi Final Solution dictates the chilling discussion of "the Colored Question" in North Carolina. An 1811 *Diary of a Resurrectionist* from London becomes the experience of a young doctor who turns body-snatcher in Boston or sterilizer of blacks in South Carolina. When Cora hears a woman scream "they're taking away my babies" in South Carolina, she assumes a traumatic flashback to slavery, but finds out that the woman "wasn't lamenting an old plantation injustice but a crime perpetrated here in South Carolina. The doctors were stealing her babies from her, not her former masters" (123). As the great yellow fever epidemic of 1878 ravages Tennessee, the neighboring state of Indiana sees the birth of the Klan, refusing to allow "Valentine Farm"—a sanctuary established for black people by black intellectuals evoking Douglass, Du Bois, and Washington. In each section, time is cross-hatched by space, as every state develops its own racial world with its own peculiarities (next to each other, yet worlds apart), until the linear time of the escaped slave and the relentless pursuer catches up.

For a number of readers, the novel has evoked some specific parallels to contemporary attacks on black lives in the United States—especially likening the slave patrollers and their demand for papers to the "stop and frisk" policies hounding unarmed black men and women today.[46] But the novel itself never resorts to such analogies, choosing instead to place what we know as the facts of actually existing slavery next to what might have been, from other times and places. Doing so does not affirm the singularity of slavery as an institution, nor seek to explain present-day black subjectivity as structured by slavery. *Underground Railroad* is far more oblique and allusive than that, since it speeds up and amalgamates various slave narratives, generating almost a collage effect since not all these experiences could have plausibly happened to a single character. Even as he makes a metaphor literal—an actual train running underneath the slave states—Whitehead overloads all the characters with symbolic, allegorical freight. Allegory presumes some ahistoricity rather than a revelation of truth about one single moment of time. The novel clearly does not just relate the story of a fugitive slave's journey to freedom: it meditates on the very state of freedom and its possibility.

Whitehead has repeatedly said that he was inspired by Jonathan Swift's *Gulliver's Travels* and Gabriel García Márquez's *One Hundred Years of Solitude*. He explains that the latter gave him a way to write about slavery's brutal excesses in a matter-of-fact tone, one that echoes the plainness of the interviews collected by the Federal Works Progress Administration in the 1930s. Drawing on Kafka and John Bunyan's *Pilgrim's Progress* as well, Whitehead frames Cora's journey as allegorical: "Any kind of adventure story where someone goes from allegorical episode to allegorical episode, and escapes at the last minute, that sort of outlandish series of events actually works for an escaped slave. You are just going from slim refuge to slim refuge trying to make it out."[47] Whitehead creates allegory in the sense described by Walter Benjamin—"Allegories are, in the realm of thoughts, what ruins are in the sense of things"—to build and destroy racial infrastructures.[48] But it is Swift who seems like the most intriguing predecessor. Whitehead notes that "I went back to *Gulliver's Travels*, to read it properly, and I was struck how alien it was. It was really about 18th-century British history and all this internecine political and religious in-fighting, but the structure is really sound."[49] Adopting the structure of a traveler in strange and often hostile lands for his neo-slave narrative, Whitehead "reboots" the story every sixty pages or so as Cora travels from state to state, revealing a different aspect of US racial regimes. Whitehead explains his decision as a result of his desired scope—not a fidelity to a single account of slavery in a single southern plantation, but a comment on the nation itself: "What if every state that she traveled through was a different state of American possibility, like in *Gulliver's Travels*?"[50]

Caesar, the character who opens the novel, urging Cora to run away, keeps a copy of Swift's book hidden in an abandoned schoolhouse on the Georgia plantation where Cora is born. The white abolitionist from whom he gets the book warns Caesar that "the book will get him killed." But Caesar knows that "if he didn't read, he was a slave" (235). Here,

Whitehead emphasizes the same inextricable connection between literacy and freedom enshrined in classic slave narratives by Douglass and others. Caesar nonetheless proposes a critique of this Talking Book: "The white man in the book, Gulliver, roved from peril to peril, each new island a new predicament to solve before he could return home. That was the man's real trouble, not the savage and uncanny civilizations he encountered—he kept forgetting what he had. That was white people all over: Build a schoolhouse and let it rot, make a home then keep straying. If Caesar figured the route home, he'd never travel again" (235). Caesar never does find the way home, strung up by Ridgeway, but Whitehead insists on Cora's journey to a possible home, even as the novel grows further and further away from realism to allegory. Reimagining the neo-slave narrative as Swiftian allegory means that Cora becomes the norm in a crazy world—the norm against which that world must be measured and judged. Swift's preferred title for *Gulliver's Travels*—*Travels through Several Remote Nations of the World*—aptly indicates the scope afforded by Whitehead's usage, neither nihilistic nor misanthropic. When Cora first finds the underground railroad—an actual rusty train underneath Georgia ("the steel ran south and north presumably, springing from some inconceivable source and shooting toward a miraculous terminus"; 67)—Lumbly, the station agent, tells her that "every state is different. Each one a state of possibility, with its own customs and ways of doing things. Moving through them, you'll see the breadth of the country before you reach your final stop" (68–69). But Cora's journey is far more fragmented and uncertain than a linear flight from south to north, slavery to freedom. Born in Georgia to a mother who died in the swamp trying to escape, and a grandmother who underwent the Middle Passage from Africa, Cora ends the novel still in flight—as she joins a set of wagons heading west to St. Louis and then California. Over the course of the novel, she stops at South Carolina, the stage for a range of liberal racist experiments to improve and then eugenicize the black race, North Carolina, which implements the final solution and lynches every black person in sight, leaving their bodies hanging as "rotten ornaments" dotting the "Freedom Trail," Tennessee, ravaged by yellow fever, and Indiana, where a black utopian community establishes a farm, only to have it massacred and burnt to the ground by neighboring "bloodthirsty whites" (209).

Several characters function as allegorical archetypes: like Ridgeway who helpfully anatomizes his own biography and formation as a principle of order chasing the principle of fugitivity. The American imperative—the core of the nation and its history and future—becomes this elemental quest. Cora will flee, will hide, will seek freedom, and Ridgeway will chase her to bring her back to brutal slavery. For Ridgeway, the fanatical slave-catcher who pursues Cora unrelentingly, the two are locked in a cosmic struggle: "I'm a notion of order. The slave that disappears—it's a notion, too. Of hope" (223). When she struggles with him to be free, strangling him with the very chains that shackle her, Whitehead describes her scream as "a train whistle echoing in a tunnel," cementing the association of the train with liberty (226). The final chapter of the novel, titled simply "The North," similarly seems more allegorical than realist, as Cora makes her improbable escape by deciding, as she descends the stairs of the "ghost station" in Indiana, that she would hold Ridgeway "close, as if in a slow dance" (302). Leaving the slave catcher to his death, she pumps the handcar "into the tunnel that no one had made, that led nowhere. She discovered a rhythm, pumping her arms, throwing all of herself into movement. Into northness. Was she traveling through the tunnel or digging it?" (303). Here, as in much of the novel, the North remains an abstract principle, not a place or destination, one that is likely to disappoint if ever attained. Rather than the endpoint, the journey itself is what the novel emphasizes as for a slave, any place has to be better than where she runs from. Cora is guided by this principle: "She trusted the slave's choice to guide her—anywhere, anywhere but where you are escaping from" (304). Cora becomes one of the mythical creators of the railroad, as well as its anointed heir.

Actual advertisements promising rewards for runaway slaves punctuate the novel, until Whitehead writes a final fictional one for Cora—an act he calls a bit of "postmodern jujutsu," titled simply "Ran Away." Clarifying that she fled her "legal but not rightful master," the ad announces that "she has stopped running" and "she was never property" (298). In doing so, Whitehead undoes the racist logic of the genre of the runaway advertisement, which blandly asserts the rights of the master and glosses over the personhood of the fugitive, noting wounds and scars (from burns or other abuse) simply as identifying markers to assist the pursuer. The runaway advertisement—which exists to capture and return to slavery—transforms into a declaration of independence at the novel's end, one that is far more meaningful than the one Michael used to recite on the Randall plantation to amuse slave owners as a "parlor trick" designed to exhibit the parity of a slave with a parrot capable of mimicry (32). Cora's independence is from America, which has tried repeatedly to enslave her, to remain her "warden," but in an echo of what Richard Wright called "the Negro"—"America's metaphor"—Cora also comes to embody the real essence of America: a nation of fugitives.[51]

Critics have rightly noted the novel's challenge to the mythology of the Underground Railroad—where white saviors overpower an evil system and guarantee freedom for the heroic fugitives.[52] Here, without a comforting binary of white savior or black victim, Whitehead indicts the historical and present-day United States. Representing whites as monstrous, patronizing, kind by turns, he builds distinct racial infrastructures in each state. A seeming utopia in South Carolina reveals biopolitical management of labor and an active eugenics program; North Carolina chooses unadulterated fascism, while Indiana provides a glimpse of sanctuary only to wrench it away. In that sense, the novel's scope is like *Invisible Man*—going through the range of alternatives open to African Americans for the shelter of home and erasing each one. All that remains is the principle of fugitivity itself. Whitehead does not prioritize plausibility, but quickly builds worlds and breaks them down. The assorted stories—about the afterlife of slavery—the management of labor, eugenics, the paternalism of uplift, the refusal of sanctuary, the massacres of black towns, sterilization, lynching—are all true, and are out of time.

Remarkably, Cora represents the antithesis of sentimental portraits of black womanhood. Whitehead departs from Harriet Jacobs's precedent in his refusal to work within the sentimental tradition. Jacobs famously manipulated the literary conventions of domestic fiction to appeal to female readers, revising the cult of true womanhood and its diktats of chastity and piety into a unique experience of the slave girl. To do so, Jacobs had to reckon with notions of motherhood and manage audience expectations about female sexuality, especially black female sexuality. In fusing the male slave narrative's elements of adventure and jeremiad with novelistic frames highlighting interiority and psychological depth, Jacobs molded Linda Brent as a suitable sentimental heroine, devoted to her children, and aspiring to her grandmother's model of piety with passion despite a calculated affair with Mr. Sands. But Whitehead's Cora comes with no such constraints. She is outside the sentimental norm, even as she is an enormously sympathetic character. Neither maternal nor romantically inclined, she withholds affection more than once from loving partners, unable to love in the face of so much trauma, and bears a great deal of rage toward her absent mother. The novel's beginning finds her inheriting her grandmother's legacy of a small garden, but where Linda Brent's grandmother becomes Jacobs's emblem of true womanhood, Cora loses first grandmother then mother, and no memory of their legacy can protect her even from her fellow slaves. That there might be community among the enslaved or traditions of solidarity is outweighed by their brutalization, as Whitehead unsentimentally speculates that a people so oppressed may not be inclined to be generous to each other. The Hob on the plantation, seemingly designated as the space for outcasts by the enslaved, repeats itself in South Carolina, as those with psychological problems are isolated in parallel ways. Cora imagines making love to Royal at the novel's very end, but only after his death, and her sublimation into allegory. Whitehead thus refuses us easy access to Cora's interiority, loading her with symbolic capital.

Even though Whitehead narrates a bleak tale, adapted from fabulist fictions like that of Márquez, he chooses a galvanizing pace, which explains why many readers find the ending uplifting. We inhabit the space of myth at the end: the ghost station and the stylized, picturesque fight between Cora and Ridgeway doesn't so much suggest that Cora is now free but that, as an allegorical compression of African American life, she represents the ongoing fugitivity of black life. Cora keeps going West, losing everyone she knows along the way, and starts over and over again. In his resolute focus on an immensely relatable young girl's experience of trauma and her resolve to flee, Whitehead transcends the divide between an affective and historicist approach to the past identified by several scholars as the central quandary facing the neo-slave narrative.[53] An unflinching look at the horrors of slavery, the novel captures philosophical concerns as well as the lived reality of the historical experience of slavery. The novel thus illuminates (by replicating) the peculiar generic mix of the slave narrative—the uneasy blend of adventure tale, a romantic quest for freedom, a bildungsroman (especially the female slave's coming of age as elucidated by Jacobs), and a jeremiad. Whitehead further highlights the world-making powers of the novel as a genre, building up and destroying whole worlds in remarkably compressed fashion. The railroad as portal almost works like a device for travel through time, not just space. No longer "a figure of speech" (300), the underground railroad nevertheless remains both whimsical and phantasmagoric. Fugitive slaves repeatedly ask the station agents, "Who built it?" only to receive the laconic reply, "Who builds anything in this country?" (67). An "underground prison" (147) or a mica mine as much as the promise of liberty, the train lurches from horror to horror, as Cora realizes that "she was a stray in every sense. The last of her tribe" (145).

In this way, Whitehead mines the speculative power of racial allegory to disturb the valence of both fable and history, thus joining (and extending) the efforts of Johnson and Beatty to corrode any comfortable revival of slavery today. All three writers showcase the shift in twenty-first-century usages of the historical past, which fail to return clear conclusions about the present. None of them revive the slave narrative in any simple fashion, but in posing the question of what slavery means in a purported postracial world, they break the commandment of the slave narrative that black art must further black progress. Johnson inverts past racisms to comic effect in *Pym* to arrive at a quotidian conclusion that the future of the world is mostly brown-skinned. Shattering all postulations of race in the present, including any attempt to whitewash the past, Beatty ends at a kind of exhilarating nihilism. In his thoughtful transformations of slavery into a range of other exploitative racial regimes of disposability, expropriation, and genocide, Whitehead serves as a bridge between such satirical excesses and the focus of my next chapter. "Talking Books (Talking Back)" traces the intensification of the variegated uses of far-flung analogies by Toni Morrison and Caryl Phillips (who rewrite Othello as surrogate for the child soldier and Holocaust survivor) and M. NourbeSe Philip and Robin Coste Lewis (who return to history to revise it beyond recognition), still further transforming the sentimental substitutions of the modern slave narrative.

4

Talking Books (Talking Back)

The history of blackness is testament to the fact that objects
can and do resist.
—Fred Moten, *In the Break*

"The trope of the Talking Book is the ur-trope of the Anglo-African tradition." So declares Henry Louis Gates Jr. in a powerful effort to create an immanent theory of an African American literary tradition in *The Signifying Monkey*.[1] The trope originates toward the end of the eighteenth century with James Gronniosaw's *A Narrative of the Most Remarkable Particulars in the Life of James Albert Ukawsaw Gronniosaw, an African Prince, as Related by Himself*:

> [My master] used to read prayers in public to the ship's crew every Sabbath day; and when I first saw him read, I was never so surprised in my life, as when I saw the book talk to my master, for I thought it did, as I observed him to look upon it, and move his lips. I wished it would do so with me. As soon as my master had done reading, I followed him to the place where he put the book, being mightily delighted with it, and when nobody saw me, I opened it, and put my ear down close upon it, in great hopes that it would say something to me; but I was very sorry, and greatly disappointed, when I found that it would not speak. This thought immediately presented itself to me, that every body and every thing despised me because I was black.[2]

Reading this confrontation of the silent book and the enslaved black man as the archetypal figure for thinking about the African American relationship to literacy, and by extension, to the project of Enlightenment itself, Gates argues that the struggle for emancipation centers squarely in the effort to demonstrate one's humanity to a world bent on denying it. If an object, a commodity, a piece of chattel could write, could will herself into existence through writing, then she was not destined to be a slave. Writing was the measure of civilizational achievement and possibility. This is why, Gates notes, Phillis Wheatley was reviewed by the "Who's Who of the French, English, and American Enlightenment," including Voltaire, Thomas Jefferson, and George Washington. Accordingly, "in the black tradition, writing became the visible sign, the commodity of exchange, the text and technology of reason."[3] Declaring the significance of the black vernacular and forms of orality to the development of African American literature, Gates centers the literate subject who proves her (or more often, his) command of humanity and potential for citizenship by evolving away from the object without knowledge of letters, enslaved as a creature unable to read, write, or think.

While John Marrant, Quobna Ottobah Cugoano, and John Jea signify on the same trope, in some ways, Olaudah Equiano instantiates the clearest transformation of object to subject in *The Interesting Narrative of the Life of Olaudah Equiano* (1789).[4] Equiano's account of his transformation from "African to Anglo-African, from slave to potential freedman, from an absence to a presence, and indeed from an object to a subject" draws its power from his mastery of the Talking Book trope. "I had often seen my master and Dick employed in reading; and I had a great curiosity to talk to the books, as I thought they did; and so to learn how all things had a beginning: for that purpose I have often taken up a book, and have talked to it, and then put my ears to it, when alone, in hopes it would answer me; and I have remained very much concerned when I found it remained silent."[5] In this sense, Gates notes that a better description is the "un–Talking Book," signaling the refusal of the desired object to reveal its secrets of textuality to an oral-centered epistemology. This constitutive contradiction frames Gates's reading of subsequent literature ranging from Zora Neale Hurston to Ishmael Reed to Alice Walker as variations on the theme of the journey to splice the dual heritage of African orality and Western literacy. Gates's emphasis on repetition as improvisation and his notions of signifying have been field-defining in their explicit equation of freedom with literacy. In the company of such critics as William Andrews, Robert Stepto, Houston Baker, Nellie McKay, Barbara Christian, Deborah McDowell, Frances Smith Foster, Richard Yarborough, and Mary Helen Washington, Gates also establishes the overriding importance of the black vernacular tradition in an attempt to carve out a distinct African American literary tradition out of its own self-representation. The story of the Talking Book, therefore, is also the story of how an African became an African American after the Middle Passage.

Equiano, for instance, creates several different speaking selves in *Interesting Narrative*, relating the story of his subjection from the distance of a free man by shifting between past and present tense, a rhetorical achievement that Gates credits with his outsize influence as the prototype of the slave narrative until 1865. In "contrasting his earlier self with the self that narrates his text," Equiano transforms his status as akin to "the watch, the portrait, and the book" as all variations of "the master's object" to a speaking subject, who masters the master's language to come into a full humanity.[6] As discussed in the introduction, slave narrators had to walk a tightrope of aiming for credibility (going so far as to claim that no use was made of their imagination in the ensuing account) while fashioning a subjectivity out of the very narrative that described their journey from bondage to freedom. This meant that scenes of instruction, of learning to read and write, acquired a great deal of symbolic weight in much of early African American writing. For Gates, such an origin story leads not to a fraught relationship between the world of print and the question of freedom, but rather to an almost indistinguishable conflation of the two.

While such a formulation of a canon has been extraordinarily influential, it has also been critiqued for its various exclusions, especially for ignoring the Native American entanglements with these founding scenes.[7] Moreover, critics have wondered about the difference gender makes in such a genealogy, and quarreled with the seeming acceptance of the definition of humanity through access to the book (often signaling the Bible in slave narratives), and asked if the divide between African orality and Western literacy can be sustained.[8] Harryette Mullen, for instance, questions the Eurocentric assumption that African cultures lacked indigenous cultures of writing and script.[9] This means not only recognizing the existence of Islamic writing systems that enslaved literate Muslim Africans brought with them in the eighteenth and nineteenth centuries, but also reconsidering how we might conceive of the larger African American relationship to the oral and the written, accounting for what Robert Farris Thompson has called "the flash of the spirit."[10] For Mullen, this also requires rethinking the distinction between spiritual and material forms of freedom and greater investigation into the kinds of secular and sacred forms of resistance that emerged in slave culture. Grey Gundaker further argues for broadening the definition of writing, pointing to ritual forms of scarring and grave marking that were retained across the African diaspora.[11] More recent critiques have argued for a need for more book history, for a theory of reading founded on print culture (recalling Douglass's passionate interest in typography, for instance, as John Stauffer and Robert Fanuzzi note), while pathbreaking research on reading habits has revealed the existence of black print counterpublics distinct from a white civil society.[12] Such historicist reconstruction challenges the conceptual parameters of Gates's approach as well, especially its normative status as the canonical account of black literature. As John Edgar Wideman wondered in an otherwise laudatory review in 1988, "What about the Talking Book trope in literature not written by blacks? Was it a common way of 'figuring' literacy vs. illiteracy? Is it important or not to establish the blackness of this trope?"[13]

Perhaps the most searching challenge to Gates's approach comes from Ronald Judy, who asks for a graver reckoning with the horror, abjection, and objectification elucidated in the slave narrative. Judy argues that Gates accepts literacy and humanity as interchangeable, instead of pursuing a critique through thanatology.[14] Such unresolved questions about the frame of the Talking Book require reopening the subject, especially because so many contemporary works return to the slave narrative as formal antecedent and inspiration. Gates's emphasis on formal reflexivity, his identification of a complex continuity across Africa and the Atlantic, across writers separated by three centuries, and his recognition (albeit partial) of the painful contradictions of equating black freedom with the acquisition of literacy continue to propel generative ways of reading African American literature. Though he does not always fully admit the power of the paradox, his question—"How can the black subject posit a full and sufficient self in a language in which blackness is a sign of absence?"—continues to refract debates about black literary traditions and canons to this day.[15]

These debates code three larger areas of critical disagreement: the valence of Enlightenment rationality as a container for black subjectivity, the black relation to the West, and the symbolic place of Africa as a possible counternarrative to modernity. The three are obviously related, and in what follows, I show how such contemporary authors as Toni Morrison, Caryl Phillips, Robin Coste Lewis, and M. NourbeSe Philip resurrect these questions to refigure the relations among liberal Enlightenment ideas of humanity, the black presence in the West, and the expansion of the African American literary tradition to a more global one across time and space. Philip's *Zong!* (2008) incorporates legal documents of slavery into a poetic collage that reshapes orality, visuality, and textuality alike, by returning to the words of the 1783 legal decision *Gregson v. Gilbert*. In *Voyage of the Sable Venus* (2015), Lewis expands the boundaries of African American literature by collecting art objects that embody black women across a range of cultures and histories into a remarkably cohesive poem. Both Morrison and Phillips return to Shakespeare's *Othello* in *Desdemona* (2012) and *The Nature of Blood* (1997), respectively, to unmoor the question of race and literacy from the sixteenth century, filling in historical lacunae but also connecting histories of racialization and slavery to current concerns about feminist and interracial coalitions. In their varied engagements with the Western aesthetic tradition, they draw on the founding trope of the Talking Book to revisit the act of literary ventriloquism and to establish surrogate selves. The Talking Book thus morphs into Shakespeare or Emily Brontë, objects of Western art or legal briefs of abolition, as the reconstructed history of slavery and colonialism collides with the Western canon.

Exposing the Talking Book as a fetish, such contemporary writers remake the relation between the objects that signify racist commodification and the literature and art that presupposes more complex representational aspirations. Just like a ventriloquist can throw her voice to make it seem like it's coming from elsewhere (from a dummy, for instance), producing the dissonance that comes from seeing an object speak and assume subjectivity, these writers throw their voices imaginatively into the Western canon to challenge us to see what new possibilities open up when they disturb received genealogies and reconstruct comparative, relational, and speculative histories.

The figure of the ventriloquist—an animate body and inanimate object sharing speech—immediately suggests deception, veiling, and masking. As Steven Connor shows in *Dumbstruck: A Cultural History of Ventriloquism*, the origin of the voice and its relation to the speaker's body have long been the central features of the art.[16] In thinking of the slave narrative as enacting a form of literary ventriloquism, I gesture to both the relationship between editor and narrator (discussed in the introduction and chapter 1) and the navigation of the subject-object duality that characterizes the slave narrator's relation to the Talking Book. Such difficulties index larger concerns about autonomy and agency, as questions persist about the degree of control a white editor had over the ostensible subject of the slave narrative. While such relations often return in the global context of humanitarianism, as we saw in chapter 1, the stakes for contemporary African American writers can often be quite different. In part, this is due to the fact that when we think of racial ventriloquism today, the relationship between a white mediator of a black experience seems to be inverted, as it frequently signals a white desire to speak black. The rich body of scholarship on minstrelsy has revealed the strange longings and the often grotesque drama of identification, disavowal, and transference at the heart of various forms of linguistic and somatic blackface.[17] But even more subtle forms of transracial identification tend to raise questions of appropriation, as speaking the other can easily become speaking for the other, reinforcing racist stereotypes.[18] Because so much of the conversation around appropriation today relies on the understanding of racial identity as a kind of property, I want to clarify at the outset that my use of the frame of literary ventriloquism on the part of Morrison and Phillips indicates something quite different, as the writers channel the figure of the ancestor in their writing, using the notion of being possessed as a figure for the creative intervention they stage. Blocking easy access to meaning or identification, they choose to travel in the Western canon to rethink our history of the figure of the "black" or the "African" in the West. In *Invisible Man*, Ralph Ellison memorably staged the dancing black "Sambo" doll to show the Harlem youth leader, Tod Clifton's need to "fall outside of *history*." The writers I discuss, in contrast, choose to fall *inside* history.[19]

The Master's Words

Falling inside history more often than not involves a deep immersion in the master's words. This does not merely mean participating in revisionist accounts of received histories, whether as sequel, riposte, or parody:

a massive undertaking in much of contemporary literature. The postcolonial project of writing back to the empire may easily be seen as the core mission of the most celebrated writers of the late twentieth century, including J. M. Coetzee, Maryse Conde, Jamaica Kincaid, V. S. Naipaul, Jean Rhys, Tayeb Salih, and Derek Walcott.[20] Such recent works as Kamel Daoud's 2013 *The Meursault Investigation* (rewriting Albert Camus's 1942 *The Stranger*) and Caryl Phillips's 2015 *The Lost Child* (responding to Emily Brontë's 1847 *Wuthering Heights*) continue such returns.[21] African American writers have similarly written back to canonical representations of slavery, often rendering the originals unrecognizable. Ishmael Reed's 1976 *Flight to Canada*, a parody of Harriet Beecher Stowe's 1852 *Uncle Tom's Cabin*, and Alice Randall's 2001 *The Wind Done Gone*, an "unauthorized parody" of Margaret Mitchell's 1936 *Gone with the Wind*, appropriate the master's words, turning a decolonizing gaze onto the romanticized accounts of slavery found in Stowe and Mitchell.[22] As examples of postmodern ventriloquism, they also cast doubt on the knowability of history, emphasizing indirection and loss instead. In doing so, they display the strategies Houston Baker names as "*the mastery of form* and the *deformation of mastery*." Baker argues that in the face of widespread stereotype, distortion, and romance, the task for the black writer at the dawn of the twentieth century "was the production of a manual of black speaking, a book of speaking *back and black*."[23]

Many twenty-first-century works that refigure the trope of the Talking Book differ from such earlier instances of revision, in part because they can take them for granted and build upon them. John Keene's *Counternarratives* revisits Mark Twain to imagine Huck Finn and Jim (with his full name, James Alton Rivers, restored) encounter each other on opposite sides of the Civil War. But this speculative history is placed within a much larger project of rethinking historical origins and trajectories, beginning with imagining the first inhabitant of Manhattan Island, and gesturing outward to farther flung histories in Brazil, Mexico, Haiti, and Africa.[24] Amitav Ghosh's *Sea of Poppies*, an Indian Ocean epic, similarly invokes a figure like Frederick Douglass only to invite us to think about slavery, indenture, and the opium trade in conjoined and intersecting ways.[25] In this chapter, I explore similarly experimental revisionist projects that move beyond the task of writing back. As Keene puts it in his earlier novella, *Annotations*, while "the uneven terrain of history remains, the challenge, however, no longer to write the unrecorded story."[26] Similarly, Morrison and Phillips are after something more ambitious and even more oblique, as they stage more subtle travels in the Western canon, not just countering or revising but imagining alternate histories, relations among races and genders, and new geographies of belonging and being. In trying to do more than correct the historical record, Morrison and Phillips also expand the analogy with slavery in unexpected ways, neither equating the contemporary racialized subject with the enslaved ancestor nor agreeing to separate past depredation from present abuse. Extending the scope of the African American literary tradition to African and Jewish histories of oppression, they dissect the ways in which similar histories may or may not allow for solidarity or friendship.

Perhaps the most striking instance of revisiting the story of slavery by ventriloquizing the master's words is M. NourbeSe Philip's *Zong!* (2008), which takes up the 1781 massacre on the slave ship, where the captain ordered that the 133 captured Africans on board be thrown overboard so that he could recoup their loss through insurance. While the incident was a flashpoint for abolitionist debates in the eighteenth century, it has since been mined by writers and poets for imagining a range of responses to the atrocity. The single extant public document relating to the case—the 1783 legal decision *Gregson v. Gilbert*—makes up the entire text of Philip's poem. Riffing on the conventions of "as told to" or "written by herself" slave narratives, Philip also lists on the title page a cocreator, "As told to the author by Setaey Adamu Boateng," explaining that the latter is "the voice of the ancestors revealing the submerged stories of all who were on board the Zong."[27] Philip's memorial and hauntological project in *Zong* unmistakably draws upon and differentiates itself from the slave narrative in its attempt to make the text of Western authority speak otherwise.

Philip's decision to use the words of the legal document is a difficult and wrenching one, not least because it seems to perpetuate the transformation of human into chattel, into property that can be compensated in material terms, rather than a life with meaning. She explains that "in *Zong!*, the African, transformed into a thing by the law, is retransformed, miraculously, back into human" (196). But this is an uneven process. Hence Philip notes her refusal to narrate a linear story—rather she outlines the impulse "through oath and through moan, through mutter, chant and babble, through babble and curse, through chortle and ululation to not-tell the story" (196). This struggle to speak, to render legible, to mourn and memorialize, to exhume or "exaqua" (201) explodes formally onto the space of the page of the book as Philip scatters, shatters words and spaces, aspiring toward a "negative space, a space not so much of non-meaning as anti-meaning" (201). Transforming the slave narrative's quest to fashion an identity out of literacy, Philip expands the absence so often glossed over, forcing the reader to come to terms with what cannot be spoken.

The confrontation of African orality and Western textuality staged by the Talking Book trope receives a stunning mutation in Philip's hands as well. Many readers have remarked on the difference in reading the poem on the page and watching Philip perform it in person. Using musical forms like the fugue and counterpoint, visually arranging words on the page to mimic the fall overboard of the enslaved, and imagining names for the murdered in various African languages as a footer running along the page are only some of the ways that Philip disrupts conventional textuality.[28] That the original text of the court case between the owners and the insurers, *Gregson v. Gilbert*, comes to only about five hundred words further underscores Philip's spatial and sonic innovation. The penultimate section, titled "Ebora" (meaning underwater spirits in Yoruba), even contains words superimposed and rendered illegible by an initial printer error, but later becomes a deliberate decision to emphasize the opacity of language. A glossary in various languages does not so much make sense of or translate foreign words but further accentuates the impossibility of our access to the lost lives on the *Zong*. Philip explicitly links her revisionist work to the uncertain passage between language and law, noting that "I deeply distrust this tool I work with—language"; hence the choice of "disorder, illogic and irrationality" in her attempt to transform the silent text of the legal brief into a book that talks back (197).

Robin Coste Lewis's National Book Award–winning *Voyage of the Sable Venus* (2015) further electrifyingly subverts such a fraught relationship with Talking Books and other objects. The seventy-nine-page title poem at the center of the poetry collection highlights the ways in which the black female figure has been represented in some forty thousand years of Western art. Lewis explains in the "Prologue" that the narrative poem is "comprised solely and entirely of the titles, catalog entries, or exhibit descriptions of Western art objects in which a black female figure is present, dating from 38,000 BCE to the present."[29] She uses both traditional artistic media like paintings, sculpture, and photography and such material objects as clocks, combs, spoons, and legs of tables that signify some kind of visual (often violent) connection to the black female body. Moreover, she realizes that in removing such labels as "slave" and "negro" in favor of "African-American" museums and libraries were sanitizing and whitewashing history, so to combat this "historical erasure of slavery," Lewis replaces the words with the original epithets (35). This project of reappropriation illuminates the production of the black woman into an art object, that then becomes a poem (not just in an ekphrastic repetition) but as a challenge to what constitutes our understanding of Western art itself and its reliance on racial and gendered violence. Such a poetics draws on ventriloquism as a central technology of dismantling the master's house, as Lewis condemns the entire history of Western art without using any extraneous words or analysis. Her narrative dexterity generates such chilling juxtapositions as "Partially Broken Young Black Girl / Presenting a Stemmed Bowl / Supported / by a Monkey" (44), revealing not only the dehumanization of the young girl but also the broken vessel of her body as art object.

Lewis reclaims her title from Thomas Stothard's 1793 "The Voyage of the Sable Venus from Angola to the West Indies," itself a grotesque parody of Botticelli's *Birth of Venus,* and a marker of the representational violence that accompanied slavery. Lewis explains in an interview that the long historical span as well as the geographical range (including various kinds of Moorish and other Oriental figures from colonial harem photographs, for example, in her catalog of black women) were deliberately corrective: "I refuse to accept 1492 as the inception of black history.... I think it's a brilliant sleight of hand to ask African Americans to think of ourselves this way, with a history that is only a few centuries old, and before that we were nothing, a blank. I refuse to agree to this fantasy, because that means we began in slavery, which is to say, as no one, and we all know that that is not true."[30]

Formally, as well, Lewis exhibits the same urge toward expansiveness, when her first catalog on ancient Greece and Rome takes the shape of Sanskrit couplets, or *shlokas,* a tradition she studied at Harvard. Continuous with her effort to expand the parameters of what is allowed within the circuit of African American literature, Lewis notes that "postcolonial literature is a great comfort for [her] as a writer because it encourages [her] to remember several borders, more than one empire, and all the bodies constantly navigating those who own them."[31] Rather than returning to slavery to create an unbroken line of continuity between past and present in the manner of Gates's literary canon, such innovative approaches in contemporary literature linger in the breaks across historical time. At the same time, they expand their spatial outlook to create histories that go back in time before Atlantic slavery and across the world to other times and places when whiteness was conceived of in relation to bodies marked as Other.

Ventriloquizing the Archive

Morrison and Phillips similarly revisit, renovate, and otherwise transform an iconic representation of blackness in Europe—Shakespeare's *Othello*—inviting a meditation on what it means to write in the wake of conquest and slavery, how the emblems of Western civilization so often denied to racialized subjects might be made their own, and how a longer and more circuitous history of race in the early modern world changes how we imagine race today. In centering whiteness in different ways, both ask us to understand the black presence in the West as an ongoing examination of whiteness as well. While it is easily possible to read Morrison and Phillips together through the lens of influence, borrowing, or dialogue across the Atlantic, I am invested in thinking about their common preoccupation with ventriloquizing the deeply equivocal figure of Shakespeare's Othello. Both writers are interested in the possible expansiveness this engagement affords, staging a more uncertain, triangulated form of relation between the West and its internal other, which speaks to the transformation of the slave narrative in the contemporary moment.

In constructing the typology of the slave narrative as a genre, James Olney notes the repetition of the phrase "a plain, unvarnished tale" in various "as told to" accounts of slavery, including John Brown, Edwin Scrantom, and James Williams. Noting that the *Oxford English Dictionary* traces the first use of the word "unvarnished" to Othello—"I will a round unvarnish'd tale deliver / Of my whole course of love"—Olney finds that it is only white sponsors, editors, and authenticators who refer to Othello to stage the accounts of slavery to follow. But no ex-slave narrator uses the word "unvarnished" to describe their own stories. In fact, slave narrators like Douglass tend to refer to Hamlet as an antecedent for their predicament, while William Lloyd Garrison invokes Othello directly in his preface to Douglass's *Narrative*. Olney concludes that because Shakespeare's Moor was noble and heroic, but "a creature of unreliable character and irrational passion," abolitionist editors invoked his precedent because of their own paternalist attitudes toward their ex-slave narrators.[32] Morrison's play *Desdemona* (2012) and Phillips's novel *The Nature of Blood* (1997) return to precisely this charged site—resituating Othello as an iconic form of blackness in the Western tradition away from its historical anchor, making him a prism for a range of contemporary concerns about race and sexuality, slavery and analogy.[33] Othello, in their hands, remains both exceptional and exemplary, allowing a ventriloquism of variegated histories.

In demonstrating how Morrison and Phillips think race through and beyond Shakespeare, I emphasize neither mimicry nor decolonization, but rather an irradiation of the canon, exposing the occluded past to light so that cracks can seep through. This is how the double bind of absence and presence that Gates located in the founding moments of the African American literary tradition may be transcended, or at least reshaped beyond recognition. My claim may seem odd, since such a strategy could arguably appear as a recentering of the master's words.[34] Moreover, choosing to ventriloquize the archive in this manner generates further quandaries, not simply because such efforts invert the conditions of production that attended the slave narrative. Scholars of slave narratives and early African American autobiographies termed their objects of study a form of literary ventriloquism precisely because so many of them were narrated to a white editor or amanuensis. In breaking through this paternalist frame, ex-slaves like Douglass, Equiano, and Jacobs claimed the right to speak for themselves, proudly authenticating their own story as written by themselves.[35] That is why the fact that contemporary black writers choose return to the prior strategy may seem tendentious. Phillips, for example, is clearly invested in historicizing and recovering the untold stories of two and a half centuries of the African diaspora.[36] Why does he seemingly reverse the progress made by Douglass, Equiano, and Jacobs, when he focalizes the story of the enslaved through the words of the master in a number of his fictions?

Many have referred to Morrison's most famous novel, *Beloved*, as an attempt to ventriloquize Margaret Garner's story. But Morrison has been clear on this point, insisting instead on a refusal to reconstruct the truth, recover a lost history, or restore agency to the historically disenfranchised.[37] Why then does she turn to a figure like Othello only to voice him entirely through Desdemona? And what happens to our interpretive frames when we think of ventriloquism as the generic optic through which we read such efforts, rather than writing back to the empire or deforming the master's words? What do we do with the fact that we do not find Manichean antagonism or anxiety, but intimacy, comfort, and dialogue?

As I show below, Morrison and Phillips both intervene in what it means to write back to the empire now and stage the malleability of the slave narrative as archive for the contemporary black writer. In extending the trope of the Talking Book beyond the slave narrative to a Shakespeare play or a Brontë novel, they also insist on opening up the terrain of the entire Western canon as implicated in these dynamics of surrogacy and deformation.

Othello especially stages the question of the relation between race and transatlantic slavery because so many have refused to talk about race in the play, arguing that it precedes Atlantic slavery. Scholars of the early modern era have probed the question of what race might signify to a seventeenth-century audience, and warned of the dangers of anachronism in harnessing conversations about blackness and slavery to explain a radically different context.[38] Kim Hall acknowledges the malleability of the term "Moor" in the early modern era, and the impossibility of stabilizing Othello's exact racial origins, since the term could refer to (as indicated by the play's performance history) a black African, a Turk, a Muslim, an Indian, or an Egyptian.[39] In recent years, scholars have variously emphasized the Iberian slave trade, piracy, conversion, Islam, and the Mediterranean theater of war as more appropriate contexts for understanding Shakespeare's representation of the Moor, arguing against race-based understandings that emerged from eighteenth-century Atlantic slavery. Others have disagreed and insisted on anachronistic reading as a useful unsettling of historical distance, especially in relation to the exigencies of the classroom.[40] The performance history of the play as well—including blackface, color-blind casting, and feminist appropriation—raises thorny questions about how to read race in *Othello*.[41]

For Peter Sellars, "Shakespeare's *Othello* is a permanent provocation, for four centuries the most visible portrayal of a black man in Western art."[42] Accordingly, a number of African American and postcolonial writers have turned to the figure of Othello, following the lead of Ben Okri, who declares that "if it did not begin as a play about race, then its history has made it one."[43] Rita Dove, Gayl Jones, Tayeb Salih, and Derek Walcott have variously revisited the play's depiction of otherness, part of a larger project of globalizing and provincializing Shakespeare.[44] As a play that has come to be seen as saying something about the relationship between a black man and a white woman, *Othello* immediately conjures up questions of sexuality and fetishism. Phillips and Morrison take up this conjunction but render it unrecognizable: their reckoning with the play makes it no longer the now familiar story about miscegenation, interracial desire, or racial stereotyping. For Phillips, *Othello* offers a conduit to Jewish history; for Morrison, an exploration of feminist alliance between black and white women, an encounter of music with poetry, Africa with the West. Their revisionism illuminates precisely this indeterminacy about the connection between race as we know it now and the history of Atlantic slavery that helped shape that concept. For writers like Phillips and Morrison, Othello is and isn't a figure for the afterlife of slavery. Which is why they place him within that history but also ventriloquize through him a more expansive range of experiences, thus probing the risks and possibilities opened up by refusing the singularity of slavery and making it a prism that refracts more.

In positioning Shakespeare's Othello as an "extravagant stranger" to use Phillips's phrase, Morrison restores the unspeakable absences in the original text, imagining Desdemona's African maid, Barbary, as the first source of stories about black warriors.[45] But her Othello is not just a jealous warrior; rather he emerges as an orphan child, rescued from slavers by a root woman, conscripted into war and rape as a child soldier, who becomes a young man haunted by his past crimes. I read Morrison's engagement with a classic figure in black British history as a conduit to a black Atlantic circuit that opens up new ways of thinking, beyond influence or intertextuality, adaptation or revision. Along similar lines, Phillips's tryst with Othello evenly draws on deliberately anachronistic African American histories of Jim Crow and the languages of Uncle Tom, opening outward in spirals toward Jewish, Israeli, European, and Ethiopian worlds. My goal in staging this encounter is also to test the ongoing viability or sufficiency of the formations of "Black Britain" and "African America" in relation to the transnational frames of the "Atlantic" or the "global" to see what kinds of possibilities for thinking relation are enabled or foreclosed. Widening the circuit beyond Britain and the United States to Venice, Africa, Germany, Phillips takes us across time— from the fifteenth and sixteenth centuries to the mid-twentieth—while Morrison deliberately displays ahistoricism, setting her entire play in the afterlife. Both stage the interplay of intimacy and distance in our access to Othello: Morrison ventriloquizing him through Desdemona, and Phillips detouring his story through several others, notably that of Eva Stern, a young survivor of a Nazi death camp. Neither writer recuperates the voice of Othello in any simple, unmediated fashion. Morrison stages a symphony of African song and European text, where neither is complete without the other, refiguring the binary of orality and textuality that characterizes the Talking Book. Phillips proposes a similar symphony but with one story following another, as echoes, repetitions, and similarities abound, indicating a "multi-directional memory," but no direct analogy or relation of substitution.[46]

Morrison and Phillips are often paired in studies of comparative slavery and the Holocaust—with the suggestion that Morrison repels the comparison Phillips embraces, insisting instead on the singularity of the memory of slavery implied by the epigraph to *Beloved*, "Sixty million and more," widely read as a reference to the six million killed in the Holocaust.[47] But in reading their engagements with Othello, no such clear difference emerges, as both writers offer a way to think about connection and difference outside of stark binaries of Atlantic/global or racial/universal. Certainly it is important to keep in mind the very different histories that structure their relative relationship to the English canon on the one hand, and to the analogy with either white feminism or with the Jewish experience. Scholars of trauma studies have further argued in favor of comparative and connected analysis of distinct historical traumas.[48]

In *The European Tribe*, Phillips describes coming to the United States and knowing that he can become a writer only after the encounter with Harlem, Detroit, Alabama, and Salt Lake City. Reading Richard Wright's

Native Son in Los Angeles, he "felt as if an explosion had taken place inside [his] head."⁴⁹ But despite such feelings of kinship, Phillips writes, "one of the aspects of black America that I have never been able to comprehend fully is the virulent anti-Semitism that seems to permeate much black thought" (53). In contrast, he "was brought up in a Europe that still shudders with guilt at mention of the Holocaust" (53). As a child, he fully identified with the Jewish experience of persecution, in part because it was the only available language to discuss marginality and oppression. Because of the pervasive silence around the violence of slavery and colonialism, Phillips writes that "I vicariously channeled a part of my hurt and frustration through the Jewish experience" (54). His Othello, accordingly, not only is framed by the central representation of the Holocaust, but also walks through the Jewish ghetto, finding kinship as a foreigner in the alienated lives he sees there.

For Phillips, Othello as a figure for the black presence in Europe helps frame his own biography in *The European Tribe*. Later, in *Nature of Blood*, Othello's story frames and helps historicize the experience of the Holocaust, fifteenth-century anti-Semitism, and the treatment of Ethiopian Jews in contemporary Israel. By placing Jewish experiences at the center of the novel, Phillips suggests that various forms of European tribalism refract black experiences and vice versa. This is why it is difficult to give credence to Hillary Mantel's objections, as she quarrels with the seeming equation of Jewish and black suffering in the novel, advancing a familiar and ethnocentric rebuke by asking Phillips not to "lay claim to other people's suffering."⁵⁰ The shifting points of view, range of styles and genres of writing, and lack of a clear marker separating these stories ensure that no definitive historical recovery attains; rather the novel tasks the reader with the tantalizing possibility of learning to read connections, with interracial romance (figured by Othello and Desdemona) as the site of this possible translation.

It is worth recalling that Morrison first thought that Shakespeare's *Othello* no longer allowed for an interesting treatment of race. It was opera and theater director Peter Sellars's deliberately anachronistic portrayal of *Othello* in 2009, shaped by the recent election of Barack Obama as the US president that changed her mind and led her to write the play. Sellars cast multiracial actors in the play, with a black Duke, a Latino Othello, a black Cassio, a white Desdemona, and a Latina Emilia.⁵¹ Morrison's *Desdemona* is itself a transnational collaboration, created by the joint contributions of Sellars, Morrison, and Malian singer and songwriter Rokia Traoré. In contrast to much of her other work, Morrison centers a white woman, Desdemona, in her account, suggesting that something more complicated than recovery, writing back to the canon, or filling in historical gaps is at work.

Both Morrison and Phillips map geographies that crisscross African America and Black Britain, even as they gesture outward to a series of possible histories and connections. Pairing Morrison and Phillips—both established and celebrated writers—one American, one Black British (by way of Saint Kitts)—also serves as an opportunity to reckon with the stakes of expanding the African American canon. Phillips is one of the few non-US writers represented in *The Norton Anthology of African American Literature* edited by Gates and Smith, while Morrison constitutes one of the most important writers of the canon.[52] Reading the two in tandem allows a probing of the relation of contemporary black literature to the Western canon in direct dialogue with the historical slave narrative and its current revival. Moreover, such efforts productively link the postcolonial project of writing back to the empire to African American deformations of the canon.

At first glance the two writers render starkly different accounts: Phillips bestowing interiority to Othello, Morrison withholding it and funneling all his words and feeling through Desdemona. Morrison emphasizes the homoerotic bond with Iago, Phillips sidesteps Iago altogether. Morrison's play centers on feminism—the relations among white feminists and women of color—the potential for sharing and its impossibility, shadowed by Morrison's manipulation of what Angela Davis has identified as "the myth of the black rapist."[53] In contrast, Phillips explores the twentieth-century experience and ongoing impact of the Nazi Holocaust (surveyed in a number of ways, most extensively in the slow going mad of Eva Stern, a survivor of a death camp who loses everyone she loves, and the story of her Zionist uncle Stephan, who fights for an underground army in Palestine only to learn that the state he fights for, Israel, denies Ethiopian refugees the same welcome it extends to others). These stories distill through a range of earlier experiences—Othello's in sixteenth-century Venice and the lynching of three Jewish men accused of the ritual murder of a Christian boy a century earlier. Pulling these strands together is a diatribe against European obsession with the purity of blood and its propensity for barbaric tribal violence. In an interview, Phillips explains the logic behind the collage that comprises *The Nature of Blood*: "What makes [*Othello*] belong is loneliness, isolation, sense of betrayal, all things that befell Jewish people in the fifteenth century and during World War II."[54] As Phillips collects such far-flung experiences in a single narrative, his collage aesthetic indicates his disinclination to recover a stable sense of an authentic history; rather his deliberate anachronisms and transhistorical juxtapositions yield a subtler sense of commingled counterhistories.

In *The European Tribe*, Phillips situates Othello as a "black European success" (45) who remains "an alien, socially and culturally" (47). Othello's true "psychological anguish" has been missed—he must "have lived on a knife-edge" (45) since "life for him is a game in which he does not know the rules" (47). Phillips consistently reads Othello through modern frames—imagining that he needed a "a close friend" (47) who could translate the rules of Venetian society. His sin is that he "relaxes" and "begins to forget that he is black" (48): "Othello relaxed, like the black man in the middle-class suburb who is suddenly surprised to see racist graffiti daubed on the side of his house" (51). Othello is an immigrant trying to assimilate, not least through marriage. Phillips muses that there is no evidence that he has any black friends or any other connection to Africa, concluding that Venetian society could accept him, but only up to a point. Once Othello marries their daughter, that invisible line is crossed. An unnamed voice forwards an Afrocentric critique of Othello in snippets at the end of the novel, calling—with deliberate anachronism—Othello "a black Uncle Tom" "fighting the white man's war for him" (180). But it seems clear that the novel doesn't share this sense of condemnation. Allying Othello to Fanon's "abandonment-neurotic" (50), or seeing him as "the Jackie Robinson of his day" (51), Phillips resolutely refuses to accept any historical distance and finds in Othello's lonely and isolated state of mind a predecessor for his own feelings of marginalization and alienation. Phillips concludes his travels by asking Europe to "perform a historical striptease" (127)—to understand that its imperial actions have generated the present crisis: "Europe is blinded by her past, and does not understand the high price of her churches, art galleries, and architecture. My presence in Europe is part of that price" (128). He marks his difference from Othello by imagining the sense of foreignness Venice must have generated in him, a theme amplified in *The Nature of Blood*. Finally, he concludes that "unlike Othello, I am culturally of the West" (128).

Phillips gives Othello first-person narration in *The Nature of Blood* and takes his readers on walks with him, marveling at the architecture of Venice, trying to fathom the rituals of courtship in his wooing of Desdemona, puzzling over the persecution of the Jewish community. It is a humanizing gesture, re-creating Othello not as a famed warrior or jealous husband but as a lonely man, evenly troubled by his staff's microaggressions and flattered by his lover's public gesture of loyalty. But, like Morrison's, as we will see below, Phillips's Othello is also a deracinated man—and that is the root of his tragic fate. At one moment, Othello recalls his homeland: "Alone on these seas, and with none of my kind or complexion for company, there is nobody with whom I might share memories of a common past, and nobody with whom I might converse in the language that sits most easily on my tongue."[55] Because Othello remains "a foreigner" (106), we see him dazzled by his own success—a former slave turned general and soldier—captivated by Venice, seduced by it just as he is by Desdemona. Pushing away the thought that he has left behind a wife and child in Africa, or that he is of royal blood, he seems to accept the ascriptions of inferiority Venice grants him on account of his experience of slavery. This is why the most remarkable moment of his account is when he visits the Jewish ghetto, and, too excited to be able to decipher the text of the letter Desdemona has written him, asks a Jewish scribe to read it to him and to pen his response. Given the long-standing association of black freedom with literacy and print in the trope of the Talking Book, this strikingly triangulates the African Othello and the European Desdemona via the figure of the Jewish scholar. The scholar has immediate "sympathy" (142) with Othello, and the two communicate almost wordlessly, two outsiders finding a connection through the exchange of print.

Phillips's return to *Othello* in several of his books is part of his larger project of inhabiting the Western canon and making it speak otherwise, visible in any number of works including *Crossing the River*, *Cambridge*, and *Lost Child*.[56] The latest novel, a purported response to *Wuthering Heights*, illustrates what I referred to earlier as the desire to render an oblique rejoinder rather than a sharp revision. One would expect the novel to restore the story of Heathcliff, a "seven-year-old dark stranger 'rescued' from the streets of Liverpool in 1771" who "was one of the first literary characters to seize [Phillips's] imagination."[57] In *The Lost Child*, Phillips does clearly locate Heathcliff in relation to slavery—many have wondered about his possible lascar or gypsy ancestry (described by Mr. Earnshaw in *Wuthering Heights* as "a gift of God; though it's as dark almost as if it came from the devil), but Phillips names him as black and situates his origin in slavery, beginning the novel with the tragic figure of the abandoned slave mother and Heathcliff as her biological child with Earnshaw.[58] But quickly (apart from brief and fascinating forays into the Brontë sisters), *The Lost Child* focuses on Monica, a white woman who marries an Afro-Caribbean immigrant. The father is mostly absent while the novel examines Monica and her two mixed-race children, highlighting themes of loneliness, abandonment, and isolation. In this sense, even as he echoes an earlier revisionist project like *Wide Sargasso Sea*, Phillips establishes a frame of intimacy rather than antagonism between the races, as the madwoman in the attic (central to feminist reclamations of *Jane Eyre*) becomes a white woman, sympathetically rendered and the center of the narrative (repeating the stance of earlier novels like *Cambridge* and *Crossing the River*). For Phillips, Monica serves as surrogate for the ex-slave mother of Heathcliff, and perhaps for Heathcliff as well. At the same time, Othello becomes a surrogate for Phillips's own feelings of marginalization from British society.

Surrogate Selves

Surrogation can be a powerful tool for collective memory and forgetting, for creating myths of origin and seeking closure through mourning as Joseph Roach has shown.[59] To better situate Phillips's meditation on whiteness and terror, race and gender, I turn to Morrison's *Desdemona*, which amplifies these fraught dynamics of substitution, ventriloquism, and exchange still further. Morrison rewrites Shakespeare's tragedy *Othello* by tapping into the power of the Greek meaning of Desdemona's name, misery, to transform the familiar story of doomed interracial romance into something much more powerful and unsettling. Recreating Desdemona's memory of her nurse, Barbary, as a sign of Africa,

Morrison not only transforms expected binaries of black and white, male and female, but also probes the very possibility of feminist connection across barriers of racial stereotype and uncovers Shakespeare's hidden connection to Africa. That the play itself is a transnational "literary and musical collaboration" is evident from the circumstances of its production (7). Opera and theater director Peter Sellars facilitated the exchange between Morrison and Malian singer and songwriter Rokia Traoré, who wrote the lyrics of the play in response to Morrison's reinvention of "lacunae and poetic ambiguities in Shakespeare" (10). On stage, English, French, and Bambara intermingle, as do song and story, as Morrison strips the characters down to just two—Desdemona and Barbary, the African maid mentioned briefly by Shakespeare and reimagined by Morrison and Traoré. As Sellars notes, "In seventeenth-century London, 'Barbary' meant Africa" (8).

Accordingly, in *Desdemona*, in any line from the play, we hear not only Morrison's distinct prose, but also that of Shakespeare, Sellars, and Traoré. This layering of histories, of ghostly figures from across the globe and from past and present, makes for a rich and deeply unsettling experience, as the play refuses to anchor itself in any stable place or perspective, offering instead a series of shifting dialogues that speak as much to the failure to translate or empathize as to its necessity. Shakespeare's *Othello*, as we all know, is full of deceit, mystification, and innuendo, and Morrison's *Desdemona* both rehearses that equivocation and its violence and stages the conditions of possibility for its transcendence. And even though one might assume that the play will unearth hidden histories, and surface silenced voices, *Desdemona* also keeps some things veiled, untranslated, unknowable. Centering women and their conflicts—with men (Desdemona and Othello, or Sa'ran and her lover), but more often, between women (Emilia/Desdemona; Barbary/Desdemona; the two mothers)—the play's feminist and antiwar politics are quite unambiguous, but its exploration of whiteness, terror, and masculinity is challenging, and relies heavily on Desdemona herself, alternately delusional and insightful, given to romanticizing, and schooled in honest truths.

It would have been fairly easy for Morrison to restore interiority to Othello, to amplify his tragic heroism, to give us unmediated access to his voice. But she chooses to do something else with the overdetermined figure. She ventriloquizes Othello (who is already a prism) through Desdemona (who has an equally prescripted destiny). As Morrison often says, literature isn't a case study or a recipe; its task, therefore, is to stage conflicts, not to resolve them. Even as the stripped-down, minimal figures on stage represent forms of oppression past and present, visions of social justice and of individual connection, engaging in honest dialogue in the afterlife, there is much that remains unspoken. The play of languages, spoken, sung, and subtitled, immediately draws our attention to the politics of who speaks, and who listens, evoking the dramatic interplay of orality and textuality so central to the African American literary tradition. The men do not speak on stage at all, while much of the dialogue is conducted in English by Desdemona with a response in Bambara or French by Traoré, or a musical response alone, with no words. The most arresting moment of the play is when Traoré responds in English for the first time to Desdemona's plea of a common experience of patriarchy. Desdemona asks "Barbary" to come closer, urging her to remember that "we shared so much" (45). But "Barbary" rejects her, clarifying that Desdemona does not even know her name: "Barbary is what you call Africa. Barbary is the geography of the foreigner, the savage." When Desdemona claims her as "my best friend," the now retitled Sa'ran clarifies "I was your slave" (45).

Though it's tempting to read this as a decolonizing of Shakespeare, as a feminist, antiracist recovery of hidden histories, the play is more estranging, and less Manichean than this suggests. Part of this has to do with how we read Traoré and Desdemona on stage—as characters within a familiar narrative, as figures or allegories for black and white femininity, as symbols of Africa and the West, or of song and music against the word. Othello finds voice only through Desdemona—signaled quite simply by a deepening of her voice, a squaring of shoulders, and a spreading of the knees. Morrison thus implies at once a feminist inversion of male ventriloquism of female voices, a surrogate self for a woman searching for heroism, a black man trapped inside a white woman's body and inside the white envelope of the slave narrative, thus usefully disturbing rigid distinctions of male and female, black and white.

In thinking of how the past relates to the present (beyond guileless narratives of progress, amnesia, or overcoming), Morrison has shown that resurrecting, and living with, pained and sometimes vengeful ghosts from the past is impossible, because they can be predatory rather than nurturing, making it no easy task to speak to the dead. Hence *Beloved*'s ambiguous ending: "this is not a story to pass on."[60]

Shakespeare often stands in for a kind of timelessness and placelessness—he is for all time, he is universal, he is classic, he is, so the story goes, Western civilization itself.[61] Morrison queries the foundation of such assumptions, probing, as she asks in *Playing in the Dark*: "What happens to the writerly imagination of a black author who is at some level *always* conscious of representing one's own race to, or in spite of, a race of readers that understands itself to be 'universal' or 'race free'?"[62] Her transformation of the question of universality can be unearthed by focusing on the scene in which Othello narrates the story of his life, an orphan taken in by a root woman, then captured by Syrians but sold to an army. As a child soldier, he finds salvation in a uniform, in fraternity, in the violent rituals of war.

Othello woos Desdemona with wondrous tales of exotic and surreal lands, with fierce armies of women—Amazons who rule nations and kingdoms. Desdemona's soul, starved of imagination, responds with fantasies of competing with these Amazons. So far, we may see this as Morrison providing flesh to Shakespeare's terse—and oblique—account of "passing strange" stories. But Othello continues, in Morrison's account, and narrates a graphic tale of his rape of two old women, along with Iago, while a young boy watches. Othello tells Desdemona (and remember, this is voiced by Desdemona), "This, my secret, will be our bond" (36).

Morrison joins Iago, Othello, and Desdemona in this narration of a war crime, a scene that combines trauma, violence, shame, guilt, voyeurism, sympathy, love, friendship, and perhaps, the possibility of absolution. The romance between Othello and Desdemona, and the homosocial bond between Iago and Othello ("the exchange of musk"; 37), arises from this conjunction of terror and storytelling. We have long understood that these relationships in Shakespeare get to the heart of the combination of risk, repulsion, and attraction among these characters, not just as individuals, but as symptoms of larger forces of whiteness and blackness, femininity and masculinity. Here, Morrison's Desdemona listens to this last confession, calls it "obscene, monstrous," but accepts it—"I always knew you / were caressing me with fingers hardened / by swords and that your hands stroking my / breasts also drew blood" (39).

Reminiscent of Frantz Fanon's powerful account of the white woman and the man of color in *Black Skin, White Masks*, Morrison ties the romance between Othello and Desdemona to the unspeakable horror of war crimes.[63] The scene opposes words to glances: the women look once and do not speak, the young child watching does not speak, the women whimper, the men groan. Iago and Othello do not speak—but the circuit of glances between them recalls Morrison's pithy phrase—"unspeakable thoughts, unspoken"[64]—"There was a look between us. Before our / decision to do no more harm our eyes met, / Iago's and mine, in an exchange of secrecy. . . . We were not only refusing to kill our own memory, but insisting on its life in another" (38). As a counter to this obscene brotherhood, all the women on stage exchange glances, words, and songs. While Iago and Othello bond as secret sharers of trauma and assault—learning to be men by killing and raping—the women enact different models of sociality, new forms of love or friendship.

This confession pivots the romance between Othello and Desdemona out of the doomed interracial love story into something else, as their love—mediated by not just desire or fetishization but by the capacity to share and listen, to accept if not to forgive (as Desdemona says, she cannot forgive him "but I can love you and remain committed to you"; 39)—touches upon even if it doesn't complete the spirals of justice, reparation, and reconciliation.

There is a long tradition of blackface in productions of *Othello*, but when Othello as child soldier is spoken by Desdemona while Barbary sings, the language of blackface or whiteface doesn't seem adequate. Morrison reclaims the celebrated warrior as a vulnerable child, an agent of terror, but also innocent, and desperate. Because Shakespeare's Othello is almost never on stage alone, and (unlike Hamlet) not given to extended soliloquy, he functions as a prism that reflects everybody else's perceptions, not somebody with a rich interior life. That Othello is a white man's fantasy about an African I think few will dispute. Or we may say, an entire culture's fantasy about another entire culture. Pairing this with Morrison's account of Desdemona—is it a recovery, or also a revelation of the phantasmatic nature of both whiteness and femininity—a fantasy that doubles, turns inside out, or exorcises Shakespeare's fantasy about Africa?

To begin to answer this, we could think of Othello alongside Son of *Tar Baby*, Milkman Dead from *Song of Solomon*, or Paul D. from *Be-*

loved, rather than next to Hamlet, Lear, or Macbeth, to unspool conversations not about blackface or love and jealousy, but about black masculinity under duress, in crisis, in search of lost roots. Like Milkman, Othello might be a man cut off from his heritage, and he may need a figure to guide him on a quest of reclamation. Like Paul D., he may have a tobacco tin, rusted shut, in place of a heart, or like Son, he might be an undocumented man, who won't give up brotherhood, who's drawn to women like honey, but who doesn't know how to fully surrender to that passion, and could be guided away into a mythical swamp.[65]

Othello would then appear as a black Atlantic figure in the manner described by Paul Gilroy—restless, coding in his musings on love and death and their conjunction, vaster stories of deracination, historical displacement, and momentous migrations.[66] If Othello is an orphan of Africa, brought to Venice, marauding the Turks in their name, what kinds of migrations or routes of war, capture, commerce, and discovery does he map? And what place is there for the woman at home? Morrison's Desdemona seems shadowed by Joseph Conrad's *Heart of Darkness* (1899) as well, as she appears as Kurtz's intended waiting in Europe—a pale shadow with her African counterpart (for whom Conrad couldn't or wouldn't invent language)—she whose delusions must be protected.[67] Even if the Thames and the Congo can be seen as secret sharers, still Desdemona must remain apart, for Conrad. But Morrison imagines intimacy instead, drawing Desdemona into the circle of Barbary and Othello, as she becomes the conduit for this dialogue between two Africans, raising the question of how we may read this engagement with whiteness.

Desdemona, whose name means misery, may say that she is not the name she did not choose, but she can never not signify whiteness. In *Playing in the Dark*, Morrison takes up whiteness in American literature, showing how its exploration of sin and guilt, its obsession with heaven and hell, its longing for the frontier, its shuttling between chaos and individualism, terror and shame relies on, and is constituted by a "dark, abiding, signing Africanist presence."[68] Exorcism, reification, and mirroring are the duties of the surrogate selves of white writers, as no American literature is free of the power of blackness. Here, what is the power of Othello's blackness, of Barbary's? How are they surrogates for Desdemona, what does she escape from or entangle with? It's worth recalling Morrison's claim that in American literature, we find a plenitude of images of blackness, and a silence around white ones: she shows how "images of blackness can be evil *and* protective, rebellious *and* forgiving, fearful *and* desirable. . . . Whiteness, alone, is mute, meaningless, unfathomable, pointless, frozen, veiled, curtained, dreaded, senseless, implacable."[69]

How might we then place Morrison's portrayal of Desdemona—the salvage of her hidden history or silenced voice—against Morrison's earlier work recovering the occluded black woman's voice? Making Desdemona a surrogate for Othello seems to reverse Morrison's foundational account of literary whiteness in *Playing in the Dark*, and such an inversion is precisely the innovation of the play. This is where it becomes significant that the entire play is set in the afterlife, removed from the vicissitudes of history. In doing so, it draws on memory—or what Morrison has theorized as "rememory"—to thwart the violence of history, offering a contrapuntal harmony of song and narrative, a call and response, that can occur only in the timelessness of after death, where the repetition of trauma can be interrupted, or at least restaged safely, as an exorcism that isn't possible, yet is needed.[70] Morrison's engagement with whiteness may tell us more about how we cannot think race without gender and vice versa, and as black art transforms the past, rather than just revising it, to make possible new openings through these imagined encounters.

Morrison's concept of rememory arguably encapsulates, if in fact it did not create that school of thought known as new historicism. Refusing, like Walter Benjamin, to accept the linear ravages of history, taking in the ruin—the catastrophe, the debris of modernity—Morrison shows the impossibility of beating back the past, or moving forward without it, the desire for redemption, and its impossibility. Rather than individual, this is a collective memory—both in its healing and in its hurting—as it registers the atrocities that are unspeakable, unspoken, to hear which we need something beyond language—what Morrison calls in *Beloved* "the right combination, the key, the code, the sound that broke the back of words."[71] Beloved as both ghost and flesh, spirit and symbol challenges the rational divisions of modern thought.

Scholars have traced Morrison's influences to everything from the Bible to Milton, Faulkner to Joyce, Woolf to Rushdie, Márquez to Coetzee. But in unmooring Othello by making him a child soldier, Morrison may be placed alongside contemporary African writers like Chris Abani, Chimamanda Adichie, and Uzodinma Iweala, who also explore the conjunction of what it means to see the figure of the child soldier today as a resurrection of the Atlantic slave. As I discussed in chapter 2, given that so many accounts of the child soldier are narrated by white editors, often women, the fraught figure of the child soldier shuttles between the poles of sentimentalism and terror. Connecting the map of the globe Shakespeare, Phillips, and Morrison construct with our world now, we may think of a character like My Luck in Abani's *Song for Night*—a child soldier whose vocal chords have been cut to prevent him from screaming when he steps on a mine, who has to learn over the course of the novel that he is in fact a ghost himself, albeit one who has to learn of his own death and spectral afterlife. Or of Iweala's *Beasts of No Nation*, written entirely in the continuous present tense—"I am wanting to kill," "I am chopping and chopping and chopping until I am looking up and it is dark."[72] As Morrison's Beloved insists in her memory of the Middle Passage, "All of it is now, it is always now."[73] But such a contention promises neither therapy nor redemption. Morrison compels looking into slavery with all the risk of the erosion of self it may entail, not to claim the horrors of the past as salvation for the present.

In reckoning with the challenge of hearing these voices outside of sentimental, gothic, or pornographic modes, beyond pity or absolute innocence or guilt, how do we emancipate the past, or reckon with its ethical claim on us? Can these figures retain the right to opacity, and escape easy analogy across time and space? What do the ghosts mean, and what do they want? What is the modernity of Shakespeare, the untimeliness of *Othello*—said to be ahead of its time, out of time, now resurrected by Morrison and Phillips, to stage perhaps the same question: Who are you to me, who am I to you? Am I symbol or spectacle, friend or foe?

In her most recent lectures, *The Origin of Others*, Morrison explicitly links her previous explorations of the African American experience to the problem of global migration. Excluding the height of the slave trade in the nineteenth century, she notes, "the mass movement of peoples in the latter half of the twentieth century and the beginning of the twenty-first is greater than it has ever been. . . . Much of this exodus can be described as the journey of the colonized to the seat of the colonizers (slaves, as it were, leaving the plantation for the planters' home), while more of it is the flight of war refugees, and (less of it) the relocation and transplantation of the management and diplomatic class to globalization's outposts."[74] Most evocative is her lapidary statement that once the final figure of displaced people is tabulated—"those running from persecution, conflict, and generalized violence in today's world"—"the number will far surpass sixty million."[75] The United Nations High Commissioner for Refugees estimates that the number of displaced persons is 65.6 million, which is probably Morrison's point of reference, but it is impossible not to hear an echo and an extension of her earlier, polemical use of the same number.[76] *Beloved* was dedicated to "sixty million and more," the estimated number of people who died during the Middle Passage, widely understood to refer to the figure of "six million" attributed to the Holocaust. In fact, right-wing critics attacked Morrison for this move, alleging that she was setting up her novel as a blackface Holocaust novel, or insinuating a comparative measure of suffering across Jewish and black people.[77] Morrison here invokes that number again to link the depredations of slavery (the subject of most of *The Origin of Others*) to the question of what makes a foreigner belong and how we might rethink the category of home and dwelling in the world. The final chapter of the book revisits the African writer Camara Laye's 1954 *Radiance of the King*, a novel that reimagines "the clichéd journey into storybook African darkness."[78] Laye's white European protagonist must encounter the fantastical Africa conjured up in so many colonial accounts before he can be deraced and experience marginality and dehumanization himself. Morrison reads this process as a white man learning what it means "to become a black slave," and suggests that all literature must find a way to bridge the gaps of racial identity, not to ignore differences of power and privilege, but to remake the meaning of what is foreign and what can be rendered as home.[79] Instead of suggesting an easy substitution—where a white man imagines what it's like to be a black slave—Morrison delves deeper, asking us to "re-discover or imagine anew what it feels like to be marginal, ignored, superfluous, foreign; to have one's name never uttered; to be stripped of history or representation; to be sold or exploited labor for the benefit of a presiding family, a shrewd entrepreneur, a local regime."[80] Insisting on estranging what we know to be fact, Morrison aligns the otherness of Beloved as the ghost of the slain child with the claim of the contemporary refugee on our imagination. The title of the final chapter, "The Foreigner's Home," asks for such an imaginative reach, as Morrison extends her gaze from the United States to the diaspora, connecting past histories of enslavement with current predicaments of forced migration.

Extravagant Strangers

There is perhaps no better way to conclude this discussion of talking back to the Talking Book than to turn to James Baldwin's iconic meditation on the black relationship to Western culture, "Stranger in the Village." Baldwin famously plumbs the depths of his fraught relation with the land of his birth and the tiny Swiss village where "from all available evidence no black man had ever set foot."[81] Confronting brutal violence back home and hostile curiosity in Switzerland, Baldwin also ponders the ontology of being black, being African (as well as the schism between these two), and their relationship to the project called the "West":

> For this village, even were it incomparably more remote and incredibly more primitive, is the West, the West onto which I have been so strangely grafted. These people cannot be, from the point of view of power, strangers anywhere in the world; they have made the modern world, in effect, even if they do not know it. The most illiterate among them is related, in a way that I am not, to Dante, Shakespeare, Michelangelo, Aeschylus, Da Vinci, Rembrandt, and Racine; the cathedral at Chartres says something to them which it cannot say to me, as indeed would New York's Empire State Building, should anyone here ever see it. Out of their hymns and dances come Beethoven and Bach. Go back a few centuries and they are in their full glory—but I am in Africa, watching the conquerors arrive.[82]

There is so much to analyze here: the poignancy of the longing for home and a place in the world; the difficulty of living in a world built on excluding one's presence; the cursed inheritance of the construct of Western civilization for its belated others; the storied history of artistic freedom African American writers found in Europe in the Jim Crow era. Baldwin is also well known for articulating the anxiety of influence among black writers in his relationship with Richard Wright. But timely as these words might be, they also seem to erase a longer black presence in Europe as well as African achievement before conquest, suggesting that an ancestral memory of whiteness transmits a kind of right of inheritance. Of course, Baldwin goes on to complicate this statement in the essay, concluding that not only has the "interracial drama acted out on the American continent" created "a new black man, it has created a new white man, too." Accordingly, he declares that "the world is white no longer, and it will never be white again."[83]

Recently, in *Known and Strange Things*, Teju Cole returns to Baldwin to dwell on the "disposability of black life" evinced in the daily killings of black people by the police.[84] A stranger in the same tiny village in rural Switzerland, Cole feels himself possessed by his ancestor as another "custodian of a black body" (5) traveling in the West. Evincing a distinct anxiety of influence, Cole is eager to mark his difference as well. While he also experiences Baldwin's "undimmed fury" (11), reacting to various accounts of police killings of unarmed black men and women, Cole finds himself puzzled by Baldwin's insistence on estrangement from the cultural achievements of Western civilization. Cole has to part ways with his ancestor: he marvels at Bach's humanity with full confidence that it is his heritage in the same way that Bessie Smith's blues songs are; he assumes the equivalence of Yoruba-language poetry to Shakespeare's sonnets, Ife sculptures to Donatello. "I'm happy to own all of it," he confirms (10).

These questions of the meaning of whiteness, home, belonging, and a place for black people in the "West" (understood as a project not a place) remain at the heart of a vast array of recent works from the African diaspora. Explicitly taking up Baldwin's suggestive question of the relation of blackness to the construct of Western civilization, writers from the new African diaspora like Cole redefine the terms of engagement, not just of black and white binaries but also between and across the African diaspora. The final chapter of *Runaway Genres* turns to these new imaginaries of race, migration, and diaspora that fully push aside the sentimental substitutions of a facile globalism, asking instead for a finer reckoning with both past and prospect.

5

We Need New Diasporas

I came from a country where race was not an issue. I did not think of myself as black and I only became black when I came to America.
—Chimamanda Ngozi Adichie, *Americanah*

"For the first time, more blacks are coming to the United States from Africa than during the slave trade." So begins Sam Roberts, chronicling recent African migrations to the United States in 2005, but suggestively framing the phenomenon by invoking the history of slavery. Implying a possible redemption of the earlier coerced movement, it is as if the voluntary migration of Africans fulfills a providential destiny, with African subjects now inhabiting, and in doing so rejuvenating, the familiar story of coming to the United States. Noting that one in three blacks in New York City is now foreign-born, Roberts suggests that this movement "is already redefining what it means to be African-American."[1] In his follow-up essay from 2014, Roberts puts the figure of legal black African immigrants at one million between 2000 and 2010.[2] He then wonders what this will mean culturally as these new immigrants identify as African or African American, and how these changing demographics will shape questions of affirmative action, reparations for slavery, and intraracial conflicts based on ethnic, religious, or linguistic differences.

That Roberts situates the issue of new African immigrants within and against the frame of Atlantic slavery is not surprising, given that most models of diaspora have tended to prioritize a similar setting. From Paul Gilroy's focus on the memory of slavery for the descendants of a black Atlantic to frequent efforts to use Countee Cullen's plangent query, "what is Africa to me?" as the pivot for thinking diaspora in relation to racial heritage or memory, to journeys organized around roots and return narratives, diaspora has largely been understood in relation to the African American experience.[3] But the Nigerian-Ghanaian writer

Taiye Selasi tells a very different story of the migration and circulation of Africans in the world, in which the history of Atlantic slavery finds no mention: "Starting in the 60s, the young, gifted and broke left Africa in pursuit of higher education and happiness abroad. . . . Some three decades later this scattered tribe of pharmacists, physicists, physicians (and the odd polygamist) has set up camp around the globe." As she continues, "Somewhere between the 1988 release of *Coming to America* and the 2001 crowning of a Nigerian Miss World, the general image of young Africans in the West transmorphed from goofy to gorgeous." The figure Selasi terms the "Afropolitan" refuses to choose any one place as home or to see itinerancy as tragic or alienating, insisting on multiple ways of being African. Selasi accordingly emphasizes complexity and situatedness: "To 'be' Nigerian is to belong to a passionate nation; to 'be' Yoruba, to be heir to a spiritual depth; to 'be' American, to ascribe to a cultural breadth; to 'be' British, to pass customs quickly."[4]

Selasi—along with such writers as Chris Abani, Chimamanda Ngozi Adichie, NoViolet Bulawayo, Teju Cole, Dinaw Mengestu, and Binyavanga Wainaina—belongs to a generation that not only heralds an African literary renaissance but also insists that new migrations demand new conceptualizations of diaspora. Most of the prominent theories of diaspora over the last two decades have been galvanized by the aspirations and contradictions of the journeys of a W. E. B. Du Bois or a Richard Wright.[5] The new visibility of African writers is a welcome antidote to such tendencies. Yet to open up the script of diaspora itself, we still need more multifaceted histories and models of what such visibility entails or enables. For Selasi, her blackness must be marked as different from a more visible and normative African American one: "Until I got to high school, my world consisted of white people and *Nigerian* people. I simply didn't think in terms of white and black. In fact, it wasn't even white people and Nigerian people. It was Nigerian and *other*." Moreover, both her parents were disaffiliated from an African American identity: "My mother doesn't call herself black. My father has spent his entire life as a sort of conscientious objector to American culture."[6]

Thus far, the figure of the contemporary African immigrant appears in this book as a refugee or child soldier, Lost Boy or kidnapped girl, seeking remedy for a subjectivity structured through trauma. For the most part, such figures experience extreme and spectacular suffering, with few scenes of ordinary life and frequent recourse to allegory and abstraction. This chapter serves to end the story of sentimental substitution inaugurated by the modern slave narrative. The fictions of the new African diaspora decisively shift away from existing templates of Atlantic slavery, insisting on new frames for fathoming contemporary patterns of migration. Moreover, they reject other available prototypes—such as the ethnic bildungsroman or the immigrant plot—to funnel their stories of arrival. In doing so, they make visible numerous critical possibilities for the study of diaspora, expanding previous geographies and weaving together race and class with location. Moving away from the concerns of previous generations—anticolonial resistance, the clash of tradition and modernity, alienation and exile—they also resist received notions of what constitutes African literature. By inviting the appreciation of varied histories and geographies of African migrations while rejecting a linear path toward immigrant assimilation in the United States, their emphasis on the varied routes of migration that have generated the new diaspora helpfully counters the hegemony of any single genealogy of blackness.

Firmly rejecting any sentimental lens through which the experiences they describe may be interpellated—whether in a humanitarian guise or a neocolonial one—these writers also rebuff models of racial formation that induct new immigrants into antiblackness. To reshape the resonant figure of the African in the West and received narratives of black difference, they illuminate hitherto marginalized histories of race by focusing on migrations other than those occasioned by the Middle Passage or Atlantic return. To do so, they have to navigate the fraught space of Africa as an overdetermined signifier of trauma on the one hand and celebratory narratives of immigrant assimilation or triumphal globalism on the other. Available genres of sentiment, horror, or romance fall short as these writers choose to return to realism.

For the new African diaspora, the ideas of race and migration generated by Atlantic slavery no longer serve as adequate containers for black subjectivity. As Selasi puts it, "The young African immigrant must locate herself along three divides: the first between blackness and whiteness; the second within blackness, between native and foreign; the third between African and American."[7] Because of such complexity, existing narratives within postcolonial or African studies must also be revised, as the traditional tendency to view locally based texts as authentic representations and those focusing on immigrant experiences as somehow less valid no longer seems applicable. That is to say, although many critics see the spectacular success of such figures as Selasi, Cole, or Adichie as somehow diluting the real African experience on the continent, such Manichean frames cannot fully account for the power of the new African narrative, which insists on thinking intermixture beyond the language of contamination or assimilation alone.

This is why despite the often middle-class protagonists at the center of these novels, we find time and again a focus on the figures that have populated this study thus far—refugees, forced migrants, and displaced and vulnerable children in the world's largest slums. Contemporary African novels thus both rehearse and reverse the Middle Passage, prompting the question of how modern experiences of being a refugee or trafficked person or child soldier relate to the historical experience of Atlantic slavery. If the Middle Passage is understood not just historically but metaphorically and conceptually as the engine that produced African Americans (transforming a "man" into a "slave," an "African" into a "Negro"), giving birth to the modern concept of race (indeed, the birth of modernity itself, as Morrison suggests), then does it not become available for theorizations of racial disposability in the present?[8] How might we understand this analogy across time and place ethically—without collapsing past experiences into the present in a melancholy vein, or conflating a range of geopolitical situations into a sentimental template of a generalized global feeling? If, as I have suggested earlier, the first tendency is visible in the literature of neo-slavery and Afro-pessimism, and the second in the human rights construct of modern slavery, then how might we position as comparative counterpoint or complement novels like *Half of a Yellow Sun*, *GraceLand*, and *We Need New Names*, all of which represent civil war, military rule, and extreme poverty and inequality in the postcolony in direct relation to the United States—either literally, through immigration to the United States as escape, however incomplete or ambivalent, or through the circulation of such texts as Frederick Douglass's *Narrative of the Life of Frederick Douglass, an American Slave*?

Such new migrations, as Selasi notes, are shaped by generation and demography: "Where our parents sought safety in traditional professions like doctoring, lawyering, banking, engineering, we are branching into fields like media, politics, music, venture capital, design."[9] And certainly, the figure of the Afropolitan may be traced in fashion, music, art, and architecture. But the stunning visibility of novelists like Adichie (whose TED Talks have made her into a household name, as her words appear in Beyoncé's video "Flawless," on Dior's T-shirts, while she serves as the face of a makeup line, and New York City chooses *Americanah* for its 2017 One Book One New York project) clearly establishes the primacy of literary fiction rather than its often assumed demise. The new African novel thus becomes the place where contemporary migrations are most forcefully mapped. And they do so in mostly realist fashion. Neither wildly experimental nor postmodern nor magic realist, they do what novels do best: map middle-class manners (Adichie), narrate stories of formation and education (Abani, Bulawayo, Cole), explore the possibility of romance (Adichie, Mengestu), chart social transitions (Mengestu), and probe the dysfunction of families and individuals (Cole, Selasi) with psychological depth and social intricacy. Capturing ordinary life (as opposed to the sublime, gothic, or fantastic), these realist novels are nonetheless revisionist to their core. Whether juxtaposing the novel with the race blog, satirizing ethnographic expectations of tribal Africa, reversing the imperial romance by situating the West as the heart of darkness, or claiming the mantle of writing the great American novel, these fictions of the new diaspora fundamentally reshape the boundaries of the American, African, and African American canons alike.

The African Immigrant in the Global Era

Precisely because such fictions depart from expected ways of narrating migration and alienation, most accounts of the new diaspora locate it as proof of the obsolescence of prior models—nationalist, black Atlantic, and Third Worldist alike. Often, the single story (to paraphrase Adichie's useful warning) that is told about the new diaspora is that of friction between African Americans and Africans.[10] For many scholars, trying to grasp how African Americans triangulate the new relations between Africans and Americans, the shift from earlier models of diaspora is complete, as conflict replaces imagined solidarity. Louis Chude-Sokei's simplistic, somewhat nihilistic reading focuses on an "overall sense of brokenness or incommensurability, of perhaps failed expectations, intra-racial threat or cross-cultural competition" something he sees as "paradigmatic" of our moment.[11] Time and again, the visibility of the African story is seen as somehow detracting from the African American one, as if the diaspora were some kind of zero-sum game, where only one community could assume center stage, in a kind of Darwinian free for all. In other words, commentators fear that the newfound visibility of the African story somehow detracts from the African American one, as African immigrants become the United States' latest model minority. Their entrepreneurship, habits of industry, and cultural values of hard work and discipline seem only to rebuke African Americans and blame them for their continuing subordination or malaise.[12] Adichie's *Americanah* (2013) has prompted the best examples of this kind of diasporic melancholy, insofar as African gain must mean African American loss. Even as the novel undermines US perceptions about Africa, it also chastises black and white Americans alike for their shared "American tribalisms."[13] As one African American character observes, revealing a schism between African American and African immigrant relationships to the United States, Ifemelu can write her blog, "*Raceteenth or Various Observations about American Blacks (Those Formerly Known as Negroes) by a Non-American Black*," "because she's African. She's writing from the outside. She doesn't really feel all the stuff she's writing about" (337).

In part, such one-dimensional readings arise because US cultural histories have usually treated immigration and slavery as two distinct stories, and their collision here presages a number of conflicts and challenges to expected ways of narrating both America and Africa. Most clearly, it signals a distinct shift in conceptions of diaspora imagined in terms of global solidarity or an "identity of passions," to use Ralph Ellison's resonant phrase.[14] Any notion of diaspora as a shared identity or politics appears as merely anachronistic, a nostalgic or romantic remnant, as the dream of pan-African freedom seems broken. If once it was easy to assume some sense of commonality—no matter the real historical differences, at least as an aspiration in black transnationalist encounters—the discourse of the new diaspora announces the obsolescence of such freedom dreams as certain scenes recur: an African immigrant being mugged by an African American, an African being blamed for slavery by an African American, or being commended by a white American for a superior work ethic or lack of a victim mentality. The fear that new immigrants will take resources away from the descendants of slaves, as well as the specter of African blame for the slave trade ensure conflict and competition as a substitute for shared notions of blackness.

For instance, Teju Cole's Nigerian-German protagonist, Julius, flinches at any attempt at connection in *Open City* (2011)—equally puzzled by an elderly black veteran celebrating Julius's achievements as a black doctor as he is traumatized after a violent attack from two young men who had earlier nodded to him in a "gesture of mutual respect based on our being young, black, male; based, in other words, on our being 'brothers.'"[15] Adichie further illuminates such conflicts even in ordinary social interactions in *Americanah*. A white woman expresses her appreciation for her Nigerian doctor and Ugandan student, who "didn't have all those issues" as the African American in the class to the novel's assertive protagonist, the aforementioned Ifemelu, a Nigerian student in the United States. Ifemelu's response is clear: "Maybe when the African American's father was not allowed to vote because he was black, the Ugandan's father was running for parliament or studying at Oxford" (207). Further pressed to explain, she continues, "I just think it's a simplistic comparison to make. You need to understand a bit more about history" (208). But earlier in the novel, such nuance escapes the four black students, as they debate the censorship of the "N-word" during a screening of *Roots*. Quickly the conversation devolves into "if you all hadn't sold us, we wouldn't be talking about any of this" (170). Even the fact that the college has two black student associations—"African Americans go to the Black Student Union and Africans go to the African Students Association" (172)—testifies to the splintering of uniform notions of blackness, unmediated by place or ethnicity.

Scholarly literature on the new diaspora emphasizes three key differences from earlier forms of migration: it is largely voluntary, rather than coerced; it is connected to globalization; it results from the failure of the postcolonial state.[16] In literary terms, however, it is the second that resonates most fully with the writers from the new African diaspora. Critiques of the global African novel swiftly emerged, some lamenting the recourse to cosmopolitan privilege and wishing for a return to the utopian solidarities of the pan-African in a kind of Bandung nostalgia, others contending that these novels retrofit for neoliberal times a commonplace story of immigrant assimilation. Leftist critics are also dissatisfied that these global African novels are too readily comprehensible, making no aesthetic or philosophical demands on the reader. The editors of *n+1* bemoan the rise of "world lite" literature, which prizes cosmopolitan ease over socialist principles, cultural hybridity over a concern with social justice.[17] Nostalgic for difficult socialist novels from the 1960s—about the challenges of getting water in a remote village or a railway strike—such critics dismiss the moment of the Afropolitan as a symptom of neoliberalism, as the global turn leaves behind the Manichean framework of the postcolonial or the pan-African. For Tim Parks, these novels are banal and belated entrants into an already exhausted narrative.[18] In contrast to such accounts are the celebratory ones, which read these fictions as yet another page in the story of American exceptionalism, transforming migration into a question of cultural assimilation alone.

Challenging such readings, I show how the literature of the new diaspora destabilizes national or ethnic categories, something that is now routine, just as it demands more complex scales of comparison and analysis sufficient to navigate local, regional, and global formations. Mengestu's *The Beautiful Things That Heaven Bears* (2007) refuses an opposition between cosmopolitan ease and immigrant trauma, providing more expansive and flexible frames to understand migrations not bounded by the history of slavery. Even novels received as either echoing an immigrant story of assimilation or reinforcing a racialized narrative of poverty porn, like Bulawayo's *We Need New Names* (2013), forge a path beyond these binaries, insisting on the intertwined nature of race and class. Abani's *GraceLand* (2004) which stages an uncertain relation to a range of past histories—of colonialism, patriarchy, and slavery—along with a sharp look at the cacophony of a globalized Nigeria, charts distinctive diasporic itineraries as often through reading world literature as through actual travel. The novel announces its distance from the slave narrative by neither asking for empathy nor fulfilling an ethnographic purpose, nor allowing a white envelope to enclose its ambiguous message. Finally, Cole's *Open City* (2011) layers the history of slavery alongside numerous other individual and collective atrocities, insisting on reading diaspora beyond linear notions of return or redemption. These fictions also inscribe the geopolitical specificity of the migrations they represent, as Ethiopia, Zimbabwe, and Nigeria appear as tangible places, not just as forerunners to an Atlantic destiny. Reading through and beyond the frame of Atlantic slavery to fathom contemporary experiences of trauma consequently enables a reckoning with the aftermath of colonialism, the dysfunction of the postcolonial state, and changing conditions of precarious labor in a neoliberal world. In moving away from well-worn frames of racial ancestry or heritage, these novels present fresh ways to conceive of race and racial formation in a global frame, as well as innovative forms of representing black humanity, agency, and futurity in the literature of migration and diaspora.

Rather than engage with these fraught dynamics of intimacy and estrangement, the response to these fictions of the so-called African literary renaissance has been to slot these as variants of the immigrant plot. Doing so disregards the specificity of each novel as any classification does, but, more importantly, also misses much of what is new about them. For instance, Mengestu's *The Beautiful Things That Heaven Bears*, rightly called "a great African novel, a great Washington novel, and a great American novel," maps the change from earlier frames for thinking about migration and displacement to ones more apt for globalization.[19] Haunted by his guilt for his father's death during the Ethiopian Red Terror of 1977–1978, the protagonist, Sepha Stephanos, gives up the dreams of an immigrant life of reinvention in the United States, choosing instead to open a store in a "poor, black, cheap, and sunk into a depression" Logan Circle, wanting nothing more but to "read quietly, and alone."[20] Refusing a recognizable narrative of immigrant hope, Sepha notes that "I did not come to America to find a better life. I came here running and screaming with the ghosts of an old one firmly attached to my back" (41). For Sepha, D.C. layers onto Addis, resembling it "if not always in substance, then at least in form" (173), as a portrait of Frederick Douglass on a building reminds him of a picture of Haile Selassie on the walls of the Capitol, and the proximity of the White House suggests a promise for change that soon becomes a guarantee of disappointment. His uncle's letters to Carter and Reagan signal the war-torn refugee's naïveté as well as the heartbreaking losses of a generation of people "for whom nothing is left of their home country" (123).

The novel's plot turns on the arrival of a white woman, Judith, and her mixed-race daughter and their elaborate renovation of a "shining big house" in a poor and decaying neighborhood, an arrival that catalyzes Sepha out of his guilt-ridden despair even as it clarifies to him his in-between position in relation to his African American neighbors and Judith (209). While he is not one of "these people"—the white gentrifiers—he has also "never really been part of Logan Circle either" (189). Just as the novel provides both a subtle account of the economic dynamics of gentrification in D.C. and a nuanced look at the longing for home that characterizes the experiences of Ethiopian immigrants, it also delivers something else, a way to think beyond the polarized framework of trauma on the one hand and cosmopolitanism on the other.

This becomes clear in Sepha's friendship with two other African immigrants—renamed "Ken the Kenyan" and "Joe from the Congo" (1). Joseph, a waiter, believes that "all of the marches in the world won't change anything anymore. We were at our best in the sixties. Africa was free. America was free. Everyone was marching to something" (220). He is forever working on a cycle of poems that would invoke Dante but must "tell the entire history of the Congo, from the rubber plantations to the first coup. Nothing can be left out" (170–171). For Joseph, Dante's *Inferno* provides the most perfect metaphor for an African's life (also providing the title of the novel), since Africans live "hell everyday with only glimpses of heaven in between" (100). But as Kenneth, the engineer, mocks him, nothing fails to be a metaphor for Africa for him. In turn, Joseph accuses Kenneth of "being a perfect immigrant," "the perfect house nigger" (182) to which Kenneth responds, "Which one is it, Joseph? The perfect immigrant or the perfect slave? You can't have it both ways" (182). Indeed, the three friends inhabit neither role well, indicating the need for more elastic frames to understand these new experiences of displacement and their relation to a variety of histories.

Even readers who recognize the novelty of this story insist on resorting to inadequate generalizations. Caren Irr, for instance, views such "African migration fiction" as a conscious shift from "themes of cultural loss and traumatic history" popularized by Toni Morrison's *Beloved* with a focus on "racial wounds." Seeing Sepha as an immigrant melancholic, Irr reads the novel, somewhat confusingly, as "anti-ideological" but "pro-political."[21] But the novel can be read in posttraumatic terms only if the only traumatic template allowed to a black writer is that of slavery and its afterlife.[22] Historical traumas of postcolonial Africa rather than transatlantic slavery plague Sepha and his friends, and it is difficult to render the two analogous without parsing the necessary differences.

With a twenty-year-old map of Africa on the wall of Sepha's failing grocery store, the three friends play a grim game, resolutely testifying to the histories that brought them there—"Name a dictator and then guess the year and country.... No matter how many we name, there are always more, the names, dates, and years multiplying as fast as we can memorize them so that at times we wonder, half-jokingly, if perhaps we ourselves aren't somewhat responsible" (8). Even as they parody the dream of African freedom in this macabre game, their friendship also evokes a pan-African tradition, albeit in ambiguous fashion. The difference from earlier accounts of liberation focused on decolonization and nation building is clear, as is the anatomy of dictatorship on the continent. But in a friendship built on the recognition of these failed aspirations, the three African migrants poignantly neither break away from the traumatic past via repression, nor do they merely replicate the life of the homeland in exile. Nor do they embrace a liberal narrative of reinvention or remain stuck in melancholy. The horror of the dictator game they play should not hide its creativity—itself a form of reckoning with an ever-present history. To see this novel as a turn away from the model of trauma, as Irr does, is to miss many of these tensions, flattening the subtlety of the novel's representation of loss, and its navigation of the overlapping presence of the past in the present and the future.

At the same time, where Selasi emphasizes easy mobility, Mengestu's characters appear haunted, as ambivalent about the place they have left as they are about their present home, evoking not just the split identity or dual allegiance common to immigrant narratives, but an unease about navigating racial formations in a world shaped by an experience (of slavery) they do not share. The burden of the traumatic past and the dead-end future make any mobility apart from endless, aimless loops around the circles of D.C. impossible. The circles of Dante's hell evoke the recursive patterns of immigrant lives, which accede to neither celebratory narratives of Afropolitanism nor an embrace of the possibilities of immigrant reinvention.

The difference of such an approach to migration emerges most sharply when contrasted to a paradigmatic diasporic novel like Caryl Phillips's *Crossing the River* (1993). Phillips begins the story of the "many-tongued chorus" of the diaspora with the primal moment of the sale of children into slavery by a mythicized African father, and concludes with the father listening to the voices of the survivors across "the far bank of the river" who are "a long way from home." The father tells them, "There are no paths in water. No signposts. There is no return."[23] Phillips himself, a poster child for a transnational wandering that yields no certainties, only encounters with ambiguities, fluid identities, and contested states, explores all the points of the Atlantic triangle that have formed him—Africa, Europe, and the Americas—ultimately to discover of each place, "I feel at home here, but I don't belong. I am of, and not of, this place."[24] Even as he searches for "a plural notion of home," he clearly situates the beginning of his journey in slavery: "All journeys have a beginning. Mine began on the west coast of Africa in a slave fortress." Although his literal biography begins with his birth in Saint Kitts, West Indies, and subsequent migration to Britain, for Phillips the primal moment of origin of the diasporic subject remains the sale into slavery in Africa. He also imagines the end of his life with distinct reference to the history of slavery, asking that his ashes should be scattered "in the middle of the Atlantic Ocean at a point equidistant between Britain, Africa and North America."[25] Rather than display a comparable "high anxiety of belonging" located in an Atlantic world, the writers of the new diaspora chart other itineraries—some that do involve a return home, like Adichie's Ifemelu; others that choose to grapple with the precarious existence of an immigrant life, like Bulawayo's Darling, with little room to even acknowledge feelings of alienation and hyphenation; or others like Abani's Elvis in *GraceLand*, poised between two equally frightening worlds, with no resolution in sight.

Poverty Pornstar

Bulawayo's *We Need New Names* (2013) similarly restages debates over the reception of African literature in a changed twenty-first-century landscape, via ten-year-old Darling, who lives in a shantytown called Paradise, and dreams of escaping to the United States. Darling's journey from Paradise to what she calls "Destroyed-Michigan" or Detroit, unfolds alongside the larger story of social and economic collapse in Zimbabwe, with forced displacement, hunger, unemployment, sexual violence, and the specter of AIDS dogging her steps and her friends'. Alternately lyrical and gothic, Bulawayo sprinkles the novel with dark humor, sarcasm, and tragic musings, illuminating the contradictions of life in her native Zimbabwe during the lost decade of the 2000s.

The response to the novel and to the prize-winning short story ("Hitting Budapest") that preceded it has been largely twofold. The first approach views it as a customary narrative of US immigration. Indeed, Bulawayo herself encourages this interpretation in the reading group guide included at the end of the novel, inviting the implied reader to see that "Darling is Zimbabwean, but it is my hope that she is also Mexican and Indian and British, that she is from anywhere else where people live and hope and dream and leave. I hope she speaks to you."[26] Inspired by what she calls "Africa and Africanness" as she may be, Bulawayo also shows that Zimbabwe's story is neither exceptional nor exorbitant but allegorical of various kinds of contemporary migrations, all of which raise the question of belonging and being at home in evocative (though perhaps somewhat conventional) ways. Bulawayo imagines a transnational community of migrants—from Sri Lanka, Mexico, India, Sudan, Ethiopia, Israel, Kazakhstan, Niger—who all become friends of the Zimbabwean migrants, since "like us, they had left their homelands behind. . . . We had never seen their countries but we knew about everything in those pictures; we were not altogether strangers" (245). The novel's occasional shift to the collective voice further emphasizes the desire to speak to a broad story of contemporary migration, where displacements often mean that "we were no longer people; we were now illegals" (244).

The second approach has centered on how Africa emerges in the twenty-first century in the Western media, through the language of atrocity. Critics worry that novels like *We Need New Names* cement a racialized and neocolonial narrative of the dysfunction of the postcolony by parading well-worn tropes like children without the supervision of adults, doing warped things like staging a mock abortion for their eleven-year-old friend whose grandfather raped and impregnated her.[27] After all, Bulawayo races us through a veritable litany of what has come to be known as poverty porn, a depressingly familiar narrative of African atrocity—featuring rape, incest, hunger, suicide, and AIDS, but also absent or sadistic adults, along with children seemingly free of any authority or supervision, wise beyond their years, and all too accustomed to brutality, so much so that their childhood games involve throwing stones at a corpse, reenacting a brutal murder of a democracy activist, or trying to perform an abortion on a pregnant friend based on their memory of the TV show *ER*. As if this wasn't enough, when the novel shifts to the United States, within a span of a few pages, it covers the threat of a school shooting by a disturbed child, the hanging of a second child bullied as a freak, an extended scene featuring three teen-aged friends watching a variety of often violent pornography only to be brought up short by a video of circumcision, and a dispute among the friends over Ebonics and Nigerian 419 scams. There is little pause for reflection as the novel hurtles through these overcrowded scenarios at an unrelenting pace.

Reading this pace not as a challenge to credibility or a form of bad realism but as symptomatic of the accelerated pace of life and the compressed attention span of contemporary consumers of culture, I propose that Bulawayo finds a way to write about trauma without satisfying voyeurism. Although some discussions, especially on literary blogs featuring Caine Prize–nominated stories, questioned the novel on these grounds, the sheer power of Darling's wry, world-weary, precocious, biting, self-absorbed narrative voice suggests that *We Need New Names* invites us to complicate a reflex reading of this sort.[28] Bulawayo's characters, however disempowered, speak with an immediacy that removes them from a static or sentimentalized role of the victim. For instance, Darling and her friends play games like "Find Bin Laden" (290) and "Country-Game" (where "everybody wants to be certain countries," like "the U.S.A. and Britain and Canada and Australia and Switzerland and France and Italy and Sweden and Germany and Russia and Greece" but "nobody wants to be the rags of countries like Congo, like Somalia, like Iraq, like Sudan, like Haiti, like Sri Lanka, and not even this one we live in—who wants to be a terrible place of hunger and things falling apart"; 51). They also invent a brutal game about the murder of democracy activist Bornfree, prompting the two BBC journalists to probe with a mixture of horror and voyeurism "what kind of game were you just playing" (146). Invoking the generation that was born free but that found itself without options, the name is, of course, grimly ironic. As the children mimic the violence of adults, miming an abortion, a break-in, or a murder, all historical events to which Bulawayo alludes acquire the raw intensity and limited attention span of child's play, indexing how much of African land and resources have become games for Western powers and how African leaders have continued the exploitation after decolonization.

We Need New Names interrupts itself at regular intervals with an explicit critique of various outsider figures—a privileged young woman visiting from London whose clean feet surprise the children or an NGO aid worker who responds to Darling's "thank you much" with a shocked silence, leading her to wonder "like maybe I just barked" (57). The children quickly realize that even though the aid workers "are giving us things, they do not want to touch us or for us to touch them" (56). The novel exposes the limits of their humanitarian stance, warning potential readers of the pitfalls of voyeuristic appreciation of suffering when it is divorced from larger social and historical contexts or from any meaningful attempt to engage the victim. Bulawayo satirizes the "NGO people" who come in a truck with random gifts but insist on taking pictures as a reward for their transaction: "They don't care that we are embarrassed by our dirt and torn clothing, that we would prefer they didn't do it; they just take the pictures anyway, take and take" (54). The pregnant Chipo draws the most attention, leading Darling to comment on her newfound celebrity: "It's like she has become Paris Hilton, it's all just click-flash-flash-click" (55). Similarly, the young woman with a necklace of Africa in the opening chapter, who is well fed, clean, and safe, assumes that the children are enamored of her camera, and proceeds to photograph them: she doesn't realize that they are looking at the food in her hand instead. In their refusal to be fixed as objects of her photographic gaze, which in turn highlights her blindness to their actual needs, the children reveal the limits of an outsider's ability to empathize or even to really see what is in front of her eyes.

Moreover, the novel's structure itself—especially in terms of temporality—critiques the mechanics of relation between an outsider and insider or between the West and Africa. The shift to a collective voice, the way that the novel replicates the temporal impatience and optimism of a child (who gets bored easily, is always ready with a mean comment, is shocked quickly but astonishingly resilient), and the way that one incident relates to the other not only departs from a conventional narrative of growth or development of a bildungsroman, but intriguingly suggests that history is neither sequential nor reliable. The promised transformation or real change will not come, and the past cannot be left behind, as Darling keeps finding her friends appear in her imagination in the American mall, thus interrupting her present in spectral fashion, and realizes that they are always a phone or Skype call away. The sole voice speaking the language of antiracist resistance to "white vultures," that of Tshaka Zulu, can emerge only through his mental illness, a voice that Darling finds incomprehensible: "It's like listening to a skipping record" (274). The novel's sense of progress may itself be seen as a kind of skipping record, with omissions of moments that would be necessary for a novel with conventional realist claims. Darling's mother and father, for instance, sporadically fade and reappear, and readers never do learn how she migrates to the United States. The novel's conclusion, especially, seems to loop back to the beginning—with a scene of the death of a dog under the wheels of a truck carrying bread—seemingly randomly, and difficult to read symbolically as a resolution of the fictionalized events.

If the novel challenges rather than reinstates racialized narratives of African atrocity through such mechanisms of internalized critique, it also expands conventional accounts of US immigration. Bulawayo has said that "this image of a kid sitting on the remains of his bulldozed home—I just couldn't get him out of my head" inspired her novel. Starting in 2005, the government program Operation Murambatsvina ("Clear Out Rubbish") destroyed entire neighborhoods in a few hours, leaving more than three hundred thousand people homeless. Although many critics have selectively lauded either the sections of the novel set in Zimbabwe or those set in the United States, Bulawayo insists that we read the two stories of internal displacement and external migration together. The novel shows the contrast between the two locations clearly, marking them as coeval but unequal: hyperinflation in Zimbabwe strips the currency of its meaning, while overdevelopment in the United States means that no real suffering is possible (as Darling mocks the Occupy protesters and the anorexic daughter in the house she cleans). Unlike in *Americanah*, interracial marriages are for green cards, not love, and there is no hope of any romance—white or black—that would rescue Darling from her financially precarious life.

Although critics have tried to read *We Need New Names* within the Afropolitan discourse, arguing that "Darling and her fellow displaced residents of Paradise [are] true Afropolitans," the novel refuses to celebrate migration, centering poverty and economic vulnerability as key facets of the characters' lives.[29] To be sure, its critique of the figure who leaves home is so powerful that even Darling is not exempt from it. When Darling describes watching a BBC program about the suffering of the people to Chipo, her friend's response is brutal: "You think watching on BBC means you know what is going on? No, you don't, my friend, it's the wound that knows the texture of the pain; it's us who stayed here feeling the real suffering, so it's us who have a right to even say anything about that or anything about anybody" (287). When Darling asserts a right to her country, Chipo continues, "You left it, Darling, my dear, you left the house burning and you have the guts to tell me, in that stupid accent that you were not even born with, that doesn't even suit you, that this is your country?" (288).

Undercutting Darling's claim to the home she has left behind, Bulawayo further highlights uneven encounters over racialization in diaspora. Darling befriends both an African American and a Nigerian girl in the United States. But friendly banter among the three teenaged girls quickly becomes a dispute with accusations of being unable to speak English (one girl speaks Ebonics), orchestrating 419 scams, or singing "tribal stuff" (222), showing how no appeal to diasporic unity will suffice. Bulawayo tells her readers that Darling's "story is my attempt to marry Zimbabwe with America, to tell a story rooted in both worlds. But even in fiction, this marriage is a difficult one."[30] Neither narrative uses Atlantic slavery as a touchstone. Instead, Darling's story invites a rethinking of the diasporic paradigm altogether, away from the slave sublime, or from the question of heritage—the paradigm that may be captured in Cullen's famous unresolved question I invoked earlier: "What is Africa to me?" Refusing to imagine diaspora solely as a conversation among Africans and African Americans, *We Need New Names* makes us reckon with class as a key factor in the lives of African immigrants to the United States, as any time a seeming cultural difference between the United States and Zimbabwe crops up (how to discipline a spoiled child, for instance, or perceptions of beauty and body image), the novel invariably shifts to the economic realities of poverty, reminding us that Darling is busy "cleaning the toilets or bagging groceries" (253) and is not likely to reach middle-class or legal immigrant status.

When compared to another Zimbabwean coming-of-age story, Tsitsi Dangarembga's *Nervous Conditions*, the differences in historical moment become even clearer.[31] If Tambu had to grow further and further away from the homestead to escape the patriarchy of her home and of colonial missionary Christianity, and thus to learn to write her story along with that of the four women in her life, Darling, who has already left behind her mother and been taken up by her aunt, cannot benefit from that upwardly mobile trajectory of the anticolonial era, including win a scholarship, learn English, adopt liberal ideas, and find a path up and away. Darling finds in the United States only another kind of subordinated position in the economy of precarity. Moreover, while both novels link the personal development of the protagonist to historical change, Bulawayo makes little reference to historical dates or persons, with almost no mention of colonial rule at all. It is difficult to understand Darling's journey without reckoning with its complex relation to such predecessors as *Nervous Conditions* and its refusal to cohere as a bildungsroman, in favor of the "skipping record" of history, as if Bulawayo's novel were unaware of the possibility of co-optation. The author refuses sentiment and positions the reader as a voyeur and outsider, eliciting neither pity nor horror nor even easy empathy. Indeed, the novel itself may be seen as commenting on the empathetic abilities and limits of readers, as well as drawing attention to the conditions of production, circulation, and reception of African literature.

In proposing and rejecting various reading models, *We Need New Names* may easily be read as an allegory of interpretation. When Darling reads *Jane Eyre*, the classic bildungsroman of feminist self-consolidation and a possible Talking Book, she says that "the long meandering sentences and everything just bored me and that Jane just kept irritating me with her stupid decisions and the whole lame story made me want to throw the book away" (228).[32] Indeed, all kinds of media compete with books—pornography on the Internet, T-shirts with Cornell University or Save Darfur on them, Morgan Freeman playing Nelson Mandela, and maps of Africa becoming either necklaces or ivory slabs—affording a steady commentary on how images of Africa circulate and are commodified. In evoking the internal rhythms of children talking to each other, or managing the puzzling demands of adults themselves at loss in a time of crisis, the novel sounds the refrain—"even a tree knows" or "even a brick knows"—indicating that there is no need for interpretation (54–55).

Bulawayo thus escapes both poverty porn and the immigrant story of reinvention, connecting Zimbabwe to the United States by showing us vulnerability and precarity in each location, foregrounding inequality in the place of easy mobility, and asking for new names over new nations. In doing so, she helps underline the ways in which neither a focus on trauma nor the Afropolitan is adequate to the new African narrative. Neither do notions of an afterlife of slavery or Gilroy's idea of the "slave sublime" as the form for representing "living memory" seem appropriate.[33] To fully reckon with such fictions, conceptions of diaspora drawn solely from the history and memory of slavery will need stretching and reshaping. To that end, I explicate the need for this dynamic through Abani's 2004 novel *GraceLand*, which showcases the critical possibilities opened up when we are attuned to the ethics of reading across time and place. In *GraceLand*, the local and the global intermesh with abandon, and a new worlding of African literature becomes possible.

Elvis Has Left Lagos

As a novel about the vivid fantasies of a sixteen-year-old child in Lagos, living in a slum with his dejected and broken father, mourning the death of his beloved mother who named him Elvis after her favorite singer, drawn into the informal economy of drug trafficking and the organ trade and threatened by the military government, *GraceLand* seems immediately relevant to this study. Because the novel ends with Elvis at the airport, seemingly set to escape Lagos for the United States, *GraceLand* is often read as marking the shift in African literature from the national to the global. But reading it in relation to Atlantic slavery, as several recent scholars have done, underscores the problems with the hegemony of Atlantic frames of analysis. Veronica Hendrick sees the novel as connecting Atlantic slavery to its story through an emphasis on indebtedness, as a "system of financial and social debt . . . connects modern situations to the slave trade." Characters assume the position of the slave trader, the local slave-trading middleman, and the human cargo—for example, the Colonel is the trader, Redemption the local middleman, and Elvis the cargo; or the World Bank is the trader, the Colonel the local leader, and the King the cargo.[34] Such an ingenious formulation leads Hendrick to see the novel as condemning global cultural influences, like Elvis's love for Elvis Presley, and thus to theorize any nonnative interaction as a form of cultural invasion. Abani, in this way, putatively laments the loss of tradition and kinship structures of the parents' generation, in the wake of which such corruption proliferates. What this reading obscures is any sense of military rule as a modern phenomenon, while it also misses the critique of tradition that forms such a powerful part of *GraceLand*. Hendrick's interpretation also requires seeing slavery itself in a fully dehistoricized fashion. Similarly, Erin Fehskens reads Elvis as repeating the path of Jamaican maroons (slaves who fled the plantations and formed hinterland communities in the early eighteenth century), seeing him as "a kind of enslaved subject."[35] Like the maroons', Elvis's journey becomes one of resistance, and he emerges as a black Atlantic hero of the kind that Gilroy so influentially envisioned. Elvis appears in flight from an oppressive Nigerian masculinity, sensitized by his revulsion at becoming part of the trade of human organs and bodies, and thus heroic in the forms of agency he displays.

But *GraceLand*, as many scholars have shown, clearly jettisons the binary of the West versus Africa, or oppressor-oppressed, or even of resistance-subordination. Highlighting the ethics of survival in the slum of a mega-city, Abani shows Lagos as a place deeply rooted in a local and global culture, cross-hatched by the diasporic but not subsumed by it, with few possibilities for heroism. Since the book's publication in 2004, scholars have appreciated Abani's precise evocation of Lagos as a mega-city continually pollinated by global culture, situated the novel as part of the third generation of Nigerian literature, which tends to turn to the United States, pondered its ambivalent politics of gender and sexuality, and mined it for its representation of the exigencies of life in a slum.[36] American, Indian, and Yugoslavian films mingle here, as do novels from across the globe, making it difficult to separate Ellison or Baldwin from Dickens or Dostoevsky. Race appears both as indigenous and imported: what emerges most powerfully is the creative adaptation of foreign culture, not any form of brainwashing. For instance, when watching Hollywood Westerns, Elvis and his friends rename all the characters Actor or John Wayne.

GraceLand maps the historical transition from country to city as its characters move from Afikpo in the 1970s to Lagos in the 1980s, without recourse to stark contrasts, as both the global city and the rural space are equally steeped in mass culture, and Elvis's fantasy world acknowledges something of the texture of contemporary media-saturated desires and longings everywhere. In tune with Abani's claim that Nigeria is "the most Western black country in Africa" (just like Los Angeles is a "Third World City"), binaries of First and Third World, or Western and non-Western, do not suffice.[37] Reading the brutal excesses of the military as repetitions of the slave-master's whipping only conceals the analysis of modern forms of power, where technology, media, and aesthetics combine in producing death and terror. Hence, the colonel who photographs his corpses, sometimes cuts off an arm or leg to capture a better image in his search for the beauty of death. Focusing on historical slavery as the interpretive frame further obscures forms of power based on oil, insofar as *GraceLand* documents the transformation of Nigeria into a modern petro-economy.

Readings focused on slavery also miss the critique of tradition that forms such a powerful part of the novel. The novel's concern with the process of inheritance of cultural traditions and genealogies emerges in its extensive use of epigraphs, detailing in an impassive, sonorous voice the ceremonies of the Igbo rituals featuring the Kola nut as the paternal inheritance, as well as recipes for dishes and healing concoctions suggesting a maternal inheritance. Placing *GraceLand* within ethnographic expectations that have long dogged African literature helps us to understand these functions. As Abani notes, the reader needs to go through the "irritating voice" of the ethnographer who thinks any single ritual can explain the culture to reach the more vivid and ambiguous story presented in the novel.[38] Both the epigraphs (reminiscent of Achebe) and Elvis's performances meet Joseph Slaughter's terms of a "parody of a parody" and should be read as ironic comments on the appropriation of cultures, as well as a gentle mocking of readerly expectations about authentic Igbo ways of being.[39] A sixteen-year-old Igbo boy dressing up in whiteface to look like Elvis Presley recalls a performer with little stability or normativity of race, gender, class, or sexuality, a white man who is himself a performing a kind of musical and choreographic blackface.

The much-discussed ending similarly speaks neither to novelistic failure of imagination (as some have charged) nor even to a sociological reflection of the turn toward the United States in third-generation Nigerian writers.[40] Even though Elvis is armed with a fake passport and new (and richly resonant) identity as Redemption, en route to the United States, he is guided more by his intimacy with "that scar, that pain, that shame, that degradation that no metaphor could contain"—as Baldwin describes the lynching of a black man in *Going to Meet the Man*—and less by his earlier fantasies of becoming an entertainer.[41] Immigration and cultural transnationalism are not presented as alternatives to the violence of the postcolony under military rule. Domestic and global economic systems are thoroughly interpenetrated, and both rely on keeping vulnerable people like Elvis marginalized. The novel thus demonstrates an alternative to the antagonism that a host of scholars imagine: African migration to the United States must necessarily be detrimental to the ongoing quest for African American freedom, or African writers must decide whether to embrace the global or Afropolitan or to focus on social justice and trauma. *GraceLand* models a new kind of worlding of the African novel as indeed of the figure of the African writer. In outlining a philosophy of history that neither instrumentalizes the past for contemporary exigencies, nor renders it frozen or static, nor a prelapsarian idyll, Abani's novel elaborates with urgency and lyricism the many folds of time inhabited by his protagonists as they ponder, endure, and battle the weight of a violent history.

A scene where, "with the air of ritual," Elvis methodically puts on his Elvis whiteface while admiring the image of a "white couple in evening dress dancing under a sky full of stars" (77) and fantasizing about putting on makeup in public without abuse or threat crystallizes the novel's richly ambiguous relation to concepts of race and diaspora. The makeup is clearly tied to both race and gender performance for Elvis, and the sponging of white talcum powder somehow softens his skin, making it more feminine and erotic, "smooth, like the silk of Aunt Felicia's stockings" (77). With blue eye makeup, deep red lips, and a wig, he feels transformed into "the real Elvis" (78), but as the fantasy fades and the makeup starts to sweat, he wonders, "What if he had been born white, or even just American?" Immediately he checks himself, noting that Redemption would label this "colonial mentality" (78). The novel thus preempts the usual allegorical reading—wanting to be white or American as a colonial hangover—and suggests its limitations as a meaningful frame for Elvis's fevered imaginative universe. Readings like those, gesturing to the antagonisms of the moment of decolonization have failed to yield meaning to contemporary Nigerian teenagers like Elvis. There is no easy path to that past language for the novelist either—as that language of resistance is placed under erasure in a sense, acknowledged as always already contaminated, co-opted, yet visible in its loss as an object of melancholy.

Moreover, by repeatedly recalling the protocols of circulation and reception, reading and interpretation, *GraceLand* allegorizes the literary relations of the contemporary world republic of letters instead of passively receiving forms from another time. The clearest sign of this is the novel's sustained intertextuality, liberally sprinkled as it is with references to and sometimes excerpts from fiction by Dickens, Achebe, Baldwin, Ellison, the Bible, and Onitsha market fiction like *Mabel the Sweet Honey That Poured Away*. When Elvis buys *Mabel* from a bookseller who reminds him of Friar Tuck from Robin Hood, he carefully tucks it "between the Dostoevsky and the Baldwin" (113) since he doesn't want to admit reading "low-class trash" (112). The narrator first glosses such popular fiction as "pamphlets, written between 1910 and 1970 . . . produced on small presses in the eastern market town of Onitsha" and then describes them as "the Nigerian equivalent of dime drugstore pulp fiction crossed with pulp pop self-help books" (112). The excerpt from *Mabel* that follows focuses on a scene of seduction, presented in the flowery language of romance. Inserting such fiction between Dostoevsky and Baldwin democratizes a world republic of letters, decenters the prestige of the acknowledged masters, and helps us view them from the point of view of the periphery. The included excerpt relates to *GraceLand* itself and its cultural project as well, signaling Elvis's seamless ability to navigate high and low culture, expressive of Abani's vision of Lagos: as violent as it is beautiful. Even if the hierarchies of an unequal system of a world republic are not so easily dismantled—such that *Mabel* can democratize Dostoevsky but not the other way round—*GraceLand* itself as a self-reflexive participant in the system can and does proffer a reading challenge to world literature.

Elvis is thus best interpreted as an allegory of the figure of the postcolonial artist (rather than of the Atlantic slave narrator), constantly learning how to read the city, eclectic in taste, violated and under perpetual threat, yet curious and open to any number of escape routes. As an artist, he suffers more, is sensitive and vulnerable, and will not survive this world. We see him always reading the city—its geography, landscape, and people, walking into a scene and immediately wondering how he would film it, if he were a director, at a remove from the action he witnesses. Yet as an artist, rather than acting as a moral conscience of society, he remains detached and exploratory. Elvis's characterization may lead us to see *GraceLand* as staging a series of debates about methods of reading—formalist, allegorical, or sociological, whereby Elvis would appear to be a formalist. When the King of the Beggars makes an impassioned speech at a rally about the evils of capitalism, Elvis notes that he can appreciate the form, the style, but the content doesn't move him: instead, he "was mesmerized by the richness of the King's voice. It was seductive, eliciting the listener's trust and he soon forgot his concerns and began to believe the king was right" (155). For Elvis, the history of struggle and anticolonial resistance only seems legible as formalism, insofar as form is the only way that he can appreciate the language of politics. Meanwhile, another character, Okon, espouses a species of naturalism, arguing that "we are who we are because we are who we were made" (312).

In reading *GraceLand* as a *kunstlerroman*, it may seem that I have arrived upon a contradiction—an insistence on new forms, yet a return to old ones. But as Anthony Appiah has forcefully argued, formal experimentation in postcolonial fiction cannot be read as the same as its counterpart in the West.[42] Paraphrasing him, we might say that Abani's kunstlerroman is not the same as Joyce's. But doing so would seem to proliferate not resolve problems, since Abani's novel clearly draws upon global culture in its fullest possible reach, making a Yugoslavian film speak as vividly to Elvis as an Onitsha pamphlet. A singular moment of magic realism in the novel—Elvis's father's death, seemingly transforming him into his totem animal of a leopard—further complicates matters, recalling the long-standing association of postcolonial literature with the genre. One may also see the novel as merely an instance of bad realism, best instantiated in the seemingly authentic and detailed recipes that really would not yield the dish they promise. To see the events of the novel as overwrought, melodramatic, or just too glossy would also not be wrong. But all these possible objections are already staged in the novel; after all, the presiding symbols here are Elvis Presley and a postcard of Las Vegas. In saying that the novel is a kunstlerroman and Elvis the figure of the artist, what matters is that Abani is writing both within and against ethnographic expectations, expanding the possibilities associated with the form, conscripting it into his vision to track an incomplete modernity rather than linear development. Wrestling with the received form, rearranging time and space to foreground questions of transmission, nodes, networks, and slippages (somewhat like the highways of Lagos), allows this global novel to be at once tragic and flippant, metafictional and realist. Elvis has been grappling throughout with how to become a man, an artist, an immigrant. But in the end, the novel, like Elvis, wants to become Redemption—to make love and poetry real, and to assert the value of life and art.

Seeing Elvis as the figure of an artist, a writer and a reader, helps to resituate the ambivalence of the ending as an opening for more stories, recalling Ellison's injunction to the reader at the close of *Invisible Man*: "On the lower frequencies, I speak for you."[43] The novel thus stages a series of reading lessons, posing questions of how readers arrive at legibility, whether they fall into the ethnographic trap set by the epigraphs or learn to read the intertexts or register the historical longing for a Messiah who never arrives. Toward the end, Abani writes, "Elvis traced patterns in the cracked and parched earth beneath his feet. There is a message in it all somewhere, he mused, a point to the chaos. But no matter how hard he tried, the meaning always seemed to be out there somewhere beyond reach, mocking him" (317).

Drift, Digression, Diaspora

Because so much of the critical dialogue about the new African narrative has bifurcated into either an advocacy of cosmopolitanism or a requirement to document trauma, Teju Cole's inventive treatment of migration and mobility in *Open City* (2011) demands further discussion precisely because it combines both paradigms. Thus far I have suggested that new and more varied conceptions of diaspora become possible when we read new African narratives of the twenty-first century. But Cole's celebrated novel seems to depart from all available templates altogether. In fact, it seems to constitute itself in direct opposition to existing accounts of black Atlantic mobility. It might seem that the novel applauds or at least participates in a kind of cosmopolitanism, cherishing unencumbered travel, on planes, on trains, and on foot, but also through its erudite protagonist's ramblings on world culture—ranging across Appiah, Bach, Barthes, Brewster, Coetzee, Said, Mahler, and Cannonball Adderley. But Julius's "aimless wandering" (3) across New York City that opens the novel seems far more melancholic about mobility than may initially seem. The patterns of bird migrations that Julius follows at the novel's opening portend something much darker, as the novel concludes with the image of dead birds crashing into the flame of the Statue of Liberty. Julius had hoped that he would be able to see "the miracle of natural immigration" (4) but finds himself weighed down with suicidal thoughts—his own, emanating from some unexplained melancholy, and those of his patients, such as a Native American professor, whose study of the horrors faced by indigenous people haunts her and leads her to suicide. Being among people in New York City's public spaces makes Julius feel only that he is "standing close to strangers, jostling them and being jostled by them for space and breathing room, all of us reenacting unacknowledged traumas, the solitude intensified" (7). Even the novel's title suggests equivocation, signaling ethical compromise and inclusiveness alike—Brussels chose "surrender" and "negotiation" during the Second World War to save itself from being "reduced to rubble" (97), while New York City's openness is most visible in its many cultures layered upon another—"each one of those past moments was present now as a trace" (54).

It is these traces that inform the novel's sustained exploration of the weight of history on the present. A sophisticated flâneur musing on the aesthetic effects of classical music, art, fiction, philosophy, and photography collides with deeply melancholic meditations on past and present violence, including Rwandan and Native American genocide, slavery in New York and Haiti, Ellis Island and 9/11, Japanese American internment, rape, and, most of all, World War II and the Jewish Holocaust. Cole insists on telling the two stories together, implicitly at least submitting that one does not exist without the other. Even though the Nigerian-German Julius may be seen as fitting an Afropolitan mold, his many encounters with the figures that have populated my study thus far—Saidu, a refugee from Liberia, Pierre, an ex-slave from Haiti, the bodies of thousands of slaves interred beneath the streets of New York in the African burial ground, groups of Congolese and Rwandan emigrants in Brussels, and, most of all, Moji, the girl from his childhood who reappears and confronts him of his teenage rape—link these disparate experiences together.

What is puzzling, however, is that while the novel does suggest—at least associatively—some kind of connection between these public worlds and Julius's private alienated self, it is difficult to discern the terms of such a correlation. Musing on the ruins of the World Trade Center, Julius ponders not just its current void, but numerous past erasures: "The site was a palimpsest, as was all the city, written, erased, rewritten" (59). Most of the novel's physical sites similarly encode past histories, in the vein of the melancholy historicism of Walter Benjamin, whose essay "On the Philosophy of History" is name-checked in the novel. In relation to representations of slavery, as we have seen, the most influential figure for such a conception of history has been Toni Morrison's conception of "rememory" forwarded in *Beloved*—the notion that what happened in the past is still there and can still impact you, even "you who never was there," making it vital to remember—like Sethe— "something she had forgotten she knew."[44]

In contrast, Julius evinces a clear distrust of memory from the very beginning, finding the birds he loves to watch so real that once they are gone he cannot quite believe they ever existed: "I couldn't trust my memory when they weren't there" (4). Indeed his self is slowly revealed to be constructed by blocking memory. If Cole's portrayal of the city as a palimpsest erects a layered edifice of a range of historical moments, Julius constitutes and continually validates his own subjectivity by repelling memory, the demands of others, and any possible connection. Erasure, rejection, alienation are his watchwords, seemingly seeking "solitude of a rare purity" (255). Even as he excavates the sediments of the city's past and claims that "I wanted to find the line that connected me to my own part in these stories" (59), he thwarts any such effort at connection—whether on the basis of race, national or African origin, or neighborly proximity. When he goes to Brussels ostensibly to seek out his estranged grandmother, for instance, he makes little attempt to locate her. The connections he does make in Brussels are fleeting and always in spaces of transit—a passenger next to him on his flight with whom he has an amiable dinner, a chance sexual encounter with an older woman he meets at a café, or an evening spent with an erudite and passionate Moroccan man, Farouq, with whom he eagerly debates politics and literature. "My instinct was for doubts and questions," he says (206). Neither his detachment nor his mobility thus attaches to a political critique. Suspicious of "overinterpreters" and "fashionable politics" and a "general inability to assess evidence" (28), he is estranged from his mother and nostalgic for his grandmother only because he shared silence rather than words with her as a child. In the end, he connects with her obliquely through Moji's accusation of rape, but this is another unexplored avenue left for the reader to travel, not explicitly delineated in the novel.

In meeting the Liberian refugee Saidu, Julius displays neither sympathy nor understanding. He fantasizes that his girlfriend, Nadège, might "fall in love" with the idea of Julius as "listener, the compassionate African who paid attention to the details of someone else's life and struggle" (70), as he himself had, but tells us in the next line that the relationship ended. He never returns to visit Saidu despite his promise and Saidu's obvious need to share his story. Julius also doubts Saidu, assuming that he was playing "an innocent refugee" when he might have been a child soldier (67). The story itself is quite stylized and formulaic and would fit the template of such tales of the loss of childhood innocence, separation from family, danger, despair, and conscription into an army unit that has recurred in previous chapters. In revealing that they have become tropes now—as an Afropolitan figure fails to connect with an equally recognizable figure of the detainee, refugee, and illegal immigrant (who may even have been a child soldier)—Cole shows how Julius neither fears nor honors any "rememory" that Saidu might evoke.

This is apiece with Julius's steady refusal to answer the call—"hey, I'm African just like you" (53)—whether it comes from an elderly veteran glad to see a black doctor, a postal worker sharing poetry about the "motherland," or a taxi driver who demands that Julius acknowledge the fact that they are "brothers" from Africa. This is also what makes it difficult to square Cole's provocative claim in an interview that *Open City* is an "African book," haunted from beginning to end by Julius's origin in Nigeria.[45] The fact that the previously published novella *Every Day Is for the Thief* also has a figure like Julius as its protagonist further tantalizes and suggests a connection between the place of origin and some larger comment on the dynamics of global identities today.[46]

Existing accounts of such mobility have tended to either celebrate rootlessness as a cosmopolitanism beyond narrow nationalist, ethnic, or racial boundaries, or to accuse figures like Julius of being a sellout, insufficiently authentic to signal "Africanness." The latter claim has been advanced with some urgency in recent years, a response to the remarkable visibility of immigrant writers like Cole, Adichie, and Bulawayo, all of whom live in the United States. Ongoing assumptions about authentic African literature as the domain of the local, preferably rural existence inform the antipathy both to Afropolitan literature and to its inverse: the literature of trauma, written to satisfy the banal sentimentalism of the "White-Savior Industrial Complex," as Cole aptly termed it.[47] Neither approach apprehends both what makes *Open City* new and the ways in which it continues previous traditions. To assess these, it is first necessary to explicate the generic choices of this unusual novel.

That *Open City* defies easy categorization by genre few will deny—its originality comes across not just in the blurring of fiction and nonfiction (an instance of a novel approximating a diary as one review states), its virtuosic intertextuality, and its stream of consciousness, but also because of the affectless protagonist and plotless narrative.[48] If a primary feature of the bildungsroman is to show a maturity from youth to adulthood, some kind of linear narrative (however arrested or incomplete) is necessary. *Open City* thwarts all expectations of such linearity, formation, or development—not just because the novel opens and closes inconclusively, but also because the key moment of revelation (Moji's accusation of rape) comes at the end and seemingly prompts no response from its otherwise compulsively voluble and introspective know-it-all narrator. The novel's nonlinear narrative—insisting on drifting and digressing—challenges the temporal logic of a bildungsroman or even of a novel more generally. Julius's *bildung* not only is a foregone conclusion at the beginning—he is overly formed, if anything—but also seems to provide no basis for an ethical or social life but only an isolated and melancholy one. *Open City* reverses the modernist epiphany and replicates the melancholy of Naipaul's arrival. But the novel rejects both melancholy and arrival as adequate containers for the horizon of the present.

Measuring it against the elements of the slave narrative helps read its generic singularity. This is not to propose that *Open City* has anything in common with a neo-slave narrative. After all, Julius would prefer not to acknowledge any call to share on the basis of race or nationality, displays no sentimentalism, offers no jeremiad or ethnography. His constant travel is neither difficult nor especially interesting. Rather, the novel's treatment of slavery and allied forms of historical violence helps clarify its distinctiveness and its peculiar negotiation of exceptionalism and exemplarity, its status as an African book, an American novel, a black Atlantic travel narrative, a quintessentially global novel. Reading its formal turns—through the genres of the imperial romance, the black Atlantic travel narrative, the modernist bildungsroman or kunstlerroman, a reverse heart-of-darkness impressionist tale, an anticolonial antiromance, and modernist flânerie—further illuminates key aspects of contemporary revisitings of slavery. This is so because *Open City* inverts the slave narrative: it rejects or repels rather than invites the reader's empathy. It layers personal and collective migrations (including those in nature: birds, bedbugs, trees), public and private histories, but refuses to allow any substitution of empathetic reader and traumatized survivor. Even though Cole has elsewhere claimed that the work of the literary is to help in "closing the empathy gap," *Open City* shows us the undoing of empathy and substitution so often thought to be performed by the global novel.[49] This is not simply the case because its first-person narrator is unable to model empathy in the face of a refugee like Saidu, but because Cole will not allow us to identify with Julius either. In the penultimate chapter, Moji reveals that this introspective man seemingly has no recollection of having raped her as a teenager, an act that has haunted her every single day since. Julius's response is to recall the stoicism of a fifteen-year-old Nietzsche rather than to turn within and remember his own actions. Reversing the modernist epiphany, Cole makes us probe the many disavowals that make up Julius's self—which mirror the complex disavowals of New York after 9/11. Reading Freud, Julius characterizes the "anxiety that cloaked the city" as a form of incomplete mourning, a pathological melancholia (209). If we analyze his own tendency to "section off," it is easy to read Julius's grief at his father's death, his unexplained anger at his German mother, his amnesiac response to Moji's presence as equally melancholic attempts that reveal his many neuroses. And it is tempting to link this neurosis to his immigrant status—the underside of the cosmopolitan traveler without affiliations. But Cole refuses to make him an allegorical figure representing the migrant, or the cultural hybrid, or the mixed-race figure (the tragic mulatto), or the been-to, or what Adichie calls the "Americanah."

Cole as a writer himself refuses such taxonomies. That the naming and categorization of the postcolonial and the American have always needed an elastic sense of nationality is especially evident in the reception of the writers of the African literary renaissance more broadly, since their distance from prior generations of African writers is clearest in their engagement with the United States. For some this is a matter of location and employment; for others the United States is the setting of their fiction, or theirs is the latest story in a long-standing genre of US immigrant writing. But for a figure like Cole, it has always been necessary to insist that he is an American writer, not a Nigerian one. Born in Michigan, he returned to Nigeria as a baby, but moved back to the United States for college at the age of seventeen. But calling him African American requires a bit of hesitation, so many commentators have settled on Nigerian American. The eclecticism of the novel's references further testifies to the histories of connection across Nigeria, Europe, and the United States. This is why it's as easy to think of *Open City* as a 9/11 novel or a New York City novel as it is to think of it as African.

As Julius recognizes that a marathon runner with no one to greet him at the close of the race is not to be pitied, it is the solitary individual—the stranger—who cannot take action who is deserving of censure. Both character and reader are thus shown the insufficiency of empathy as the means to imagine relation. The novel relentlessly probes the relation of empathy to memory, especially of pain, violence, and suffering. Cole explicitly links the language of healing and psychotherapy to art, which can take one out of one's own body.

Open City thus tests the ability of culture to perceive, process, and absorb atrocity. At times it seems like Cole literalizes the chilling game imagined in Margaret Atwood's *Oryx and Crake* (2003), pitting humanistic achievement against human capacity for evil. In the near future dystopia, Atwood plots a trading game called Blood and Roses "along the lines of Monopoly."[50] On the side of Blood, we have such large-scale human atrocities as massacres and genocides, and on the side of Roses, human achievements—*"monuments to the soul's magnificence"* ranging from *Mona Lisa* to the Ninth Symphony and *Crime and Punishment*. The game verifies a commonly held notion of literature and culture—that it speaks to the noble side of humanity, and can somehow rebut or counter atrocities. To play the game, once the dice is rolled, either a Blood or a Rose item pops up: "If it was a Blood item, the Rose player had a chance to stop the atrocity from happening, but he had to put up a Rose item in exchange. The atrocity would then vanish from history, or at least the history recorded on the screen." The game is won by acquiring or retaining as many human achievements as possible. At once a parody of capitalist exchange and humanism alike, the game also conjures up common conceptions of the value of the humanities, and the difficulty of knowing how violence may be reckoned with or that age-old question—how to produce art in the face of events like the Holocaust or the slave trade. No wonder Atwood concludes the section with the pithy statement "it was a wicked game."[51]

In *Open City*, Cole plays the same game, without accepting the premise—a game that one doesn't play by the rules, but plays to show that the rules are stacked—that perhaps is the dilemma for the postcolonial observer. Julius mulls the same question that troubled Coetzee's Elizabeth Costello: "Why show torture?" (31). How might an observer apprehend the "unspeakable" if empathy is not the answer? Everywhere the weight of the past presses as atrocity and art abound. But the novel doesn't suggest balance, questioning equivalences and substitutions throughout—Farouq's, Moji's, and Julius's own. This is why the unraveling of plot enables both avoidance and a moving on. Moreover, Cole suggests these options not as oppositions, rather as one thought following the next, echoing the frame of walking in the city and letting places, people, interactions seep into one's consciousness. Cole reveals 9/11 as a moment that locked an entire country in Freud's melancholia and offers a dense layering of other histories of violence, a palimpsest revealing one truth after another, and urges us only to learn to read, to interpret, and to question. *Open City* models the insufficiency of older languages—those of psychotherapy for trauma, the arts as generating empathy, cosmopolitan exchange as a response to difference, racial and diasporic solidarity, the enigmas of immigrant arrival. But even as it parodies or seems startled by the casual use of phrases like "the victimized Other," it doesn't hold up the alternative as unblemished, as Julius's own unreliable memory and narration destabilizes any anchor the novel may have had.

The novel persists in this refusal to adhere to standard racial characterizations. When Julius finds himself at an ATM machine, only to realize that he cannot remember his code, he recognizes that "his mind was empty, subject to a nervous condition," but rather than evoking Frantz Fanon or Tsitsi Dangarembga, he feels "as though [he] had become a minor character in a Jane Austen novel" (161). That Cole's intelligent young black psychiatrist does not evoke Fanon as antecedent is remarkable enough without a clear jab to the reader not to make these assumptions. Similarly, one may wish to turn to Du Bois's theorization of double consciousness as a psychic condition brought about by the competing pulls of race and nationality, but Julius does not feel accessible through that frame either. Cole, like Du Bois before him, wears his cosmopolitanism with ease—he "sits with Shakespeare and he winces not."[52] But he also shows fracture—whether in a mugging that begins as a friendly nod among young black men and turns into a violent attack, or in Julius's constant irritation at being hailed as an African. However, Julius himself also searches for connections as his memory of his father's burial is juxtaposed to his walks around the African burial site. But because the narrative style relies on digression, Cole stops short of suggesting an analogy, but insinuates layering, co-constitution, or homology.

This is why when Julius meets a Haitian man, seemingly out of time, recalling "the terror of Bonaparte and the terror of Boukman" (72), and narrating his escape from slavery and the difficult hesitant journey to freedom in New York, Cole's antecedent doesn't seem to be slavery's most famous ghost—Morrison's *Beloved*—who is vengeful and loving at once, making demands on the present that threaten to swallow it up whole. Cole's ghostly slave allows Julius to make spectral connections—he sees an apparition of "the body of a lynched man dangling from a tree" (75)—"as time became elastic and voices cut out of the past into the present" (74). In this way, the novel layers one historical atrocity onto another, one memory onto another, just as the city itself does. In its suggestion of a relation between public and private trauma—without an analogy—*Open City* models a possible response to the question: how to write "about atrocity without flinching" (165). It isn't enough to just say "suffering is suffering" (181) or that art is universal despite the exclusively white spaces of museum or concert hall Julius attends. The novel thus insists that we cannot read with the hope of arriving at either trauma or cosmopolitanism. Instead, we have to begin with them and to begin with their mutual constitution. Rather than favoring politics over aesthetics or debating poverty porn against Afropolitan style, *Open City* models a subtle relation between public and private trauma without substituting one for the other. "A book suggests conversation," Cole tells us at the very beginning, and the substance of the novel's invitation to many openings (through its lush intertextuality), many paths, leads not to understanding but to dialogue (5). One of the key aspects of slavery's revival I have been tracing is the notion of history as repetition. Cole's novel probes that form of melancholic historicism, creating a palimpsest that obscures rather than reveals, recommending erasures and blind spots rather than insight. In this way, Cole submits a kind of rehearsal of new historicism of the Morrison moment that might well serve as a requiem.

Afropolitan Blues

In closing, it is worth returning to the much-debated notion of the Afropolitan, to weigh its capacity to signal a new, re-formed diasporic framework explicitly removed from the trauma or victimhood associated with slavery. To critics who chastise the figure as a "polite, corporate, glossy" form of consumerism that markets an exotic African identity to the West, Selasi clarifies that she was writing from a "stranded place," not a utopian one, from feelings of pain, alienation, and nonbelonging, not celebration.[53] As a reaction to normative associations of Africa with atrocity, the Afropolitan emerges out of a desire to counteract what Selasi calls "the media's portrayals (war, hunger)" and the "New World trope of bumbling blue-black doctor" as she seeks to define African culture beyond "filial piety and pepper soup."[54]

Other scholars have similarly sought to dissociate the Afropolitan from an idiom of privilege and elitism. In her recent introduction to a special issue on the subject, Carli Coetzee seeks to "reboot" the term so that it may prompt the "beginning of an activist scholarly agenda in which 'the Afropolitan' is reimagined to include the stealthy figure crossing the Mediterranean by boat, and the Somali shopkeeper in a

South African township."⁵⁵ This is a difficult burden for any single term to bear, and the problem of class appears immediately, as it is crucial to differentiate coerced and voluntary movements. It may thus perhaps be best not to extend the term of Afropolitan to all African migrants but to recognize it as an apt label for a subset of writers, artists, and elite travelers whose movements are not likely to be controlled by the state. It would then allow middle-class African narratives to come into view and thus help stratify false notions of African authenticity. In noting that the new African diaspora comprises professional skilled migrants and their children, Selasi wryly observes that "no one wants to ask, 'why does the middle-class caged bird sing?'"⁵⁶ But it is surely too limiting to require all African literature to be focused on the village, outside of global flows, and centered on refugees or child soldiers. It should be not only easy but essential for critics to grant Selasi the freedom to write about the dynamics of a family, instead of Africa as a whole; to seek affinities with Indopolitans or writers of fiction about dysfunctional families in lieu of sociological accounts about war or underdevelopment; to remember the complexity and nuance of fiction beyond the reduction of categories of race, nation, or ethnicity.

The term also begs questions about its historicity. For Achille Mbembe, the potential of the Afropolitan lies precisely in his claim that in contrast to "institutionalized and ossified" anticolonial nationalists, African socialists, and pan-Africanists, Afropolitans are global migrants who "measure up against not the village next door, but the world at large," and who can appreciate cultural mixing and border crossing.⁵⁷ Similarly, Chielozona Eze notes that Marcus Garvey's slogan "Africa for the Africans" was a call for resistance to imperialism that was also premised on racial exclusion, appreciating instead the universalist, nonethnic, nonracial basis of Afropolitanism.⁵⁸

Despite such efforts, the relation between the Afropolitan and the pan-African remains vexed. What makes the Afropolitan a twenty-first-century figure, removed from the efforts of previous global black thinkers like Edward Blyden and W. E. B. Du Bois, who also sought to imagine an expansive, universal identity for African-descended peoples? Indeed, many scholars of the new diaspora, like Paul Zeleza, turn to Du Bois and his sense of double consciousness (albeit reframing it as multiple consciousness) to define the dynamics they observe in migrant communities. Along similar lines, introducing *The New African Diaspora*, Isidore Okpewho begins his story with Olaudah Equiano. In contrast, many of the proponents of the Afropolitan locate it squarely as a contemporary figure, born to the generation that migrated in the 1960s and enabled by the acceleration of migration in the wake of postcolonial state failures. But the claim of exception in the new century remains unresolved, as the newness of the Afropolitan requires some sense of its relation to prior forms of travel and circulation, many of which also assumed cosmopolitanism as a touchstone, sought to produce universal rather than racial or ethnic art, and refused the primacy of the nation as a marker of cultural identity. When Selasi claims Goethe, Edward Said, and Chinua Achebe in her quest for a non-African literature, it is difficult not to query the differences between now and then, especially because the elite migrant has been at the core of the entire field of postcolonial studies: indeed, the notion of cosmopolitan humanism has appeared in the thinking of everyone from Said to Frantz Fanon and Bishop Desmond Tutu. The figure of the African in the West is also one we have seen before, everywhere from Ama Ata Aidoo's Ghanaian protagonist being hailed as a black girl in a German airport to Fanon realizing his blackness when he moves to France from Martinique.[59] Invoking Stuart Hall on the postcolonial, we may well ask, "When was the Afropolitan?" and speculate about what thinking "at the limit" today might entail.[60]

A discourse still in formation, often loosely defined, and prone to polemic disavowal more than thoughtful engagement, the Afropolitan remains tricky as a sociological category. It does, however, afford immense possibilities for analyzing the global African novel, not least because it requires the recognition of class as a key feature of any possible mobility, reshaping our understanding of the home and the world, the nation and the globe. It also asks us to unpack the very category of African literature, naming a continent in a way that rarely happens to Europe or Asia, as Selasi argues, as well as asking for a clarification of our scales of analysis in the broad shift from national literature to world literature. The Afropolitan likewise names and helps generate the shift from the politics of the postcolonial moment to the more uncertain dynamics of the global. In lieu of criticizing or celebrating the likes of Selasi, more challenging is grasping what it might mean to read the global from the vantage point of the Afropolitan. It is in this sense of exploration that

Selasi insists that African literature does not exist, as she opens up Africa itself as an abstraction, a place, an overloaded sign.

Many of the novels of the new diaspora make this abstraction concrete: for Adichie in *Americanah*, Lagos names a specific longing to which Ifemelu will return and "sp[i]n herself into being" (586). Meanwhile, in *We Need New Names*, Darling cannot return to Paradise, nor Sepha to Ethiopia in *The Beautiful Things That Heaven Bears*. In *GraceLand*, the American journey is neither assured nor necessarily hopeful. *Open City* evinces little anxiety about belonging, roots, or return. These very different representations of travel and migration require more calibrated forms of analysis, always differentiating between coercion and freedom, and making class as necessary as culture, tradition, or nation.

New diaspora fictions are thus neither just anatomies of failure of the postcolony, nor belated American immigrant narratives, nor "lite" global narratives, nor poverty porn. They are elegant excavations of how the past appears in the present, meditations on space and time, deliberations over the ways books, people, and authors circulate in a world republic of letters, unequal yet interconnected. Their self-reflexivity makes it difficult to capture their concerns with abstractions like diaspora, immigration, or globalization, through recourse to ready oppositions. Older models of diaspora, from pan-African to black Atlantic ones, did often implement US hegemony as Africa continued to be narrated in terms that prioritized diasporic desires and assumptions. But now, the new diaspora writes back and advances the conversation beyond pan-Africanism and Bandung humanism. Framing the debate as a question of reception—what does the Western audience want?—does not always allow for more complex ways of imagining past, present, and future, kinship and distance, history and memory in these narratives. To do so, it behooves us to move away from the temptation to slot these fictions into preexisting plots and to recognize the need for new forms. The fear that the new African narrative will displace or silence a more politically challenging African American one seems to be ill-founded and does justice to neither tradition. Sepha's melancholy, Darling's precarity, Elvis's uncertainty, and Julius's many disavowals ensure that no triumphal, romantic, or comforting narrative of migration survives. Rejecting rather than reaffirming liberal visions of US multiculturalism, these fictions trouble diaspora itself as a frame—commonly based on Atlantic slavery as primal origin or notions of racial identification, as new forms of migration, belonging, and risk emerge. Finally, in highlighting often middle-class stories of ordinary life, they shift the conversation from the catastrophic to the mundane, from melodrama to realism. At the same time, they do not favor opacity in the manner of much previous postcolonial narrative. The stray moments of magic realism—the leopard as an ancestor's totem in *GraceLand*, the Haitian ghost in *Open City*—serve only to underscore the primacy of realism for the most part. In fact, one could argue that Bulawayo's occasional shifts into lyricism in the collective moments of narration don't have the force or immediacy of Darling's vivid voice. The return to realism not only eschews the romance of so many popular stories of migration but also signals the shift in the postcolonial novel from the era of nation building that tended to favor allegorical, magic realist, or fabulist approaches in the vein of a Ben Okri, J. M. Coetzee, or Salman Rushdie.

This is why I suggest that new diaspora fictions exact new and transformed frames, insofar as they unhook diaspora from slavery and take us beyond the assimilation mandated by the immigrant plot or the melancholy sounded by critics nostalgic for easier moments of opposition. The tendency to read these new fictions either as a sign of friction between new and old diasporas or as variants of a preexisting immigrant plot obscures the new forms of connection, critique, and optimism on display. The temporal imagination of the new diaspora as often rehearses as reverses the US immigrant plot, in which the past is to be left behind except as a memory and the United States is the inevitable end of the journey. At the very least, they evince more complex and varied temporalities, other ways of processing narratives of historical trauma. In relation to pan-Africanism, for example, we often find not just antagonism, disavowal, or a requiem—a shift, yes, but perhaps not a break. We also find more uncertain, creative forms of connection being voiced, not just a single note of longing for earlier forms of solidarity. Baldwin, himself a diasporic figure, becomes the locus of such longings in both Abani's and Adichie's imagination. Moreover, as the contours of the new diaspora intersect with model minority formation, with postracialism and color blindness, and with the precarity of labor in the United States, as they do in *We Need New Names*, they help move us away from a nation-centered frame and toward a differentiated and unequal one, often making possible a greater engagement with intertwined questions of race and class. Inviting us to resist the temptation to dismiss the long history of colonialism, resistance, and decolonization as a flat endless narrative of failure, these fictions diagnose instead why the older frames faded away, or how they persist and help shape newer imaginaries. To fully understand these new narratives, the postcolonial state and the US racial state must be read together, as must the histories of colonialism and slavery, to reckon with how the new diaspora relates to the old one, as an alternative to just announcing its supersession. Jettisoning the nation as a utopian horizon, showing that race is always about place, and that historical traumas can yield responses other than the sublime—what Adichie calls the "small redemptions of Lagos" (515)—these fictions shift diaspora into the realm of quotidian encounters and displacements, no less meaningful for being ubiquitous and ongoing, but still revealing the creativity such mobilities make possible.

Epilogue

What We Talk about When We Talk about Slavery

If he didn't read, he was a slave.
—Colson Whitehead, *The Underground Railroad*

In 2018, the Southern Poverty Law Center published a study, "Teaching Hard History: American Slavery," the result of an extended survey of high school seniors, history textbooks, and social studies teachers, only to find that students were ignorant of most basic facts about slavery: they could not name the date of emancipation, identify slavery as the cause of the Civil War, or understand that slavery was legally sanctioned by the courts and the Senate or that it was a source of profit for the entire nation. The study concludes that even when the subject is taught in the US classroom, it is only to emphasize stories about heroism (mostly of white abolitionists with occasional mention of such black leaders as Harriet Tubman and Frederick Douglass) or to acknowledge slavery as a lamentable interruption in an otherwise progressive unfolding of the nation's destiny. No corresponding history of racism or white supremacy was taught alongside slavery.[1]

And yet even as such amnesia and distortion continue, the revival of slavery as the dominant frame for thinking about black life and politics this book has outlined also holds true, generating in some arenas the near hegemony of slavery as the lens for thinking about trauma. This peculiar climate—omnipresence yet disavowal, widespread fatigue with an underexplored subject seen as surfeit—has something to do with official narratives of national identity at this uncertain historical juncture, but also with deeply held convictions in African American cultural production—in nationalist narratives of slavery as emasculation for example, or in the ongoing imperative for positive or empowering representations. Perhaps lingering constructs about slavery as the site of the breakdown of the black body formulated by nationalists have yet to be exorcized fully, though much of the avowed task of writers like Octavia Butler, Gayl Jones, Toni Morrison, and Sherley Anne Williams has been to move beyond the facile dismissal of stereotypes of Uncle Toms, Sambos, and Mammies.

My own informal survey of UCLA students over the years has found something similar. Even students who sign up for a class called "Remembering Slavery, Remaking Race" worry about how an attention to the subject cements stereotypes about victimhood. Kanye West's recent suggestion that black people who still talk about slavery forget that it's a choice taps into some of this climate of reluctance to acknowledge the true import and legacy of the historical institution. The film *12 Years a Slave* (2013) raised similar concerns among the public, with many Academy voters admitting that they hadn't watched the film before voting, and several columns in the press expressing fatigue with the sight of black bodies in pain.

Readers often share such assumptions, consistently expressing exhaustion with the neo-slave narrative. In a review of Yaa Gyasi's *Homegoing*, for example, Diana Evans writes, "If there must be a purpose to the creation of yet another slave narrative other than to show how cruel, unfair, debased and horrific slavery was, it should be to convey the impact of it on modern life."[2] This explains the response to a novel like Colson Whitehead's *Underground Railroad*, which has gained acclaim precisely because it allows for easy parallels across police killings today and slave patrollers of the past. But the claim—that the only real relevance of "yet another slave narrative" is to explain the present—takes a remarkably instrumentalizing approach to the subject, diminishing both the varied roles of literary fiction and the dynamic interplay across past and present landscapes of racialization. No such sense of critical exhaustion is in fact warranted, since we still have too few books about slavery, not too many. Comparison with any other historical atrocity would immediately prove my point. There is also no real reason why a focus on past oppression might lead to a neglect of present suffering.

The exhaustion with slavery expressed by so many must thus itself be seen as symptomatic of the unresolved residue of the array of affective and material histories slavery conjures. Today the political value of slavery, as a world historical event that forces disciplinary knowledge to reorganize itself—for history to confront the limits of knowledge, for novels to break their own frame—is everywhere visible. New efforts by various universities and corporations to acknowledge the role of the institution in their founding and success, memorial and restitution projects that rescript the valence of mourning and melancholy, activist campaigns to demand reparations, innovative cultural vocabularies of grief and remembrance, and ongoing theorizations of maroonage ensure that slavery remains a part of our present and future.

I have written this book with the sense that attention to the growing body of work on slavery and its afterlife will yield configurations of race and futurity that go beyond the impasses usually attributed to it—the divide between melancholic historicism and postracial progress for example, or between optimism and pessimism as modes of apprehending black existence. As slavery emerges now—whether as a history that hasn't been processed, an analog for contemporary systemic inequality, or a sign for the ontology of blackness—it opens up paths either to particularity or to comparison. As I have suggested, no simple answer obtains to the question of whether exploitation across the globe today is the same as slavery. The same could be said about whether forms of antiblack racism in the United States today are continuous with slavery or distinct from it. The questions themselves remain important, though, and in refusing to resolve into a simple yes or no, open up richly suggestive routes of inquiry into the ongoing role of storytelling in conceptions of human freedom.

The global circulation of slavery in literary fiction ranges beyond the fecund epistemic field I sketch here: across post-apartheid South African explorations of history and memory, Caribbean and South Asian interrogations of indentured labor and the coolie trade, the rising prominence of the Indian Ocean as a critical nexus, and feminist discussions of concubinage in a number of sites. Such a miscellany not only testifies to the malleability of the slave narrative as archive, but also reveals the ways in which an encounter with the slave past manufactures forceful accounts of the possibility of freedom. If the survey conducted by the Southern Poverty Law Center found that slavery as taught in high schools emphasizes resistance over an actual reckoning with its true horror, contemporary literature about slavery makes it impossible to do so. Asking the reader to linger in the pain, it also allows flight into the speculative, making visible other, better worlds. In rejecting sentimentalism, the writers here variably draw upon corrosive satire, ghostly haunting, or lyrical ambiguity. Whether we turn to Teju Cole's drone-like narrator with seemingly no feelings or memory in *Open City* or Paul Beatty's absurd recourse to the farcical in *The Sellout*—in disallowing empathy as the primary response to suffering, something much more complex emerges: an expansive sense of the connections of space to history, and an undoing of all the contradictions of postracialism, stretching its incoherence to a logic beyond the literal. Even without such extremes, conventional realist forms of writing like Chris Abani's *GraceLand* surface subjectivities that demand a reaction beyond the substitution so often achieved by the sentimental. The Talking Book of the slave narrative morphs into a tattered copy of Douglas's narrative in *Half of a Yellow Sun*, or into rap cassettes in *A Long Way Gone*. Olaudah Equiano's fear that the master's book will not speak to him materializes as the damaged books of Mat Johnson's *Pym* that finance the odyssey into the heart of whiteness. Imagining more complex forms of relation than analogy or substitution sometimes means reclaiming the enunciative possibilities of Rotten English, at other times a refusal of instrumentalizing human rights approaches, or satire that will not cohere into a blueprint for social change.

In this book's introduction I considered the logic of analogy visible in the construction of the contemporary Mediterranean refugee as the resurrection of the Atlantic slave. As I write this epilogue in the summer of 2018, the United States is in the grip of yet another migrant crisis, as Trump's zero-tolerance policy at the border separates children from their parents, exacerbating an already draconian US policy of family detention. These separations feature a classic sentimental tableau as the weeping child torn from her mother pulls at our heartstrings. Yet it has led to widespread outrage and collective mobilization, as abolishing ICE becomes a leftist watchword and commenters in the media recall everything from scenes of slave auctions to Native American dispossession to Japanese American internment. Tayari Jones, reading Nelson Mandela's letters from prison, confesses that "I can't help seeing, in the image of Mr. Mandela's daughter begging for her father's return, the children weeping at our southern border."[3] Amid a political landscape of rising xenophobic nationalisms and closing borders, numerous descendants of the Jewish Holocaust urge welcoming Syrian refugees, recalling their own experiences of forced migration. As we struggle to make sense of the massive historical disavowals and distortions of racial and colonial pasts in Europe, the United States, and across the world, understanding current crises in relation to past histories of detention and dispossession may help clarify both similarity and difference. Analogy could thus serve as a path to particular histories, which in turn could benefit from comparative literacies prompted by the writers who turn to slavery. What we talk about when we talk about slavery is thus the Atlantic past, the global present, and everything in between.

ACKNOWLEDGMENTS

When I first started working on a study of the neo-slave narrative, my thoughts were straightforward: efforts to render Atlantic slavery metaphorical or to analogize it to other forms of exploitation dehistoricized it. As I dug deeper into the seemingly limitless body of contemporary work on the subject, I came to see that much more was in play. Some comparisons were generative, while others made visible so many unstated assumptions about race as we understand it today, in travel and in translation, that it was indeed worth writing a book on the subject. My thinking deepened through numerous spirited and exacting conversations with friends and colleagues whom it is a pleasure to acknowledge here.

Earlier version of parts of chapters 1 and 5 appeared as "African Atrocity, American Humanity: Slavery and Its Transnational Afterlives" in *Research in African Literatures* 45.3 (Fall 2014): 48–71, and "We Need New Diasporas" in *American Literary History* 29.4 (Winter 2017): 640–663, and are republished with permission of Indiana University Press and Oxford University Press, respectively. A few paragraphs from the introduction appeared as "The Logic of Analogy: Slavery and the Contemporary Refugee" in *Humanity: An International Journal of Human Rights, Humanitarianism, and Development* 8.3 (Winter 2017): 543–546, and are published with permission of the University of Pennsylvania Press.

My sincere thanks to NYU Press and Eric Zinner for supporting this project with enthusiasm, rigor, and care, to Dolma Ombadykow for consistent assistance, and to the two readers whose wonderfully engaged and sophisticated analyses of my work helped me fathom what my book accomplished and what remained to be done.

I am grateful to the American Council of Learned Societies for providing an ACLS fellowship that enabled necessary time off for research and writing. My thanks also go to UCLA Academic Senate's Council on Research for Faculty Research Grants that facilitated research trips to plantations in the US South and to slave memorials in Liverpool and London. I have been fortunate in the institutional sustenance of my university and the Departments of African American Studies and English. I am thankful for the material and intellectual support of deans Darnell Hunt and David Schaberg. The backing of various chairs over the years of writing this book was crucial: my thanks to Ali Behdad, Lowell Gallagher, Cheryl Harris, Marcus Hunter, and Robin Kelley. Their visionary leadership in a time of seemingly permanent crisis has been necessary and inspiring. Our incredible staff—Janet Bishop, Rick Fagin, Jeanette Gilkison, Feng Huang, Michael Lambert, Adrian Lozano, Abigail Martinez, Janel Munguia, Steven Schweitzer, Eboni Shaw, and Bronson Tran—deserve special thanks, as without their assistance much of what we do would be impossible.

Colleagues at UCLA who have informed my thinking in numerous ways include Anurima Banerji, Ali Behdad, Michael Cohen, Aisha Finch, Sarah Haley, Grace Hong, Carrie Hyde, Rachel Lee, Francoise Lionnet, Purnima Mankekar, Kathleen McHugh, Uri McMillan, Sean Metzger, Shana Redmond, Michael Rothberg, Stephanie Bosch Santana, Mark Seltzer, Aparna Sharma, Jenny Sharpe, Shu-mei Shih, and Justin Torres.

Fred D'Aguiar's vibrant friendship feels like a gift no one could deserve. Helen Deutsch shared every moment of the writing of this book, and much of what is here is a credit to her intelligent encouragement. In and out of restaurants and shops in LA, over text, email, and phone, our conversations have punctuated all my thoughts. Jonathan Grossman sets the standard for what one wants from a colleague. Thank you especially for being the first to read my introduction so carefully, and for helping me come up with my title. Robin Kelley's guidance and example in many venues have been especially crucial. His voracious intellectual and political commitments illuminate and inspire in equal measure. Saree and Christina Makdisi make living in these times more bearable (not to mention tastier). Harryette Mullen brings her signature calm and charm to my life. For keeping me supplied with the best fountain pens and inks, and offering just the right combination of skepticism and hope, conviviality and caution, my thanks to Richard Yarborough.

Sangeeta Ray's fabulous presence in my life is a welcome reminder of the joys of academic life and also what lies beyond. Thank you for reading and responding so generously to my work. I treasure our friendship. Angela Naimou's delightful energy and deep intellect show me how lucky I am to count her as a comrade and interlocutor. For a meticulous and enthusiastic reading of the introduction, my thanks to Zahid Chaudhary, as well as for always knowing how to have fun. For keen counsel and deep friendship, especially over oysters and wine, my thanks to Debarati Sanyal. For scrupulous readings of several chapters, I am indebted to Samantha Pinto. Numerous felicitous conversations with Wendy Belcher, Madhu Dubey, Christopher Freeburg, Gordon Hutner, Michael LeMahieu, John Marx, and Tunji Osinubi helped me at various stages.

For asking probing questions along the way and providing the reassurance I needed to pursue this project, my thanks to Chris Abani, Anjali Arondekar, Gabeba Baderoon, Daphne Brooks, J. Dillon Brown, Kerry Bystrom, Eleni Coundouriotis, Elizabeth Swanson Goldberg, Jeanne-Marie Jackson, John Njenga Karugia, Jodi Kim, Sanjay Krishnan, Aida Levy-Hussen, Anne-Marie McManus, Alexandra Moore, Rolland Murray, Kinohi Nishikawa, Crystal Parikh, Monica Popescu, Ato Quayson, Vaughn Rasberry, Roger Reeves, Melvin Rogers, Emilio Sauri, Frank Schulze-Engler, Nayan Shah, Joey Slaughter, Kathy-Ann Tan, Karen Tongson, Francoise Verges, and Jini Kim Watson. I am grateful for the mentorship of Simon Gikandi in several forms over the years and for his extraordinary scholarship, which has shown me the true potential and resonance of postcolonial approaches.

Though we often think of writing as a solitary endeavor, invitations to share my work were instrumental in guiding my thinking, and this book feels collaborative. My sincere thanks to all the people and institutions who hosted me over the last few years: Wendy Belcher at Princeton, Hector Hoyos at Stanford, Min-Jung Kim and the English Language and Literature Association of Korea at Busan, Sarah Fekadu-Uthoff at Washington University in St. Louis and Ludwig-Maximilians-Universität, Jonathan Eburne and Courtney Morris at Penn State, and David Theo Goldberg and Asia Theories Network for the Seoul Workshop on "The Politics of Dread." At the Catholic University of Eichstätt-Ingolstadt, I received invaluable feedback and encouragement from Nathalie Aghoro, George Lipsitz, Judith Misrahi-Barak, Angela Naimou, Shailja Patel, Kerstin Schmidt, Nicole Schneider, Christina Sharpe, and Rinaldo

Walcott. At the University of Maryland, College Park, discussions about "Forming Black Britain" with Peter Kalliney, Ankhi Mukherjee, Caryl Phillips, Sangeeta Ray, Anthony Reed, Christina Walter, Mary Helen Washington, and Edlie Wong greatly informed my chapter on Talking Books. At UIUC, conversations with Aliyyah Abdur-Rahman, Gershun Avilez, and Anthony Reed helped shape my sense of the contours of the twenty-first-century African American literary field, while Gordon Hutner's inimitable editorial prowess and cheerful acuity brought my concerns into sharper focus. Endless gratitude to the visionary Peter Sellars for giving me the chance to read a paper about Toni Morrison directly to her. It will remain the pinnacle of my scholarly life.

For generative dialogues about transnational American studies, my thanks to Jessica Berman, Russ Castronovo, John Alba Cutler, Wai Chee Dimock, Shelley Fisher Fishkin, David James, Crystal Parikh, María Josefina Saldaña-Portillo, and Johannes Voelz. Thank you to Christopher Hager and Cody Marrs for getting me to think about the timelines of American literature. For their collective passion for the creative and artistic endeavors that make life in times of crisis livable, I am grateful to Elise Archias, Jonathan Eburne, Amy Elias, Sarah Evans, Gloria Fisk, Tatiana Flores, Mark Goble, Sheri-Marie Harrison, Joseph Jeon, Angela Naimou, Ignacio Sanchez Prado, and Lisa Uddin. The Association for the Study of the Arts of the Present is a unique space for convivial discussion across disciplines that too often divide us, and I cherish working on it with you. The remarkable editorial collective at *Contemporary Literature* has shaped my work in profound ways over the last few years: my thanks to Elizabeth Anker, Steven Belletto, Eileen Ewing, Janice Ho, David James, Michael LeMahieu, John Marx, Mary Mekemson, Angela Naimou, Brian Reed, and Thomas Schaub.

I am indebted to several stellar graduate students for research assistance: my thanks to Lillian Lu, Sydney Miller, Eric Newman, Arielle Stambler, Brandy Underwood, and Jordan Wingate. It has been a privilege to work with some truly fantastic students on their dissertations as I wrote this book. Will Clark, Lauren Dembowitz, Dominique Haensell, Elyan Jeanine Hill, Renee Hudson, Jessica Lee, Sydney Miller, Eric Newman, Erica Onugha, Stacey Shin, Brynn Shiovitz, and Comfort Udah: I look forward to your exceptional scholarship making its way into the world. I have written a book arguing against sentimentality, but nothing makes me more sentimental than working with you.

My deepest thanks to all the students who took classes with me on the subject of slavery. In bringing such passion and commitment to a difficult and often depressing topic, you catalyzed my research and thinking, bestowing hope and energy. I especially appreciate the students in my "Remembering Slavery, Remaking Race" seminar, where many of my final thoughts coalesced.

The debts I accumulated in conceiving and completing this book go beyond the usual academic ones. Because the years of writing this book brought so many challenges, I am thankful to those kind souls who held me together when it was difficult to go on. For counsel and healing, my thanks to Anurima Banerji, Helen Deutsch, Madhu Dubey, Lowell Gallagher, Praseeda Gopinath, and Sangeeta Ray. For coming over on a difficult summer morning, eternal thanks to Helen Deutsch and Michael Meranze, Grace Hong and Victor Bascara, Lowell Gallagher, Jonathan Grossman, Marc Major, Saree Makdisi, Rishi Manchanda, and Harryette Mullen. For continued kindness that summer, thanks also to Mrinalini Chakravorty, Fred D'Aguiar, Jay Gellar, Kamla Mankekar, Asha Nadkarni, Leila Neti, and Shilpa Sayana. To Nathalie Kramer and Devika Wikremesinghe I owe thanks of a different sort, but no less vital. Speaking of a different kinds of thanks, I would be remiss if I didn't mention the two beauties, Foxy and Raphy, who actually lived this book with me, constantly occupying any available keyboard, screen, notebook, or lap. My mother, Krishna Goyal's big-hearted fortitude and her endless capacity for love never cease to earn my gratitude. I am lucky to be your daughter.

Anish Mahajan lived this book intimately with me, quashing doubts and hesitations, knowing when I needed to binge-eat-garden-shop-watch; for knowing too that I could not pause to take a break. For fragments of joy amid many pains that attended the writing of this book, for relentless encouragement in the face of my usual despondence, for showing me that the glass wasn't half empty (nor indeed broken), for accompanying me in disturbing visits to plantations in Alabama, Georgia, and South Carolina, where a whitewashed memory of slavery still prevails, for sharing the infinite joy of the monsoons in Delhi all those years ago, thank you. The blood clot of the bougainvillea that has shaped my romance with LA would be nothing without you.

    I dedicate this book to my father, Madan Lal Goyal, who did not live to see it, whose last words to me were to finish my book, who—in the face of unceasing challenges throughout his life—did not bend, and did not break. He used to ask me often: out of all the novels you read, have you ever seen a character like me? A little bit Okonkwo, some Biswas, maybe, but no, papa, not really. There is no one like you.

NOTES

INTRODUCTION

1. Toni Morrison and Robert Richardson, "A Bench by the Road," *World: Journal of the Unitarian Universalist Association* 3.1 (January–February 1989): 4–5, 37–41.
2. Quoted in William Andrews, *To Tell a Free Story: The First Century of Afro-American Autobiography, 1760–1865* (Urbana: University of Illinois Press, 1986), 5.
3. Frederick Douglass, *Narrative of the Life of Frederick Douglass, an American Slave* (1845; Oxford: Oxford World's Classics, 1999); Colum McCann, *Transatlantic* (New York: Random House, 2013); Chimamanda Ngozi Adichie, *Half of a Yellow Sun* (Toronto: Knopf, 2006); Helen Oyeyemi, *Boy, Snow, Bird* (New York: Riverhead Books, 2014).
4. W. E. B. Du Bois, *Black Reconstruction in America 1860–1880* (1935; New York: Free Press, 1998), 727.
5. For a comprehensive account of the transnational turn in American studies, see Shelley Fisher Fishkin, "Crossroads of Cultures: The Transnational Turn in American Studies—Presidential Address to the American Studies Association, November 12, 2004," *American Quarterly* 57.1 (March 2005): 17–57.
6. That these genres appear as distinct at times and blur elsewhere is a given. As Jacques Derrida notes, in "The Law of Genre," trans. Avital Ronell *Critical Inquiry*, 7.1 (Autumn 1980): 55–81, if "as soon as genre announces itself, one must respect a norm, one must not cross a line of demarcation, one must not risk impurity, anomaly, or monstrosity," it must also be said that equally quickly, contamination would arise: "a counter-law, an axiom of impossibility that would confound its sense, order, and reason" (57). The madness of genre, then, for Derrida, entails "participation without belonging" (59).
7. M. NourbeSe Philip and S. A. Boateng, *Zong!* (Middletown, CT: Wesleyan University Press, 2008); Fred D'Aguiar, *Feeding the Ghosts* (New York: Harper Collins, 1997).
8. Ian Baucom, *Specters of the Atlantic: Finance Capital, Slavery, and the Philosophy of History* (Durham, NC: Duke University Press, 2005).
9. Paul Gilroy, *The Black Atlantic: Modernity and Double Consciousness* (Cambridge, MA: Harvard University Press, 1993).
10. Christina Sharpe, *In the Wake: On Blackness and Being* (Durham, NC: Duke University Press, 2016), 15, 21.

11. *Qu'ils reposent en revolte (Des figures de guerre)* [May they rest in revolt (figures of war)], dir. Sylvain George (France: Noir Productions, 2010).
12. Forensic Architecture, "Drift," www.forensic-architecture.org.
13. Philip Hoare, "'The Sea Does Not Care': The Wretched History of Migrant Voyages," *Guardian*, April 21, 2015, www.theguardian.com.
14. See Giorgio Agamben, *Homo Sacer: Sovereign Power and Bare Life*, trans. Daniel Heller-Rozen (Stanford, CA: Stanford University Press, 1995), 123, and Angela Naimou, *Salvage Work: U.S. and Caribbean Literatures amid the Debris of Legal Personhood* (New York: Fordham University Press, 2015).
15. Toni Morrison, *Beloved* (New York: Vintage, 1988), 235.
16. David Blight, "Frederick Douglass, Refugee," *Atlantic*, February 7, 2017, www.theatlantic.com.
17. Saidiya Hartman, *Lose Your Mother: A Journey along the Atlantic Slave Route* (New York: Farrar, Straus and Giroux, 2008), 133.
18. Adam Withnall, "African Union Criticizes U.S. for Taking Many of Our People as Slaves and Not Taking Refugees," *Independent*, January 30, 2017, www.independent.co.uk.
19. Hannah Arendt, "We Refugees," in *Altogether Elsewhere: Writers on Exile*, ed. Marc Robinson (London: Faber and Faber, 1996), 110–119, 110.
20. Ben Carson's historical revision—calling slaves immigrants to deny the reality of abuse and torture—thus hit an inadvertent analogical nerve.
21. Michel Foucault, *The Order of Things: An Archaeology of the Human Sciences* (New York: Vintage, 1994), 21.
22. Ibid., 22, 21.
23. Frank B. Wilderson III, *Red, White and Black: Cinema and the Structure of U.S. Antagonisms* (Durham, NC: Duke University Press, 2010), 7, 37. For recent critiques, see Greg Thomas, "Afro-Blue Notes: The Death of Afro-Pessimism (2.0)?," *Theory & Event* 21.1 (January 2018): 282–317, and J. Kehaulani Kauanui, "Tracing Historical Specificity: Race and the Colonial Politics of (In)Capacity," *American Quarterly* 69.2 (June 2017): 257–265.
24. We will find, for instance, that Morrison's centering of a white woman—Desdemona—in her adaptation of *Othello* reads differently from a similar structure of ventriloquism and surrogacy in Susan Minot's *Thirty Girls*. Where the latter promises easy access, the former insists on the unknowable.
25. Ann Laura Stoler, *Duress: Imperial Durabilities in Our Times* (Durham, NC: Duke University Press, 2016), 7.
26. Lisa Lowe, *The Intimacies of Four Continents* (Durham, NC: Duke University Press, 2015).
27. Stephanie Smallwood, *Saltwater Slavery: A Middle Passage from Africa to American Diaspora* (Cambridge, MA: Harvard University Press, 2007).
28. George W. Bush, "Full Text: Bush's UN Address; Speech to the United Nations General Assembly," *BBC News*, September 23, 2003, http://news.bbc.co.uk.
29. Stoler, *Duress*, 15.

30 Ahmadou Kourouma, *Allah Is Not Obliged*, trans. Frank Wynne (2000; New York: Anchor Books, 2007), 83.
31 Toni Morrison, *Playing in the Dark: Whiteness and the Literary Imagination* (New York: Vintage, 1992), 50.
32 James Olney, "'I Was Born': Slave Narratives, Their Status as Autobiography and as Literature," *Callaloo* 20 (Winter 1984): 46–73, 53; Douglass, *Narrative*, 34.
33 See ibid., 62–65, for a discussion of the etymology of this phrase.
34 Ibid., 48.
35 For a recent assessment of the question, see Sarah Meer, "Slave Narratives as Literature," in *The Cambridge Companion to Slavery in American Literature*, ed. Ezra Tawil (Cambridge: Cambridge University Press, 2016), 70–85.
36 Around one hundred slave narratives were published between 1830 and 1860. While those by Douglass and Jacobs have become representative texts now, narratives by Moses Roper, Henry Bibb, William and Ellen Craft, Henry Box Brown, William Wells Brown, James W. C. Pennington, Josiah Henson, and Solomon Northup are also well known. Pioneering scholarship on the slave narrative includes Marion Wilson Starling, *The Black Slave Narrative: Its Place in American History* (Boston: G.K. Hall, 1981), Andrews, *To Tell a Free Story*, Dickson D. Bruce Jr., *The Origins of African American Literature, 1680–1865* (Charlottesville: University of Virginia Press, 2001), Frances Smith Foster, *Witnessing Slavery: The Development of Antebellum Slave Narratives* (Madison: University of Wisconsin Press, 1994), Bernard Bell, *The Afro-American Novel and Its Tradition* (Amherst: University of Massachusetts Press, 1987), and John Blassingame, *The Slave Community: Plantation Life in the Antebellum South* (New York: Oxford University Press, 1972). Major studies of slavery and literature include Deborah McDowell and Arnold Rampersad, eds., *Slavery and the Literary Imagination* (Baltimore: Johns Hopkins University Press, 1989), John Sekora and Darwin Turner, eds., *The Art of Slave Narrative* (Macomb: Western Illinois University Press, 1982), Henry Louis Gates Jr., *The Signifying Monkey: A Theory of African-American Literary Criticism* (New York: Oxford University Press, 1988), Robert Stepto, *From Behind the Veil: A Study of Afro-American Narrative* (Urbana: University of Illinois Press, 1991), Hazel Carby, *Reconstructing Womanhood: The Emergence of the Afro-American Woman Novelist* (New York: Oxford University Press, 1995), and Saidiya Hartman, *Scenes of Subjection: Terror, Slavery, and Self-Making in Nineteenth-Century America* (New York: Oxford University Press, 1997). More recently, excellent introductions to the state of the field may be found in Audrey Fisch, ed., *The Cambridge Companion to the African American Slave Narrative* (Cambridge: Cambridge University Press, 2007), and Tawil, *Cambridge Companion to Slavery*. Oral histories collected from 1936 to 1938 by the Federal Writers' Project of the Works Progress Administration offer an unmatched resource for first-person accounts. Documenting the American South, a digital project by the University of North Carolina, http://docsouth.unc.edu, carries full versions of most US slave narratives.

37 Olney, "I Was Born," 46.
38 Ibid., 62.
39 Andrews, *To Tell a Free Story*, 3.
40 Quoted in Olney, "I Was Born," 58.
41 John Sekora, "Black Message/White Envelope: Genre, Authenticity, and Authority in the Antebellum Slave Narrative," *Callaloo* 32 (1987): 482–515.
42 Frederick Douglass, *My Bondage and My Freedom*, ed. William Andrews (Urbana: University of Illinois Press, 1987), 220.
43 Valerie Smith, *Self-Discovery and Authority in Afro-American Narrative* (Cambridge, MA: Harvard University Press, 1987), 30.
44 Gates and Valerie Smith contend that "just as the eighteenth-century slave narrators revised the trope of the talking book, writers in the black tradition have repeated and revised figures, tropes, and themes in prior works, leading to formal links in a chain of tradition that connects the slave narratives to autobiographical strategies employed a full century later in works such as Richard Wright's *Black Boy*, Claude Brown's *Manchild in the Promised Land*, Ralph Ellison's *Invisible Man*, and Toni Morrison's *Beloved*." Henry Louis Gates Jr. and Valerie Smith, eds., *The Norton Anthology of African American Literature*, 3rd ed. (New York: Norton, 2014), xliv.
45 Houston Baker, introduction to Frederick Douglass, *Narrative of the Life of Frederick Douglass, an American Slave* (1845; New York: Penguin, 1986), 12; Stepto, *From Behind the Veil*.
46 Andrews, *To Tell a Free Story*, 17.
47 Frederick Douglass, *Life and Times of Frederick Douglass* (1881, 1892), in *Frederick Douglass: Autobiographies*, ed. Henry Louis Gates Jr. (New York: Library of America, 1994), 939.
48 Harriet Jacobs, *Incidents in the Life of a Slave Girl* (1861; New York: Oxford University Press, 1988), 5, 302, 85.
49 Edward Jones, *The Known World* (New York: HarperCollins, 2003); Caryl Phillips, *Crossing the River* (New York: Vintage, 1993); Morrison, *Beloved*.
50 Saidiya Hartman, interview with Frank B. Wilderson III, "The Position of the Unthought," *Qui Parle* 13.2 (2003): 183–201, 184; Gilroy, *Black Atlantic*, 38.
51 Stephen Best, "On Failing to Make the Past Present," *Modern Language Quarterly* 73.3 (2012): 453–474.
52 Morrison, *Playing in the Dark*, 50–51.
53 Toni Morrison, "The Site of Memory," in *Inventing the Truth: The Art and Craft of Memoir*, ed. William Zinsser (Boston: Houghton Mifflin, 1995), 83–102, 90–91.
54 For critiques of the neo-slave turn, see Kenneth Warren, *What Was African American Literature?* (Cambridge, MA: Harvard University Press, 2011), Charles Johnson, "The End of the Black American Narrative," *American Scholar* 77.3 (2008): 32–42, and David Scott, *Omens of Adversity: Tragedy, Time, Memory, Justice* (Durham, NC: Duke University Press, 2014). For a recent reexamination of these questions, see *The Psychic Hold of Slavery: Legacies in American Expres-*

sive Culture, ed. Soyica Diggs Colbert, Robert J. Patterson, and Aida Levy-Hussen (New Brunswick, NJ: Rutgers University Press, 2016).
55 Morrison, foreword to *Beloved*, xvii, xix.
56 Arna Bontemps, *Black Thunder* (Boston: Beacon, 1992).
57 Quoted in McDowell, "Negotiating between Tenses: Witnessing Slavery after Freedom—*Dessa Rose*," in McDowell and Rampersad, *Slavery and the Literary Imagination*, 144.
58 Sherley Anne Williams, *Dessa Rose* (New York: HarperCollins, 1986); Angela Davis, "Reflections on the Black Woman's Role in the Community of Slaves," *Massachusetts Review* 13.1/2 (Winter/Spring 1972): 81–100.
59 David Bradley, *The Chaneysville Incident* (New York: Harper & Row, 1981); Octavia Butler, *Kindred* (Boston: Beacon, 1979); Gayl Jones, *Corregidora* (Boston: Beacon, 1975).
60 Alex Haley, *Roots: The Saga of an American Family* (1976; Philadelphia: De Capo Press, 2014).
61 Hortense Spillers, "Mama's Baby, Papa's Maybe: An American Grammar Book," in *Black, White, and In Color* (Chicago: University of Chicago Press, 2003), 203–229, 221.
62 Ibid., 207.
63 Hartman, *Scenes of Subjection*, 3.
64 Saidiya Hartman, "Venus in Two Acts," *Small Axe*, June 26, 2008, 1–14, 11.
65 Hartman, *Scenes of Subjection*, 100.
66 McDowell, "Negotiating between Tenses," 144.
67 Ishmael Reed, *Flight to Canada* (New York: Simon & Schuster, 1976); Alice Randall, *The Wind Done Gone* (Boston: Houghton Mifflin, 2001).
68 Bernardine Evaristo, *Blonde Roots* (New York: Riverhead Books, 2008).
69 Arlene Keizer, *Black Subjects: Identity Formation in the Contemporary Narrative of Slavery* (Ithaca, NY: Cornell University Press, 2004), 5. Keizer argues that the generation of writers from the 1960s and 1970s explicitly references the memories of African American grandparents who had experienced slavery, hoping to serve as witnesses to living memory.
70 Ashraf Rushdy, *Neo-slave Narratives: Studies in the Social Logic of a Literary Form* (New York: Oxford University Press, 1999). This remains the most comprehensive account of the social and political context that shaped the neo-slave narrative. The term originates in Bernard Bell's *The Afro-American Novel*, defined as residually oral accounts focusing on the journey to escape from bondage. Subsequent uses have expanded the scope to include a range of explorations of slavery by contemporary writers.
71 Timothy Spaulding explores questions of postmodernism and political agency in *Re-forming the Past: History, the Fantastic, and the Postmodern Slave Narrative* (Columbus: Ohio State University Press, 2005), and Madhu Dubey shows how black writers since the 1970s remain ambivalent about the trope of the book in an era of urban crisis in *Signs and Cities: Black Literary Postmodernism* (Chicago:

University of Chicago Press, 2003). Glenda Carpio's *Laughing Fit to Kill: Black Humor in the Fictions of Slavery* (New York: Oxford University Press, 2008) examines dark humor, wit, and stereotype in African American art. Lisa Woolfork's *Embodying American Slavery in Contemporary Culture* (Urbana: University of Illinois Press, 2008) takes up trauma theory to focus on the body, zeroing in on time travel, scars, and reenactments of slavery in such works as *Kindred, Stigmata,* and *Sankofa*. Keizer's *Black Subjects* argues that contemporary narratives of slavery offer theories of subjectivity, reading Toni Morrison, Derek Walcott, Paule Marshall, Carolivia Herron, and Charles Johnson in dialogue with more established theories of subject formation by Jameson, Althusser, and Brecht and in various psychoanalytic accounts. Christina Sharpe's *Monstrous Intimacies: Making Post-slavery Subjects* (Durham, NC: Duke University Press, 2010) also takes up subjectivity, arguing that post-slave subjectivity is characterized by the repetition of the brutal scenes of violence, often sexualized, from the past. Focusing on Douglass and Essie Mae Washington-Williams, Bessie Head and Sarah Baartman, James Hammond and Gayl Jones, Isaac Julien and Kara Walker, Sharpe meditates on "the sadomasochism of everyday black life" (123). Salamishah Tillet's *Sites of Slavery: Citizenship and Racial Democracy in the Post–Civil Rights Imagination* (Durham, NC: Duke University Press, 2012) argues that representations of slavery today are ways to manage the paradox of African American positioning within the nation: possessing full citizenship yet experiencing civic estrangement. Tillet elaborates this paradox through readings of continuing debates over reparations in the United States, heritage tourism at slave forts in West Africa, and post-civil-rights-era imaginings of the legacy of Thomas Jefferson, Sally Hemings, and Harriet Beecher Stowe. Kimberley Juanita Brown explores representations of enslaved women's bodies in literature and visual culture in *The Repeating Body: Slavery's Visual Resonance in the Contemporary* (Durham, NC: Duke University Press, 2015).

72 See Best, "On Failing."
73 Caryl Phillips, *Cambridge* (New York: Vintage, 1991).
74 Mat Johnson, *Pym: A Novel* (New York: Spiegel & Grau, 2011), 159. Of course, as we see in chapter 3, Johnson is simply posing this stance to subvert it.
75 See Hartman, "Venus," for the necessity of "critical fabulation" (11).
76 Mohamedou Ould Slahi, *Guantánamo Diary*, ed. Larry Siems (New York: Little, Brown, 2015), 314. I discuss this analogy at length in "The Genres of *Guantánamo Diary*: Postcolonial Reading and the War on Terror," *Cambridge Journal of Postcolonial Literary Inquiry* 4.1 (2017): 69–87, 2017.
77 Hartman, *Scenes of Subjection*; Orlando Patterson, *Slavery and Social Death: A Comparative Study* (Cambridge, MA: Harvard University Press, 1982).
78 Ishmael Beah, *A Long Way Gone: Memoirs of a Boy Soldier* (New York: Farrar, Straus and Giroux, 2007).
79 Douglass, *Narrative*, 63.
80 Patterson, *Slavery and Social Death*.

81 See, for instance, the Victims of Trafficking and Violence Prevention Act of 2000, William Wilberforce Trafficking Victims Protection Reauthorization Act of 2008, and Trafficking Victims Protection Reauthorization Act of 2013. www.state.gov/j/tip/laws.
82 Susan Minot, *Thirty Girls* (New York: Knopf, 2014).
83 Beah, *Long Way Gone*, 51.
84 Ishmael Beah, *Radiance of Tomorrow* (New York: Farrar, Straus and Giroux, 2014).
85 Adichie, *Half of a Yellow Sun*, 360.
86 Ibid., 424–425.
87 Gayatri Chakravorty Spivak, *A Critique of Postcolonial Reason: Toward a History of the Vanishing Present* (Cambridge, MA: Harvard University Press, 1999), 284. For a compelling articulation of how cultural forms exceed geographic boundaries precisely through aesthetic innovation, see Samantha Pinto, *Difficult Diasporas: The Transnational Feminist Aesthetic of the Black Atlantic* (New York: New York University Press, 2013).
88 Alain Mabanckou, *Letter to Jimmy*, trans. Sara Meli Ansari (Berkeley: Soft Skull Press, 2014).
89 Morrison, *Playing in the Dark*, 38; Gilroy, *Black Atlantic*.
90 For a foundational account of the postcolonial and the global, see Simon Gikandi, "Globalization and the Claims of Postcoloniality," *South Atlantic Quarterly* 100.3 (2001): 627–658. For a spirited defense of the useful promiscuity of the postcolonial, see Sangeeta Ray, "Postcolonial Studies," in *The 2014–2015 Report on the State of the Discipline of Comparative Literature* (American Comparative Literature Association, March 3, 2014), https://stateofthescipline.acla.org.
91 David Damrosch, *What Is World Literature?* (Princeton, NJ: Princeton University Press, 2003).
92 Franco Moretti, "Conjectures on World Literature," *New Left Review* 1 (January–February 2000): 54–68; Wai Chee Dimock, "Genre as World System: Epic and Novel on Four Continents," *Narrative* 14.1 (2006): 85–101.
93 I discuss Slahi in relation to the slave narrative in "Genres of *Guantánamo Diary*."
94 Mark Jerng, *Racial Worldmaking: The Power of Popular Fiction* (New York: Fordham University Press, 2018), 2, 3.
95 Tzvetan Todorov, "The Origin of Genres," *New Literary History* 8.1 (Autumn 1976): 159–170, 163.
96 John Frow, *Genre* (London: Routledge, 2015), 169.
97 Todorov, "Origin," 161.
98 Charles Johnson, *Oxherding Tale* (1982; New York: Scribner, 2005), 119.
99 Wai Chee Dimock, "Introduction: Genres as Fields of Knowledge," *PMLA* 122.5 (2007): 1377–1388, 1378, 1380.
100 Todorov, "Origin," 161.
101 Aida Levy-Hussen, *How to Read African-American Literature: Post–Civil Rights Fiction and the Task of Interpretation* (New York: New York University Press, 2016).

102 Martha Nussbaum, *Not for Profit: Why Democracy Needs the Humanities* (Princeton, NJ: Princeton University Press, 2016); Lynn Hunt, *Inventing Human Rights: A History* (New York: Norton, 2007); David Palumbo-Liu, *The Deliverance of Others: Reading Literature in a Global Age* (Durham, NC: Duke University Press, 2012); Debjani Ganguly, *This Thing Called the World: The Contemporary Novel as Global Form* (Durham, NC: Duke University Press, 2016). For a powerful argument about the intertwined, almost indistinguishable nature of law and literature, see Joseph Slaughter, *Human Rights, Inc.: The World Novel, Narrative Form, and International Law* (New York: Fordham University Press, 2007).
103 Suzanne Keen, *Empathy and the Novel* (Oxford: Oxford University Press, 2007).
104 Octavia Butler, *Parable of the Sower* (1993; New York: Grand Central, 2000), 10.
105 Ibid., 337.
106 Ibid., 141, 292.
107 Ibid., 115.
108 Jean Comaroff and John Comaroff, *Theory from the South: Or, How Euro-America Is Evolving toward Africa* (London: Routledge, 2016).
109 Octavia Butler, *Parable of the Talents* (New York: Grand Central, 2000), 223.

CHAPTER 1. SENTIMENTAL GLOBALISM

1 "Act to End Slavery Now," Anti-Slavery International, www.antislavery.org. The quoted phrases are from a pamphlet published by the organization in tandem with its 2007 Fight for Freedom campaign.
2 "About Us," Free the Slaves, www.freetheslaves.net.
3 See www.endslaverynow.org, www.freetheslaves.net, www.antislavery.org, www.walkfreefoundation.org, www.csi-usa.org, www.notforsalecampaign.org, www.iabolish.org.
4 Pheng Cheah, *Inhuman Conditions: On Cosmopolitanism and Human Rights* (Cambridge, MA: Harvard University Press, 2007), 3.
5 Estimates about the approximate number of modern slaves remain disputed. The Global Slavery Index, sponsored by the Australia-based Walk Free Foundation (www.globalslaveryindex.org), estimated that there were 29.8 million modern slaves in 2013, 35.8 million in 2014, and 45.8 million in 2016. The US State Department identified the total number of survivors of slavery at 44,000. Since the UN definition is deliberately vague, it is impossible to determine which exploitative conditions meet the bar for meeting the label of modern slavery. The most frequently used statistic—27 million—comes from Kevin Bales. The International Labor organization revised it to 20.9 million in 2012. Critics have repeatedly questioned the method of data collection and the lack of transparency. See Glenn Kessler, "Why You Should Be Wary of Statistics on Modern Slavery and Trafficking," *Washington Post*, April 24, 2015, www.washingtonpost.com.
6 See the Global Slavery Index and President Barack Obama's speech to the Clinton Global Initiative ("Remarks by the President to the Clinton Global Initiative" [Obama White House, September 25, 2012], https://obamawhitehouse.archives.

gov) arguing that domestic abuse, the use of the child soldier, forced prostitution, and abuse in sweatshops should be known by their "true name" as modern slavery. Steve McQueen, director of the Academy Award–winning film *12 Years a Slave*, dedicated his Oscar to the 21 million people who still suffer slavery today.
7   Quotations from www.antislavery.org.
8   Mende Nazer, with Damien Lewis, *Slave: My True Story* (New York: Public Affairs, 2003), 337, 340.
9   Rachel Lloyd, *Girls Like Us: Fighting for a World Where Girls Are Not for Sale, an Activist Finds Her Calling and Heals Herself* (New York: HarperCollins, 2011), 97.
10 Zana Muhsen, with Andrew Crofts, *Sold: One Woman's True Account of Modern Slavery* (London: Time Warner Books, 1991), 50.
11 Examples include Somaly Mam, *The Road of Lost Innocence: The Story of a Cambodian Heroine* (New York: Random House, 2009); Grace Akallo and Faith McDonnell, *Girl Soldier: A Story of Hope for Northern Uganda's Children* (Grand Rapids, MI: Chosen Books, 2007).
12 Kevin Bales, *Disposable People: New Slavery in the Global Economy* (Berkeley: University of California Press, 1999), 6–7.
13 Toni Morrison, *Playing in the Dark: Whiteness and the Literary Imagination* (New York: Vintage, 1992).
14 Nazer, *Slave*, 311.
15 Notably President George W. Bush is often hailed as a champion against trafficking since he signed HR 972, the Trafficking Victims Protection Reauthorization Act of 2003, and the PROTECT Act.
16 Kevin Bales and Zoe Trodd, eds., *To Plead Our Own Cause: Personal Stories by Today's Slaves* (Ithaca, NY: Cornell University Press, 2008).
17 See Jean-Robert Cadet, with Cynthia Nassano Cadet, *Restavec: From Haitian Slave Child to Middle-Class American* (Austin: University of Texas Press, 1998) and, with Jim Luken, *My Stone of Hope: From Haitian Slave Child to Abolitionist* (Austin: University of Texas Press, 2011). A similar dynamic appears in Beatrice Fernando, *In Contempt of Fate: The Tale of a Sri Lankan Sold into Servitude Who Survived to Tell It: A Memoir* (Merrimac, MA: Bearo Press, 2004), and Nazer, *Slave*, 2003.
18 Gloria Steinem, foreword to *Enslaved: True Stories of Modern Day Slavery*, ed. Jesse Sage and Liora Kasten (New York: Palgrave Macmillan, 2006), x.
19 Nazer, *Slave*, 345–346.
20 Brenda Stevenson, "What the History of Slavery Can Teach Us about Slavery Today," *UCLA Newsroom*, August 19, 2013, www.newsroom.ucla.edu.
21 Bales, *Disposable People*, 260.
22 "Invisible Children," Kony 2012, http://invisiblechildren.com/kony.
23 Joseph Slaughter, *Human Rights, Inc.: The World Novel, Narrative Form, and International Law* (New York: Fordham University Press, 2007).
24 Elizabeth Bernstein, review of *To Plead Our Own Cause: Personal Stories by Today's Slaves*, ed. Kevin Bales and Zoe Trodd, *Contemporary Sociology* 38.5 (2009): 437–439.

25 Elizabeth Bernstein, "Militarized Humanitarianism Meets Carceral Feminism: The Politics of Sex, Rights, and Freedom in Contemporary Antitrafficking Campaigns," *Signs: Journal of Women in Culture and Society* 36.1 (2010): 45–71.
26 Bales, *Disposable People*.
27 For example, a series of articles reporting the trafficking of Nigerian women on the BBC website from 2000 to 2010, as Tryon P. Woods shows, constructs African culture as "the locus of criminality and barbarism" ("Surrogate Selves: Notes on Anti-Trafficking and Anti-Blackness," *Social Identities* 19.1 [2013]: 120–134, 123). Other cogent critiques include that of Samuel Martinez, "Taking Better Account: Contemporary Slavery, Gendered Narratives, and the Feminization of Struggle," *Humanity: An International Journal of Human Rights, Humanitarianism, and Development* 2.2 (Summer 2011): 277–303. See also Joel Quirk and Julia O'Connell Davidson, eds., *Beyond Trafficking and Slavery Short Course Volume 1* (Open Democracy), www.opendemocracy.net.
28 Michelle Alexander, *The New Jim Crow: Mass Incarceration in the Age of Colorblindness* (New York: New Press, 2012); Douglas Blackmon, *Slavery by Another Name: The Re-enslavement of Black Americans from the Civil War to World War II* (New York: Anchor Books, 2008).
29 Kevin Bales and Ron Soodalter, *The Slave Next Door: Human Trafficking and Slavery in America Today* (Los Angeles: University of California Press, 2009).
30 Moreover, as Samuel Martinez points out in a review, most of the slaveholders are immigrants or diplomats living in the United States ("Book Review, *The Slave Next Door: Human Trafficking and Slavery in America Today*, by Kevin Bales and Ron Soodalter," *Connecticut Journal of International Law* 25 [2009]: 119–124).
31 Bales and Soodalter, *Slave Next Door*, 137.
32 Ibid., 137.
33 Nicholas Kristof's ongoing series of *New York Times* articles since January 2004 reinforce this narrative of rescue, going so far as to purchase and so "liberate" child sex workers in Cambodia. For a trenchant critique, see Kathryn Mathers, "Mr. Kristof, I Presume?," *Transition* 107 (2012): 14–31.
34 Janie Chuang, "The Challenges and Perils of Reframing Trafficking as 'Modern-Day Slavery,'" in Quirk and O'Connell Davidson, *Beyond Trafficking and Slavery*, 26–29, www.opendemocracy.net.
35 Bridget Anderson, "Trafficking," in *The Oxford Handbook of Refugee and Forced Migration Studies*, ed. Elena Fiddian-Qasmiyeh, Gil Loescher, Katy Long, and Nando Sigona (Oxford: Oxford University Press, 2014). Also see Miriam Ticktin, "Thinking Beyond Humanitarian Borders," *Social Research* 83.2 (Summer 2016): 255–271.
36 Aihwa Ong, *Neoliberalism as Exception: Mutations in Citizenship and Sovereignty* (Durham, NC: Duke University Press, 2006), 195.
37 Johannes Fabian, *Time and the Other: How Anthropology Makes Its Object* (New York: Columbia University Press, 2002).
38 Kevin Bales, *Understanding Global Slavery: A Reader* (Los Angeles: University of California Press, 2005), 16.

39 Richard Miniter, "The False Promise of Slave Redemption," *Atlantic*, July 1999, www.theatlantic.com.
40 Nazer, *Slave*, 311.
41 "Remarks by the President at the 50th Anniversary of the Selma to Montgomery Marches" (Obama White House, March 7, 2015), https://obamawhitehouse.archives.gov.
42 Francis Bok, with Edward Tivnan, *Escape from Slavery: The True Story of My Ten Years in Captivity—And My Journey to Freedom in America* (New York: St. Martin's, 2003), further citations in text; Dave Eggers, *What Is the What: The Autobiography of Valentino Achak Deng, A Novel* (New York: Vintage, 2006), further citations in text.
43 Mahmood Mamdani, *Saviors and Survivors: Darfur, Politics, and the War on Terror* (New York: Doubleday, 2009).
44 John Sekora, "Black Message/White Envelope: Genre, Authenticity, and Authority in the Antebellum Slave Narrative," *Callaloo* 32 (1987): 482–515.
45 Harriet Jacobs, *Incidents in the Life of a Slave Girl* (1861; New York: Oxford University Press, 1988), 173.
46 Toni Morrison, *Beloved* (New York: Vintage, 1988), 235.
47 James Dawes, *That the World May Know: Bearing Witness to Atrocity* (Cambridge, MA: Harvard University Press, 2007).
48 On Douglass and sentimentalism, see Arthur Riss, "Sentimental Douglass," in *The Cambridge Companion to Frederick Douglass*, ed. Maurice Lee (Cambridge: Cambridge University Press, 2009), 103–117.
49 See Gabriel Sherman, "The Fog of Memoir: The Feud over the Truthfulness of Ishmael Beah's *A Long Way Gone*," *Slate Magazine*, March 6, 2008, https://slate.com.
50 John Stauffer, *The Black Hearts of Men: Radical Abolitionists and the Transformation of Race* (Cambridge, MA: Harvard University Press, 2001), 1.
51 I draw here on the influential scholarship of Shirley Samuels, ed., *The Culture of Sentiment: Race, Gender, and Sentimentality in Nineteenth-Century America* (New York: Oxford University Press, 1992), Jane Tompkins, *Sentimental Designs: The Cultural Work of American Fiction, 1790–1860* (New York: Oxford University Press, 1985), Philip Fisher, *Hard Facts: Setting and Form in the American Novel* (New York: Oxford University Press, 1986), Ann Douglas, *The Feminization of American Culture* (New York: Farrar, Straus and Giroux, 1998), Cindy Weinstein, *Family, Kinship, and Sympathy in Nineteenth-Century American Fiction* (New York: Cambridge University Press, 1995), and Jennifer Williamson, *Twentieth-Century Sentimentalism: Narrative Appropriation in American Literature* (New Brunswick, NJ: Rutgers University Press, 2013).
52 Lloyd Pratt, "'I Am a Stranger with Thee': Frederick Douglass and Recognition after 1845," *American Literature* 85.2 (June 2013): 247–272, 261. Pratt traces Douglass's attempts to shape alternatives to this "sympathetic transfer" (262). For a robust critique of pre–Civil War sympathy as narcissistic and appropriative in this

manner, see Pratt, *The Strangers Book: The Human of African American Literature* (Philadelphia: University of Pennsylvania Press, 2015).
53 Lauren Berlant, "Poor Eliza," *American Literature* 70.3 (September 1998): 635–668, 641.
54 Hortense Spillers, "Changing the Letter: The Yokes, the Jokes of Discourse, or Mrs. Stowe, Mr. Reed," in *Slavery and the Literary Imagination*, ed. Deborah McDowell and Arnold Rampersad (Baltimore: Johns Hopkins University Press, 1989), 28.
55 William Andrews, *To Tell a Free Story: The First Century of Afro-American Autobiography, 1760–1865* (Urbana: University of Illinois Press, 1986).
56 Hazel Carby, *Reconstructing Womanhood: The Emergence of the Afro-American Woman Novelist* (New York: Oxford University Press, 1995); Claudia Tate, *Domestic Allegories of Political Desire* (New York: Oxford University Press, 1993).
57 Richard Wright, "How Bigger Was Born," in *Native Son* (New York: Harper & Row, 1993), 435.
58 Recall here Ben Lerner (another luminary of the new sincerity movement) who explains his decision to write "another Brooklyn novel by a guy with glasses" about "eating bluefin tuna" by contrasting it to "the model of fiction that's like 'The way I deal with the political is that I pretend to have access to the mind of a nine-year-old boy in Sudan." Interview with Emily Witt, *Guardian*, January 3, 2015.
59 See Thomas Jones, "This Is Not That Place," *London Review of Books*, June 21, 2007, www.lrb.co.uk.
60 David Amsden goes on to say, like many other reviewers, that Eggers "is, famously, a lost boy himself" as his memoir showed both innocence and wit, "the bipolar urge to create community (*Please understand me!*) only to reject it (*You'll never understand!*)." "Truly Heartbreaking," *New York Magazine*, October 30, 2006, https://nymag.com.
61 Sidonie Smith and Julia Watson, "Witness or False Witness: Metrics of Authenticity, Collective I-Formations, and the Ethic of Verification in First-Person Testimony," *Biography* 35.4 (2012): 590–626, 590.
62 I have found only one negative review to date: Lee Siegel ("The Niceness Racket," *New Republic*, April 19, 2007) objects to Eggers's takeover of Deng's life, seeing Eggers as "the sincere young father of post-postmodern half-irony" or "sincerony."
63 Elizabeth Twitchell, "Dave Eggers's *What Is the What*: Fictionalizing Trauma in the Era of Misery Lit," *American Literature* 83.3 (2011): 621–648, 628, 634.
64 David Palumbo-Liu, *The Deliverance of Others: Reading Literature in a Global Age* (Durham, NC: Duke University Press, 2012).
65 Eggers's *A Heartbreaking Work of Staggering Genius* (New York: Simon & Schuster, 2000), an account of the death of the author's mother and father and his surrogate parenting of his eight-year-old brother, perfected his solipsistic style, where he constantly tells the audience how to read the book, at the same time acknowledging that this instruction is intensely annoying. The book is prefaced with "Rules and Suggestions for Enjoyment of This Book," an extended discussion

of "the major themes," metaphors, and symbols, and a flow chart of emotional consequences of death. It also is punctuated by coy asides about the way in which Eggers is milking the misery of his own family for personal fame.

66 See John Ernest, "Beyond Douglass and Jacobs," 218–231, and Robert Reid-Pharr, "The Slave Narrative and Early Black American Literature," 137–149, both in *The Cambridge Companion to the African American Slave Narrative*, ed. Audrey Fisch (Cambridge: Cambridge University Press, 2007).
67 Didier Fassin, "Humanitarianism as a Politics of Life," *Public Culture* 19.3 (2007): 499–520.
68 Slaughter, *Human Rights, Inc.*, 3–4.
69 Joel Quirk, *The Anti-Slavery Project: From the Slave Trade to Human Trafficking* (Philadelphia: University of Pennsylvania Press, 2011).
70 See Ania Loomba, "Race and the Possibilities of Comparative Critique," *New Literary History* 40.3 (2009): 501–522.
71 Amitav Ghosh, *Sea of Poppies* (New York: Picador, 2008), *River of Smoke* (New York: Picador, 2011), *Flood of Fire* (New York: Picador, 2015).
72 For critiques of modern slavery in this vein, see Woods, "Surrogate Selves"; Jared Sexton, "Don't Call It a Comeback: Racial Slavery Is Not Yet Abolished," *Beyond Slavery and Trafficking*, June 17, 2015, www.opendemocracy.net.
73 Paul Gilroy, *The Black Atlantic: Modernity and Double Consciousness* (Cambridge, MA: Harvard University Press, 1993).
74 David Harvey, *A Brief History of Neoliberalism* (Oxford: Oxford University Press, 2005).
75 See Lynn Hunt, *Inventing Human Rights: A History* (New York: Norton, 2007) and Samuel Moyn, *The Last Utopia: Human Rights in History* (Cambridge, MA: Harvard University Press, 2010).
76 Chris Abani, *Becoming Abigail* (New York: Akashic Books, 2005), further citations in text.

CHAPTER 2. THE GOTHIC CHILD

1 Chris Blattman, quoted in Allison Mackey, "Troubling Humanitarian Consumption: Reframing Relationality in African Child Soldier Narratives," *Research in African Literatures* 44.4 (Winter 2013): 99–122, 100.
2 Julie Bosman, "Disturbing Memoir Outsells Literary Comfort Food at Starbucks," *New York Times*, March 10, 2007.
3 Dave Eggers, "The Witness: Ishmael Beah," *Vanity Fair* 49.7 (2007): 179. The phrase is also reprinted on the back of *A Long Way Gone*.
4 Ishmael Beah, *A Long Way Gone: Memoirs of a Boy Soldier* (New York: Farrar, Straus and Giroux, 2007); Uzodinma Iweala, *Beasts of No Nation* (New York: Harper Perennial, 2005); *Beasts of No Nation*, dir. Cary Fukunaga (Netflix, 2015); Chris Abani, *Song for Night* (New York: Akashic, 2007); Delia Jarrett-Macauley, *Moses, Citizen and Me* (London: Granta, 2005); Emmanuel Dongala, *Johnny Mad Dog* (2002; New York: Picador, 2006); Joshua Dysart, *Unknown Soldier*, vol.

1 (New York: Vertigo, 2009); China Keitetsi, *Child Soldier: Fighting for My Life* (Johannesburg: Jacana Media, 2005); Ahmadou Kourouma, *Allah Is Not Obliged*, trans. Frank Wynne (2000; New York: Anchor Books, 2007); Grace Akallo and Faith McDonnell, *Girl Soldier: A Story of Hope for Northern Uganda's Children* (Grand Rapids, MI: Chosen Books, 2007); Emmanuel Jal, with Megan Lloyd Davies, *War Child: A Child Soldier's Story* (New York: St. Martin's Griffin, 2009); and Susan Minot, *Thirty Girls* (New York: Knopf, 2014).

5 *Blood Diamond*, dir. Edward Zwick (Warner Bros. Pictures, 2006); Jessica Dee Humphreys and Michel Chikwanine, *Child Soldier: When Boys and Girls Are Used in War* (Toronto: Kids Can Press, 2015).

6 Ishmael Beah, "The Making, and Unmaking, of a Child Soldier," *New York Times Magazine*, January 14, 2007, www.nytimes.com.

7 Jal, *War Child*, 254.

8 On human rights fiction as a genre, see Joseph Slaughter, *Human Rights, Inc.: The World Novel, Narrative Form, and International Law* (New York: Fordham University Press, 2007), Elizabeth Anker, *Fictions of Dignity: Embodying Human Rights in World Literature* (Ithaca, NY: Cornell University Press, 2012), and James Dawes, *That the World May Know: Bearing Witness to Atrocity* (Cambridge, MA: Harvard University Press, 2007). On human rights discourses more broadly, see Wendy Hesford, *Spectacular Rhetorics: Human Rights Visions, Recognitions, Feminisms* (Durham, NC: Duke University Press, 2011). For a recent consideration of human rights in relation to US writers of color, see Crystal Parikh, *Writing Human Rights: The Political Imaginaries of Writers of Color* (Minneapolis: University of Minnesota Press, 2017).

9 See Eleni Coundouriotis, "The Child Soldier Narrative and the Problem of Arrested Historicization," *Journal of Human Rights* 9.2 (2010): 191–206; Jacqueline Bhabha, "The Child: What Sort of Human?," *PMLA* 121.5 (October 2006): 1526–1535; Alexandra W. Schultheis, "African Child Soldiers and Humanitarian Consumption," *Peace Review* 20.1 (January–March 2008): 31–40, www.tandf.co.uk/; Maureen Moynagh, "Human Rights, Child-Soldier Narratives, and the Problem of Form," *Research in African Literatures* 42.4 (Winter 2011): 39–59, doi:10.2979/reseafrilite.42.4.39.

10 For a detailed history of Boko Haram, see Alexander Thurston, *Boko Haram: The History of an African Jihadist Movement* (Princeton, NJ: Princeton University Press, 2017).

11 Adaobi Tricia Nwaubani, "Media Turns Boko Haram into Superstar Monsters," *CNN*, May 19, 2014, www.cnn.com.

12 Adaobi Tricia Nwaubani, "Diaries Offer Hope to Family of Chibok Bride in Captivity" (Thomson Reuters Foundation, September 28, 2017), www.reuters.com.

13 Helon Habila, *The Chibok Girls: The Boko Haram Kidnappings and Islamist Militancy in Nigeria* (New York: Columbia Global Reports, 2016), 71.

14 Ibid., 71.

15 Akallo and McDonnell, *Girl Soldier*, 21, further citations in text.

16 The notes at the end of the children's book by Humphreys and Chikwanine, *Child Soldier*, similarly address the reader who might be wondering: "What can you do?" The response is clear: "Learn and Share! Get Involved! Raise Money!" After all, abolition was an international human rights movement based on reading.
17 John Sekora, "Black Message/White Envelope: Genre, Authenticity, and Authority in the Antebellum Slave Narrative," *Callaloo* 32 (1987): 482–515.
18 Judith Butler, *Frames of War: When Is Life Grievable?* (London: Verso, 2016).
19 Habila, *Chibok Girls*, 110.
20 Kamari Maxine Clarke, "The Rule of Law through Its Economies of Appearances: The Making of the African Warlord," *Indiana Journal of Global Legal Studies* 18.1 (2011): 7–40. For a thorough discussion of the dynamics of recruiting child soldiers, including a detailed account of the LRA, see Bernd Beber and Christopher Blattman, "The Logic of Child Soldiering and Coercion," *International Organization* 67 (2013): 65–104.
21 Minot, *Thirty Girls*, 141, further citations in text. Minot's earlier nonfiction account, "This We Came to Know Afterward," first appeared in *McSweeney's* and was republished later in Paul Theroux, ed., *The Best American Travel Writing* (Boston: Houghton Mifflin, 2001), 199–227. Minot documents her own travel to Uganda in 1996 after learning about the abduction of the Aboke girls.
22 Marie Arana, "*Thirty Girls* by Susan Minot, Follows U.S. Journalist into Horrors of Uganda's War," *Washington Post*, February 10, 2014, www.washingtonpost.com.
23 Jane Ciabattari, "Harrowing Memories, Intersecting Lives in *Thirty Girls*" (National Public Radio, February 12, 2014), www.npr.org; Diana Wagman, "Lost Girls," *Los Angeles Review of Books*, February 12, 2014, https://lareviewofbooks.org.
24 Lea Carpenter, "Susan Minot on Africa, Joseph Kony, and the Limits of Writing about Love," *Daily Beast*, February 10, 2014, www.thedailybeast.com.
25 Wagman, "Lost Girls."
26 Carpenter, "Susan Minot."
27 As David Rosen points out, children have been involved in war for centuries, including the American Civil War and the two world wars, yet the production of the child soldier as a distinctly Africanized figure occurred only at the end of the twentieth century. Comparing Andrew Jackson to Ishmael Beah, Rosen traces the changing path of the child soldier as hero of the American Revolution to victim of the civil war in Sierra Leone, explaining that we were "willing to read a political and social context into the violent acts of children in the past, but strip away this context in the present" (*Child Soldiers in the Western Imagination: From Patriots to Victims* [New Brunswick, NJ: Rutgers University Press, 2015], 133).
28 Ibid., 157, 163, 171.
29 Ibid., 178.
30 Iweala, "About the Book," in *Beasts of No Nation*, 7, further citations in text.
31 The title of the novel also points to a different gothic heritage. Fela Kuti's song "Beasts of No Nation" (in *Beasts of No Nation*, Kalakuta Records, 1989, compact

disc) was written in 1986 to protest apartheid in South Africa; the gothic album cover portrays Ronald Reagan, Margaret Thatcher, and Ian Botha as horned beasts with blood dripping from their fangs.

32 See Gabriel Sherman, "The Fog of Memoir: The Feud over the Truthfulness of Ishmael Beah's *A Long Way Gone*," *Slate Magazine*, March 6, 2008, https://slate.com.

33 Critics of the child soldier figure include Hesford, *Spectacular Rhetorics*; Coundouriotis, "Child Soldier Narrative"; and Aaron Bady, "The Last Child Soldier," *Los Angeles Review of Books*, November 11, 2015, https://lareviewofbooks.org.

34 Beah's love of African American music hints at alternate stories of connection across transnational landscapes instead of the memoir's dominant frame of African migration to the United States through human rights rescue. After watching a video of Sugarhill Gang's "Rapper's Delight," Beah becomes a fan of 1990s rap: "I was impressed with the fact that the black fellows knew how to speak English really fast, and to the beat" (6). Rejecting the "good English" of the BBC that his father wants, Beah prefers perfecting his moves like "the running man" (7) and mimicking rap lyrics. This education in black music is precisely what comes to his rescue at various moments in his journey, signaling (as I discuss in chapter 4) how the rap cassettes become something like the "Talking Book" of the Atlantic slave narrative.

35 Eleni Coundouriotis, *The People's Right to the Novel: War Fiction in the Postcolony* (New York: Fordham University Press, 2014).

36 Ibid., 192, 203. Along similar lines, see Dinaw Mengestu, "Children of War," *New Statesman*, June 14, 2007, www.newstatesman.com, Moynagh, "Human Rights," 41, and Barbara Harlow, "Child and/or Soldier? From Resistance Movements to Human Rights Regiments," *CR: The New Centennial Review* 10.1 (Spring 2010): 195–215.

37 Christopher Hitchens, "African Gothic," *Vanity Fair*, June 4, 2007, www.vanityfair.com.

38 Leslie Fiedler, *Love and Death in the American Novel* (New York: Criterion Books, 1960), 125.

39 Ibid., xxii.

40 Ibid., 127.

41 See, for instance, Teresa Goddu, *Gothic America: Narrative, History, and Nation* (New York: Columbia University Press, 1997); Justin Edwards, *Gothic Passages: Racial Ambiguity and the American Gothic* (Iowa City: University of Iowa Press, 2003); Russ Castronovo, "The Pit and the Gothic Chiasmus," *Poe Studies* 36.1–2 (2003): 118–121; and Saidiya Hartman, *Scenes of Subjection: Terror, Slavery, and Self-Making in Nineteenth-Century America* (New York: Oxford University Press, 1997).

42 Robin Bernstein, *Racial Innocence: Performing American Childhood from Slavery to Civil Rights* (New York: New York University Press, 2011), 2, 4, 32, 60.

43 Teresa Goddu, "The African American Slave Narrative and the Gothic," in *A Companion to American Gothic*, ed. Charles Crow (New York: John Wiley, 2014), 71–83, 72.

44 See Henry Louis Gates Jr. and Hollis Robbins, *In Search of Hannah Crafts: Critical Essays on "The Bondswoman's Narrative"* (New York: Basic Books, 2004); Jennifer Greeson, "'The Mysteries and Miseries' of North Carolina: New York City, Urban Gothic Fiction, and *Incidents in the Life of a Slave Girl*," *American Literature* 73.2 (2001): 277–309; and Laura Doyle, *Freedom's Empire: Race and the Rise of the Novel in Atlantic Modernity, 1640–1940* (Durham, NC: Duke University Press, 2008).

45 Maisha Wester, *African American Gothic: Screams from Shadowed Places* (New York: Palgrave Macmillan, 2012).

46 Goddu, *Gothic America*, 73. Lizabeth Paravisini-Gebert points out that eighteenth-century gothic fiction was directly responding to debates about slavery as well as anxieties prompted by colonialism. "Colonial and Postcolonial Gothic: The Caribbean," in *The Cambridge Companion to Gothic Fiction*, ed. Jerrold E. Hogle (Cambridge: Cambridge University Press, 2002), 229–258.

47 Doyle, *Freedom's Empire*, 255, 257. A similar dynamic replicates itself in the child soldier genre–navigating the racism of the frame while inviting the sympathy of the reader.

48 In contrast, there have been several excellent discussions of the bildungsroman as genre. See Madelaine Hron, "*Ora na-azu nwa*: The Figure of the Child in Third-Generation Nigerian Novels," *Research in African Literatures* 39.2 (Summer 2008): 27–48; Annie Gagiano, "Reading *The Stone Virgins* as Vera's Study of the Katabolism of War," *Research in African Literatures* 38.2 (Summer 2007): 64–76; and Brenna Munro, "Locating 'Queer' in Contemporary Writing of Love and War in Nigeria," *Research in African Literatures* 47.2 (Summer 2016): 121–138.

49 Scholars in queer studies like Lee Edelman (*No Future: Queer Theory and the Death Drive* [Durham, NC: Duke University Press, 2004]) and Elizabeth Stockton (*The Queer Child, or Growing Sideways in the Twentieth Century* [Durham, NC: Duke University Press, 2009]) argue that the figure of the child as the repository of heteronormative futurity codes deep cultural narratives about the history and destiny of imagined communities. Brenna Munro takes up the question of queerness in relation to Nigerian literature in "Locating 'Queer' in Contemporary Writing."

50 Philip Holden, "The Postcolonial Gothic: Absent Histories, Present Contexts," *Textual Practice* 23.3 (2009): 353–372.

51 Eve Kosofsky Sedgwick, *The Coherence of Gothic Conventions* (New York: Methuen, 1986), 13, 12.

52 Franco Moretti, *Signs Taken for Wonders: Essays in the Sociology of Literary Forms* (London: Verso, 1983), 83.

53 Ken Saro-Wiwa, *Sozaboy: A Novel in Rotten English* (1985; New York: Longman, 1994). The novel was first published in Nigeria in 1985. For the political uses of language, see Michael North, "Ken Saro-Wiwa's *Sozaboy*: The Politics of 'Rotten English,'" *Public Culture* 13.1 (Winter 2001): 97–112.

54 Abani, *Song for Night*, 35, further citations in text.

55 Among many sensitive readings of the novel, for trauma as paradigm, see Hamish Dalley, "Trauma Theory and Nigerian Civil War Literature: Speaking 'Something That Was Never in Words' in Chris Abani's *Song for Night*," *Journal of Postcolonial Writing* 49.4 (2013): 445–457; for an examination of orality, see Madhu Krishnan, "The Storyteller Function in Contemporary Nigerian Narrative," *Journal of Commonwealth Literature* 49.1 (2014): 29–45; and for the novel as a challenge to legalistic human rights frameworks through reciprocity, see Alexandra Schultheis Moore and Elizabeth Swanson Goldberg, "Let Us Begin with a Smaller Gesture," *Ariel: A Review of International English Literature* 45.4 (October 2014): 59–87.

56 Chinua Achebe, "The African Writer and the English Language," in *Morning Yet on Creation Day* (New York: Anchor/Doubleday, 1975); Ngugi wa Thiong'o, *Decolonizing the Mind: The Politics of Language in African Literature* (London: James Currey, 1981); Gayatri Chakravorty Spivak, "Can the Subaltern Speak?," in *Can the Subaltern Speak: Reflections on the History of an Idea*, ed. Rosalind Morris (New York: Columbia University Press, 2010), 21–78; and J. M. Coetzee, *Foe* (New York: Penguin, 1988).

57 Chris Abani, interview with Yogita Goyal, "A Deep Humanness, a Deep Grace," *Research in African Literatures* 45.3 (Fall 2014): 227–240, 236.

58 Ibid., 236.

59 Ibid., 236.

60 One antecedent for the return of the murdered child in *Beloved* was the *abiku* or *ogbanje* figure of West African literature. Abani similarly draws on that trope of the child who will not leave the earth to indict the larger society that has failed him.

61 In contrast, that any such considerations of language and translation, rotten or otherwise, could not form a part of the historical African American slave narrative is a given. For someone like Douglass, demonstrating his skill at rhetoric and facility with such classical forms as the apostrophe was a vital part of proving his fitness for freedom.

62 Toni Morrison, *Beloved* (New York: Vintage, 1988), 202.

63 Ibid., 213.

64 Ibid., 248.

65 Kourouma, *Allah Is Not Obliged*, 5, further citations in text.

66 What appears as "Black Nigger African Natives" reads in the French original as "noirs nègres indigènes d'Afrique," while "blablabla" becomes "bullshit story." For a discussion of the politics of translation, see Vivian Steemers, "The Effect of Translating 'Big Words': Anglophone Translation and Reception of Ahmadou Kourouma's Novel *Allah n'est pas obligé*," *Research in African Literatures* 43.3 (Fall 2012): 36–53.

67 Some readers have found these definitions tedious. Aminatta Forna finds the "decision to include frequent glossary entries" "irksome" and awkward in her review ("Welcome to the Jungle," *Guardian*, August 11, 2006). For readings that emphasize the achievement of the novel, see Stephen Gray, "Two African Child Soldiers:

The Kourouma and Dongala Contretemps," *Research in African Literatures* 44.3 (Fall 2013): 152–159, and John Walsh, "Coming of Age with an AK-47: Ahmadou Kourouma's *Allah n'est pas obligé*," *Research in African Literatures* 39.1 (Spring 2008): 185–197.
68 Saro-Wiwa, "Author's Note," in *Sozaboy*.
69 Forna, "Welcome to the Jungle."
70 See Slaughter, *Human Rights, Inc.*
71 Ishmael Beah, *Radiance of Tomorrow* (New York: Farrar, Straus and Giroux, 2014).
72 Bernard Ashley, *Little Soldier* (1999; New York: Scholastic Books, 2002), 11.
73 See Hesford, *Spectacular Rhetorics*.

CHAPTER 3. POST-BLACK SATIRE
 1 Key and Peele, "Auction Block," YouTube, February 2012, www.cc.com.
 2 Paul Beatty, *The Sellout* (New York: Farrar, Straus and Giroux, 2015), 95, further citations in text.
 3 Colson Whitehead, "Finally, a Thin President," *New York Times*, November 5, 2007, www.nytimes.com.
 4 Colson Whitehead, "Visible Man," *New York Times*, April 24, 2008, www.nytimes.com.
 5 Colson Whitehead, "What to Write Next," *New York Times*, October 29, 2009, www.nytimes.com. I should clarify that Everett has not yet written a neo-slave narrative, though in a conversation with me he did joke that he will do so soon and title it "Percival Everett's Long Overdue Novel about Slavery."
 6 Percival Everett, *Erasure* (Minneapolis: Graywolf Press, 2001), 261, 2.
 7 Paul Beatty, ed., *Hokum: An Anthology of African-American Humor* (New York: Bloomsbury, 2006), 7.
 8 Ibid., 10, 11.
 9 The best scholarly exemplar of this shift remains Kenneth Warren's polemical declaration of the end of African American literature as a category constituted by protest in *What Was African American Literature?* (Cambridge, MA: Harvard University Press, 2011).
10 Thelma Golden, introduction, *Freestyle* exhibition catalogue (New York: Studio Museum in Harlem, 2001), 14–15.
11 Bertram D. Ashe, "Theorizing the Post-Soul Aesthetic: An Introduction," *African American Review* 41.4 (2007): 609–623, 613–614, doi:10.2307/25426980.
12 Ibid., 620.
13 Derek Conrad Murray defines post-blackness as "a queering of blackness" in "Post-Black Art and the Resurrection of African American Satire," in *Post-Soul Satire: Black Identity after Civil Rights*, ed. Derek C. Maus and James J. Donahue (Jackson: University Press of Mississippi, 2014), 6. In "Theorizing the Post-Soul Aesthetic," Bertram Ashe notes that "these artists and texts trouble blackness, they worry blackness; they stir it up, touch it, feel it out, and hold it up for examination" (614). Darryl Dickson-Carr focuses on intragroup satire as a chief modality

of African American satire in his landmark study, *African American Satire: The Sacredly Profane Novel* (Columbia: University of Missouri Press, 2001). For a recent exploration of the relation between post-blackness and the 1960s and 1970s Black Arts movement, see Margo Crawford, *Black Post-Blackness: The Black Arts Movement and Twenty-First-Century Aesthetics* (Champaign: University of Illinois Press, 2017).

14 Trey Ellis, "The New Black Aesthetic," *Callaloo* 38 (Winter 1989): 233–243; Mark Anthony Neal, *Soul Babies: Black Popular Culture and the Post-Soul Aesthetic* (New York: Routledge, 2002); Touré, *Who's Afraid of Post-Blackness? What It Means to Be Black Now* (New York: Free Press, 2011). Neal terms such figures as R. Kelly, Jill Scott, Paul Beatty, Chris Rock, and Aaron McGruder "Soul Babies" and suggests that they avoid elitism, nostalgia, and artistic cliques, succeeding in highlighting the variety and heterogeneity of black culture. "Soul babies" understand the subversive possibilities of pop culture and are eager to navigate the gap between black leadership and the masses. Aldon Nielsen likens "post-soul" to "postcolonial" arguing that neither "post" signifies the end of the phenomenon it supersedes, and goes on to locate the new developments in a longer history of debate in African American aesthetics—from the Harlem Renaissance to the Black Arts movement—showing that "the new resembles the old" (607). He also cautions against the "generalized postmodern lite" (608) being mistaken for true innovation and experimentation with form. See Aldon Lynn Nielsen, "Foreword: Preliminary Postings from a Neo-soul," *African American Review* 41.4 (Winter 2007): 601–608.

15 Ellis, "New Black Aesthetic," 235.

16 Ibid., 239.

17 Maus and Donahue, *Post-Soul Satire*, 5. For a succinct account of post-soul satire, see Derek C. Maus, "'Mommy, What's a Post-soul Satirist?' An Introduction" in the same volume, xi–xxiii.

18 Paul C. Taylor, "Post Black Old Black," *African American Review* 41.4 (Winter 2007): 625–640, doi:10.2307/25426981.

19 Christina Sharpe, *In the Wake: On Blackness and Being* (Durham, NC: Duke University Press, 2016).

20 See, for instance, Touré, *Who's Afraid of Post-Blackness*. For a recent critique, see Houston A. Baker Jr. and K. Merinda Simmons, *The Trouble with Post-Blackness* (New York: Columbia University Press, 2015).

21 Charles Johnson, "The End of the Black American Narrative," *American Scholar* 77.3 (2008): 32–42, 42, 32, https://theamericanscholar.org.

22 Toni Morrison, *Beloved* (New York: Vintage, 1988). I should clarify that Morrison does not hold up fidelity to history as an absolute, as her creative adaptation of Margaret Garner's story shows. Rather, my point is that reading *Beloved* should generate some sense of what historical slavery was like—precisely the norm that the satires I discuss in this chapter flout.

23 Saidiya Hartman, "The Time of Slavery," *South Atlantic Quarterly* 101.4 (Fall 2002): 757–777, 759.

24 Dickson-Carr, *African American Satire*, 3.
25 Glenda Carpio, *Laughing Fit to Kill: Black Humor in the Fictions of Slavery* (New York: Oxford University Press, 2008), 4, 70.
26 Steven Weisenburger, *Fables of Subversion: Satire and the American Novel, 1930–1980* (Athens: University of Georgia Press, 1995), 3, 14, 16.
27 Everett, *Erasure*, 225, 43.
28 Ibid., 212.
29 Ibid., 193.
30 James McBride, *The Good Lord Bird* (New York: Riverhead Books, 2013).
31 Baz Dreisinger, review, "Marching On," *New York Times*, August 15, 2013, www.nytimes.com.
32 Héctor Tobar, "'The Good Lord Bird' Is a Twisted Take on an Abolitionist's Story," *Los Angeles Times*, August 30, 2013, http://articles.latimes.com.
33 Beatty, *Hokum*, 10.
34 Jared Sexton, "People-of-Color-Blindness: Notes on the Afterlife of Slavery," *Social Text* 103.28.2 (Summer 2010): 31–56; Frank B. Wilderson III, *Red, White and Black: Cinema and the Structure of U.S. Antagonisms* (Durham, NC: Duke University Press, 2010).
35 Octavia Butler, *Kindred* (Boston: Beacon, 1979).
36 Mat Johnson, *Pym: A Novel* (New York: Spiegel & Grau, 2011), 88, further citations in text.
37 Mat Johnson himself taught at Bard College for several years.
38 Edgar Allan Poe, "Introductory Note," in *The Narrative of Arthur Gordon Pym of Nantucket and Related Tales* (Oxford: Oxford University Press, 1994).
39 Toni Morrison, *Playing in the Dark: Whiteness and the Literary Imagination* (New York: Vintage, 1992), 32, 59.
40 For a critique of the novel's ending, returning us to two heterosexual men at the end of the story, see Michelle Wright, who chides Jaynes for his fixation on establishing the blackness of mixed-race characters in *Physics of Blackness: Beyond the Middle Passage Epistemology* (Minneapolis: University of Minnesota Press, 2015).
41 Kiese Laymon, review of *The Sellout*, *Los Angeles Times*, February 26, 2015, http://articles.latimes.com.
42 Colson Whitehead, *The Underground Railroad* (New York: Doubleday, 2016), 165, further citations in text.
43 See, for instance, Rebecca Carroll's review in the *Los Angeles Times* ("Colson Whitehead's *The Underground Railroad* Is Timely, Necessary, and Shattering," August 26, 2016), where she notes that "I had vivid, brutal nightmares every night for the first few days after I started reading the book—always some variation of me and my son being kidnapped and enslaved, my son watching me get raped by a slave master with my neck in a noose, while my husband, who is white, was left to wonder whether we were dead or alive, or if he himself would be murdered for miscegenation." For a critical take on such visceral responses, see Thomas Chatterton Williams, "Fried Fish," *London Review of Books* 38.22 (November 17, 2016): 21–22.

44 Colson Whitehead, *The Intuitionist* (New York: Anchor Books, 1999), 230.
45 Whitehead had originally thought that the Underground Railroad would transport characters to a different era—something like time travel by train—but ultimately decided to stage the entire novel in 1850.
46 As Kathryn Schulz puts it, "Behind the slave-catcher we can almost glimpse the police officer misusing lethal force; behind the manacles on the walls of a train depot, the bars of mass incarceration" ("The Perilous Lure of the Underground Railroad," *New Yorker*, August 22, 2016, www.newyorker.com).
47 Michelle Dean, "Colson Whitehead," *Guardian*, August 17, 2016, www.theguardian.com.
48 Walter Benjamin, *The Origin of German Tragic Drama* (London: New Left Books, 1977).
49 Mark Reynolds, "Colson Whitehead: Making It," *Bookanista*, www.bookanista.com.
50 Megan O'Grady, "Colson Whitehead on His Spectacular New Novel, *The Underground Railroad*," *Vogue*, August 2016, www.vogue.com.
51 Richard Wright, *White Man, Listen!*, in *Black Power: Three Books from Exile* (New York: Harper Perennial, 2008), 734.
52 See, for instance, Schulz, "Perilous Lure," and Julian Lucas, "New Black Worlds to Know," *New York Review of Books*, September 29, 2016. Lucas suggests that a sanitized slave memory is becoming ubiquitous in a time of rising antiblackness and resilient white supremacy because slavery offers a comfortable story of closure. Whitehead challenges that construction of the underground railroad by refusing to present a white savior or a clear road leading to freedom.
53 See, for instance, Madhu Dubey, "Speculative Fictions of Slavery," *American Literature* 82.4 (December 2010): 779–805. Dubey argues that the "proliferating subgenre of speculative fiction meets neoslave narrative" (779) emphasizes an affective, antihistoricist, visceral identification with the enslaved. Such fictions challenge national narratives of racial progress by evincing a strong sense of pessimism about the future, Dubey argues, instantiated most clearly in numerous scenes of reading that do not return knowledge, let alone freedom, to the descendants of slaves. In contrast, Whitehead's novel, though speculative in many of the same ways, clearly situates reading as the link to freedom, imagining, for instance, "the biggest collection of negro literature this side of Chicago" in the library at Valentine farm, a fragile vision of a black utopian community (273).

CHAPTER 4. TALKING BOOKS (TALKING BACK)
1 Henry Louis Gates Jr., *The Signifying Monkey: A Theory of African-American Literary Criticism* (New York: Oxford University Press, 1988), 131.
2 Quoted in ibid., 136. The date of Gronniosaw's *Narrative* remains disputed since several editions were published between 1770 and 1840. While Gates usually refers to 1770 as the date of publication, others have argued for 1772.
3 Gates, *Signifying*, 129, 132.

4   Olaudah Equiano, *The Interesting Narrative of the Life of Olaudah Equiano, or Gustavus Vassa, the African* (1789; New York: Broadview, 2001).
5   Quoted in Gates, *Signifying*, 155.
6   Gates, *Signifying*, 155–156.
7   For a detailed recent appraisal of Gates, see Katy Chiles, "From Writing the Slave Self to Querying the Human: The First Twenty-Five Years of *The Signifying Monkey*," *Early American Literature* 50.3 (2015): 873–890.
8   Drawing on Sylvia Wynter and Hortense Spillers, Alexander Weheliye argues for a new conception of the human in *Habeas Viscus: Racializing Assemblages, Biopolitics, and Black Feminist Theories of the Human* (Durham, NC: Duke University Press, 2014).
9   Harryette Mullen, "African Signs and Spirit Writing," *Callaloo* 19.3 (Summer 1996): 670–689.
10 Robert Farris Thompson, *Flash of the Spirit: African and Afro-American Art and Philosophy* (New York: Random House, 1983).
11 Grey Gundaker, *Signs of Diaspora, Diaspora of Signs: Literacies, Creolization, and Vernacular Practice in African America* (Oxford: Oxford University Press, 1998).
12 Leon Jackson underscores the need for more book history in "The Talking Book and the Talking Book Historian: African American Cultures of Print—The State of the Discipline," *Book History* 13 (2010): 251–308. For insightful discussions of print culture, see John Stauffer, *The Black Hearts of Men: Radical Abolitionists and the Transformation of Race* (Cambridge, MA: Harvard University Press, 2001); Robert Fanuzzi, *Abolition's Public Sphere* (Minneapolis: University of Minnesota Press, 2003); Joanna Brooks, "The Early American Public Sphere and the Emergence of a Black Print Counterpublic," *William and Mary Quarterly* 3rd ser., 62 (2005): 67–98; Christopher Hager, *Word by Word: Emancipation and the Act of Writing* (Cambridge, MA: Harvard University Press, 2013); and Elizabeth McHenry, *Forgotten Readers: Recovering the Lost History of African-American Literary Societies* (Durham, NC: Duke University Press, 2002).
13 John Edgar Wideman, "Playing, Not Joking, with Language," *New York Times*, August 14, 1988, www.nytimes.com.
14 Ronald A. T. Judy, *DisForming the American Canon: African Arabic Slave Narratives and the Vernacular* (Minneapolis: University of Minnesota Press, 1993).
15 Gates, *Signifying*, 169.
16 Steven Connor, *Dumbstruck: A Cultural History of Ventriloquism* (Oxford: Oxford University Press, 2000).
17 Eric Lott, *Love and Theft: Blackface Minstrelsy and the American Working Class* (New York: Oxford University Press, 1993); Susan Gubar, *Racechanges: White Skin, Black Face in American Culture* (New York: Oxford University Press, 1997).
18 For a foundational reading of the structures of such imaginaries, see Cheryl Harris, "Whiteness as Property," *Harvard Law Review* 106.8 (1993): 1709–1795. Recent discussions of racial ventriloquism have centered on figures as varied as Rachel Dolezal, Quentin Tarantino (Jelani Cobb, "Tarantino Unchained," *New Yorker*,

January 2, 2013, www.newyorker.com), and the Star Wars movie franchise, especially *The Phantom Menace* (Patricia Williams, "Racial Ventriloquism," *Nation*, June 17, 1999, www.thenation.com). For a recent examination of these forms of transracial identification, racial drag, and masquerade, see Jennifer Glaser, *Borrowed Voices: Writing and Racial Ventriloquism in the Jewish American Imagination* (New Brunswick, NJ: Rutgers University Press, 2016).

19   Ralph Ellison, *Invisible Man* (New York: Vintage, 1947), 434.
20   For a thorough examination of the project of postcolonial revision, see Ankhi Mukherjee, *What Is a Classic? Postcolonial Rewriting and Invention of the Canon* (Stanford, CA: Stanford University Press, 2014). Examples of postcolonial revision include Maryse Conde, *Windward Heights* (Soho Press, 1999), Tayeb Salih, *Season of Migration to the North* (Oxford: Heinemann African Writers, 1969), J. M. Coetzee, *Foe* (New York: Penguin, 1986), and Jean Rhys, *Wide Sargasso Sea* (New York: Penguin, 1966).
21   Kamel Daoud, *The Meursault Investigation*, trans. John Cullen (2013; New York: Other Press, 2015); Caryl Phillips, *The Lost Child* (New York: Farrar, Straus and Giroux, 2015).
22   Ishmael Reed, *Flight to Canada* (New York: Simon & Schuster, 1976); Alice Randall, *The Wind Done Gone* (Boston: Houghton Mifflin, 2001).
23   Houston A. Baker Jr., *Modernism and the Harlem Renaissance* (Chicago: University of Chicago Press, 1987), 15, 24.
24   John Keene, *Counternarratives* (New York: New Directions Books, 2015).
25   Amitav Ghosh, *Sea of Poppies* (New York: Picador, 2008).
26   John Keene, *Annotations* (New York: New Directions Books, 1995), 31.
27   M. NourbeSe Philip, *Zong!* (Middletown, CT: Wesleyan University Press, 2008), further citations in text.
28   See Jenny Sharpe, "The Archive and Affective Memory in M. NourbeSe Philip's *Zong!*," *Interventions: International Journal of Postcolonial Studies* 16 (2014): 465–482. See also Christina Sharpe, *In the Wake: On Blackness and Being* (Durham, NC: Duke University Press, 2016).
29   Robin Coste Lewis, *Voyage of the Sable Venus and Other Poems* (New York: Knopf, 2015), 35, further citations in text.
30   Leah Mirakhor, interview with Robin Coste Lewis, "A Door to Robin Coste Lewis's Los Angeles," *Los Angeles Review of Books*, April 24, 2016, https://lareviewofbooks.org.
31   Ibid.
32   James Olney, "'I Was Born': Slave Narratives, Their Status as Autobiography and as Literature," *Callaloo* 20 (Winter 1984): 46–73, 63.
33   Toni Morrison, *Desdemona* (London: Oberon Books, 2012); Caryl Phillips, *The Nature of Blood* (New York: Vintage, 1997).
34   I suggest something along these lines regarding Phillips's *Cambridge* in *Romance, Diaspora, and Black Atlantic Literature* (Cambridge: Cambridge University Press, 2010).

35 See William Andrews, *To Tell a Free Story: The First Century of Afro-American Autobiography, 1760–1865* (Urbana: University of Illinois Press, 1986).
36 The phrase is from the blurb printed on the front of *Crossing the River* (New York: Vintage, 1993). The back of the book carries an endorsement that refers to Phillips as "master ventriloquist."
37 Toni Morrison, *The Origin of Others* (Cambridge, MA: Harvard University Press, 2017).
38 See Daniel Vitkus, "Turning Turk in *Othello*: The Conversion and Damnation of the Moor," *Shakespeare Quarterly* 48 (1997): 145–176, and Emily Weissbourd, "I Have Done the State Some Service: Reading Slavery in *Othello* through Juan Latino," *Comparative Drama* 47.4 (Winter 2013): 529–551.
39 Kim Hall, introduction to William Shakespeare, *Othello, the Moor of Venice: Texts and Contexts* (Boston: Bedford/St. Martin's, 2007).
40 A sample of the large body of early modern scholarship discussing questions of race, place, religion, gender, sexuality, lineage, and exoticism would include Kim F. Hall, *Things of Darkness: Economies of Race and Gender in Early Modern England* (Ithaca, NY: Cornell University Press, 1995), Arthur Little Jr., *Shakespeare Jungle Fever: National-Imperial Re-visions of Race, Rape, and Sacrifice* (Stanford, CA: Stanford University Press, 2000), Ania Loomba and Jonathan Burton, eds., *Race and Early Modern England: A Documentary Companion* (New York: Palgrave Macmillan, 2007), Virginia Mason Vaughan, *Performing Blackness on English Stages, 1500–1800* (Cambridge: Cambridge University Press, 2005), and Ayanna Thompson, *Passing Strange: Shakespeare, Race, and Contemporary America* (New York: Oxford University Press, 2011).
41 See Thompson, *Passing Strange*; Paula Vogel, *Desdemona: A Play about a Handkerchief* (New York: Dramatists Play Service, 1994).
42 Peter Sellars, foreword to Toni Morrison, *Desdemona* (London: Oberon Books, 2012), 7–11, 7.
43 Ben Okri, "Leaping Out of Shakespeare's Terror: Five Meditations on *Othello*," in *A Way of Being Free* (London: Phoenix, 1997), 71–87.
44 Rita Dove, *Sonata Mulattica: A Life in Five Movements and a Short Play: Poems* (New York: Norton, 2009); Gayl Jones, *Mosquito* (Boston: Beacon, 1999); Salih, *Season of Migration*; Derek Walcott, "Goats and Monkeys," in *Collected Poems 1948–1984* (New York: Farrar, Straus and Giroux, 1986).
45 Caryl Phillips, *Extravagant Strangers: A Literature of Belonging* (London: Vintage, 1998).
46 Michael Rothberg, *Multidirectional Memory: Remembering the Holocaust in the Age of Decolonization* (Palo Alto, CA: Stanford University Press, 2009).
47 Toni Morrison, *Beloved* (New York: Vintage, 1988).
48 Cathy Caruth, *Unclaimed Experience: Trauma, Narrative, and History* (Baltimore: Johns Hopkins University Press, 1996).
49 Caryl Phillips, *The European Tribe* (New York: Vintage, 1987), 7, further citations in text.

50　Hilary Mantel, "Black Is Not Jewish," *Literary Review* 224 (February 1997). In contrast, critics like Stef Craps applaud Phillips for precisely his gesture of alliance in "Linking Legacies of Loss: Traumatic Histories and Cross-Cultural Empathy in Caryl Phillips's *Higher Ground* and *The Nature of Blood*," *Studies in the Novel* 40.1–2 (2008): 191–202. For a broader look at the ethics of representation, see Michael Rothberg, *Traumatic Realism: The Demands of Holocaust Representation* (Minneapolis: University of Minnesota Press, 2000). For a recent exploration of these questions, see Bryann Cheyette, "Against Supersessionist Thinking: Old and New, Jews and Postcolonialism, the Ghetto and Diaspora," *Cambridge Journal of Postcolonial Literary Inquiry* 4.3 (September 2017): 424–439.

51　See Thompson, *Passing Strange*, 169–181, for a reading of the play.

52　Henry Louis Gates Jr. and Valerie Smith, eds., *The Norton Anthology of African American Literature* (New York: Norton, 2014).

53　Angela Davis, "Rape, Racism, and the Myth of the Black Rapist," in *Women, Race, and Class* (New York: Vintage, 1983), 172–201.

54　Quoted in Wendy Zierler, "My Holocaust Is Not Your Holocaust: Facing Black and Jewish Experience in *The Pawnbroker*, *Higher Ground*, and *The Nature of Blood*," *Holocaust and Genocide Studies* 18.1 (Spring 2004): 46–67, 62.

55　Phillips, *Nature of Blood*, 159, further citations in text.

56　Caryl Phillips, *Crossing the River* (New York: Vintage, 1993), and *Cambridge* (New York: Vintage, 1991).

57　Caryl Phillips, *The Atlantic Sound* (New York: Knopf, 2000), 115.

58　Emily Brontë, *Wuthering Heights* (New York: Penguin Classics, 2002), 77.

59　Joseph Roach, *Cities of the Dead: Circum-Atlantic Performance* (New York: Columbia University Press, 1996).

60　Morrison, *Beloved*, 324.

61　For a recent discussion of the universality of Shakespeare, see Thompson, *Passing Strange*, 21–44.

62　Toni Morrison, *Playing in the Dark: Whiteness and the Literary Imagination* (New York: Vintage, 1992), xii. She further warns, "A criticism that needs to insist that literature is not only 'universal' but also 'race free' risks lobotomizing that literature, and diminishes both the art and the artist" (12).

63　Frantz Fanon, *Black Skin, White Masks*, trans. Charles Lam Markmann (New York: Grove Press, 1967).

64　Morrison, *Beloved*, 235.

65　Toni Morrison, *Song of Solomon* (New York: Knopf, 1996); *Tar Baby* (New York: Plume, 1981).

66　Paul Gilroy, *The Black Atlantic: Modernity and Double Consciousness* (Cambridge, MA: Harvard University Press, 1993).

67　Joseph Conrad, *Heart of Darkness*, 5th ed. (New York: Norton, 2016).

68　Morrison, *Playing in the Dark*, 5.

69　Ibid., 59.

70　Morrison, *Beloved*, 43.

71 Ibid., 308.
72 Uzodinma Iweala, *Beasts of No Nation* (New York: Harper Perennial, 2005), 47, 51.
73 Morrison, *Beloved*, 248.
74 Morrison, *Origin of Others*, 93–94.
75 Ibid., 98.
76 "Figures at a Glance" (UNHCR, May 13, 2018), www.unhcr.org.
77 Stanley Crouch put it crudely: the book "seems to have been written in order to enter American slavery into the big-time martyr ratings contest, a contest usually won by references to, and works about, the experience of Jews at the hands of Nazis" ("Aunt Medea," review of *Beloved*, *New Republic*, October 19, 1987, 38–43).
78 Morrison, *Origin of Others*, 104.
79 Ibid., 109.
80 Ibid., 109.
81 James Baldwin, "Stranger in the Village," in *Collected Essays* (New York: Library of America, 1998), 117–129, 117.
82 Ibid., 121.
83 Ibid., 129.
84 Teju Cole, *Known and Strange Things* (New York: Random House, 2016), 15, further citations in text.

CHAPTER 5. WE NEED NEW DIASPORAS

1 Sam Roberts, "More Africans Enter U.S. Than in Days of Slavery," *New York Times*, February 20, 2005, www.nytimes.com.
2 Sam Roberts, "Influx of African Immigrants Shifting National and New York Demographics," *The New York Times*, September 1, 2014, www.nytimes.com.
3 Paul Gilroy, *The Black Atlantic: Modernity and Double Consciousness* (Cambridge, MA: Harvard University Press, 1993); Countee Cullen, "Heritage," in *My Soul's High Song: The Collected Writings of Countee Cullen*, ed. Gerald Early (New York: Anchor Books, 1991), 104–108.
4 Taiye Selasi (Taiye Tuakli-Wosornu), "Bye Bye Babar," *Callaloo* 36.3 (Summer 2013): 528–530.
5 See Yogita Goyal, *Romance, Diaspora, and Black Atlantic Literature* (Cambridge: Cambridge University Press, 2010).
6 Taiye Selasi, "From That Stranded Place" (2015), interview with Aaron Bady, *Transition* 117 (2015): 148–165, 158–159.
7 Taiye Selasi, "A Portrait of the Artist as a Young African Immigrant," *New York Times Style Magazine*, May 8, 2017, www.nytimes.com.
8 Morrison observes that "modern life begins with slavery. . . . From a woman's point of view, in terms of confronting the problems of where the world is now, black women had to deal with 'post-modern' problems in the nineteenth century and earlier" in an interview with Paul Gilroy, "Living Memory: A Meeting with Toni Morrison," in *Small Acts: Thoughts on the Politics of Black Cultures* (London: Serpent's Tail, 1993), 178.
9 Selasi, "Portrait of the Artist."

10. Chimamanda Ngozi Adichie, "The Danger of a Single Story" (TED Talks, July 2009), www.TED.com.
11. Louis Chude-Sokei, "The Newly Black Americans: African Immigrants and Black America," *Transition* 113 (2014): 52–71, 70.
12. Amy Chua and Jed Rubenfield, the so-called Tiger Mom and her husband, situate Nigerians as the new model minority in *The Triple Package: How Three Unlikely Traits Explain the Rise and Fall of Cultural Groups in America* (New York: Penguin, 2014), showing how neoliberal forms of racism as competition structure such notions, reviving old racisms in the name of transcending them.
13. Chimamanda Ngozi Adichie, *Americanah: A Novel* (New York: Knopf, 2013), 187, further citations in text. I discuss *Americanah* at greater length in "Africa and the Black Atlantic," *Research in African Literatures* 45.3 (2014): v–xxv.
14. Ralph Ellison, "Some Questions and Some Answers," in *Shadow and Act* (1953; New York: Vintage, 1995), 261–272, 263.
15. Teju Cole, *Open City* (New York: Random House, 2011), 212, further citations in text. The latter moment appears in Dave Eggers's *What Is the What* (New York: Vintage, 2006), and may be traced back further to Derek Walcott's "Blues," in *Selected Poems* (London: Faber and Faber, 2007), reminding us again that these questions have appeared in earlier historical moments as well, most notably in response to Caribbean migrants to the United States.
16. Paul Zeleza provides extensive discussion of the two diasporas and their historical relation by seeing them as a series of flows and counterflows in "Diaspora Dialogues: Engagements between Africa and Its Diasporas," in *The New African Diaspora*, ed. Isidore Okpewho and Nkiru Nzegwu (Bloomington: Indiana University Press, 2009: 31–60). Isidore Okpewho, "Introduction: Can We Go Home Again?," in Okpewho and Nzegwu, *New African Diaspora*, 3–30, distinguishes the older diaspora as precolonial and the new one as postcolonial. There are frequent discussions in the media about the impact of new African migrations on affirmative action and reparations, as well as the fact that foreign black students might outnumber African Americans in universities. Nathan Hare, for instance, claims that "I have nothing against immigrants, but there are sociological realities we have to look at. . . . We are the ex-slaves and inhabitants of the slums. They are coming in without that" (quoted in Okpewho, "Introduction," 12).
17. "World Lite," *n+1 Magazine* 7 (2013): np.
18. Tim Parks, "The Dull New Global Novel," *New York Review of Books*, February 9, 2010, www.nybooks.com.
19. See Rob Nixon, "African, American," *New York Times*, March 25, 2007, www.nytimes.com.
20. Dinaw Mengestu, *The Beautiful Things That Heaven Bears* (New York: Riverhead, 2007), 35, 40, further citations in text.
21. Caren Irr, *Toward the Geopolitical Novel: U.S. Fiction in the Twenty-First Century* (New York: Columbia University Press, 2014), 50, 53.
22. See Saidiya Hartman, *Lose Your Mother: A Journey along the Atlantic Slave Route* (New York: Farrar, Straus and Giroux, 2008).

23 Caryl Phillips, *Crossing the River* (New York: Vintage, 1993), 1, 235, 236, 237.
24 Caryl Phillips, *A New World Order* (New York: Vintage, 2002), 6.
25 Ibid., 304, 305.
26 NoViolet Bulawayo, *We Need New Names* (New York: Back Bay Books, 2013), 4, further citations in text.
27 See Helon Habila's review of the novel, "*We Need New Names* by NoViolet Bulawayo—Review," *Guardian*, June 20, 2013, www.theguardian.com. Bulawayo's funny response on a Facebook post, about becoming a "poverty pornstar," provides the title to this section and is discussed on the literary blog *Brittle Paper*. "Caine Prizes and Poverty Pornstars—Bulawayo Takes Swipe at Habila," *Brittle Paper*, December 2, 2013, https://brittlepaper.com.
28 Several bloggers reviewed Bulawayo's "Hitting Budapest," which won the 2011 Caine Prize. See Aaron Bady, "Blogging the Caine: 'Hitting Budapest' by NoViolet Bulawayo," *Zunguzungu*, June 3, 2011, https://zunguzungu.wordpress.com.
29 Chielozona Eze, "We, Afropolitans," *Journal of African Cultural Studies* 28.1 (2016): 114–119, 117.
30 Bulawayo, *We Need New Names*, reading group guide, 4.
31 Tsitsi Dangarembga, *Nervous Conditions* (Seattle: Seal Press, 1989).
32 See Gayatri Chakravorty Spivak, "Three Women's Texts and a Critique of Imperialism," *Critical Inquiry* 12.1 (Autumn 1985): 243–261.
33 Gilroy, *Black Atlantic*, 187.
34 Veronica Hendrick, "Negotiating Nigeria: Connecting Chris Abani's *GraceLand* to Africa's Past," in *Emerging African Voices: A Study of Contemporary African Literature*, ed. Walter P. Collins (Amherst, NY: Cambria Press, 2010), 75–99, 93, 94.
35 Erin Fehskens, "Elvis Has Left the Country: Marronage in Chris Abani's *GraceLand*," *College Literature* 42.1 (Winter 2015): 90–111, 92.
36 See Susan Andrade, "Representing Slums and Home: Chris Abani's *GraceLand*," in *The Legacies of Modernism: Historicising Postwar and Contemporary Fiction*, ed. David James (Cambridge: Cambridge University Press, 2012), 225–242; Adeleke Adeeko, "Power Shift: America in the New Nigerian Imagination," *Global South* 2.2 (2008): 10–30; Sarah Harrison, "'Suspended City': Personal, Urban, and National Development in Chris Abani's *GraceLand*," *Research in African Literatures* 43.2 (Summer 2012): 95–114; and Matthew Omelsky, "Chris Abani and the Politics of Ambivalence," *Research in African Literatures* 42.4 (Winter 2011): 84–96.
37 Scott Timberg, "Living in the Perfect Metaphor," *Los Angeles Times*, February 18, 2007, http://articles.latimes.com.
38 Amanda Aycock, "Becoming Black and Elvis: Transnational and Performative Identity in the Novels of Chris Abani," *Safundi: The Journal of South African and American Studies* 10.1 (2009): 11–25, 14.
39 Joseph Slaughter, "World Literature as Property," *Alif* 34 (2014): 1–35, 11.
40 See Andrade, "Representing Slums," and Adeeko, "Power Shift."
41 Chris Abani, *GraceLand* (New York: Picador, 2004), 320, further citations in text.

42 Kwame Anthony Appiah, "Is the Post- in Postmodernism the Post- in Postcolonial?," *Critical Inquiry* 17.2 (Winter 1991): 336–357.
43 Ralph Ellison, *Invisible Man* (New York: Vintage, 1947), 581.
44 Toni Morrison, *Beloved* (New York: Vintage, 1988), 43, 73.
45 Teju Cole, interview with Aaron Bady, *Post45*, January 19, 2015.
46 Teju Cole, *Every Day Is for the Thief* (2007; New York: Random House, 2014).
47 Teju Cole, "The White Savior Industrial Complex," *Atlantic*, March 21, 2012, www.theatlantic.com.
48 James Wood, "The Arrival of Enigmas," *New Yorker*, February 28, 2011.
49 Cole, interview with Bady.
50 Margaret Atwood, *Oryx and Crake* (Toronto: McClelland and Stewart, 2003), 78.
51 Ibid., 79.
52 W. E. B. Du Bois, *The Souls of Black Folk* (1903; Oxford: Oxford World's Classics, 2007), 76.
53 Emma Dabiri, "Why I'm Not an Afropolitan," *Africa Is a Country*, January 21, 2014, https://africasacountry.com; Selasi, "From That Stranded Place," 159.
54 Selasi, "Bye Bye Babar," 529, 530. As Simon Gikandi notes, an Afropolitan idiom may allow "alternative narratives of African identity in search of a hermeneutics of redemption." He accordingly redefines the term: "To be Afropolitan is to be connected to knowable African communities, nations, and traditions; . . . to live a life divided across cultures, languages, and states. It is to embrace and celebrate a state of cultural hybridity—to be of Africa and of other worlds at the same time" ("On Afropolitanism," in *Negotiating Afropolitanism: Essays on Borders and Spaces in Contemporary African Literature and Folklore*, ed. Jennifer Wawrzinek and J. K. S. Makokha [Amsterdam: Rodopi, 2011], 9–11, 9).
55 Carli Coetzee, "Introduction," *Journal of African Cultural Studies* 28.1 (2016): 101–103, 103.
56 Selasi, "From That Stranded Place," 160.
57 Achille Mbembe, "Afropolitanism," in *Africa Remix: Contemporary Art of a Continent*, ed. Simon Njami and Lucy Duran (Ostfildern: Hatje Cantz, 2007), 26–29.
58 Eze, "We, Afropolitans."
59 Taiye Selasi, "African Literature Doesn't Exist," *Savannah Review*, no. 2 (November 2013): 53–66.
60 Stuart Hall, "When Was the Postcolonial: Thinking at the Limit," in *The Postcolonial Question: Common Skies, Divided Horizons*, ed. Iain Chambers and Lidia Curti (London: Routledge, 1996), 242–260.

EPILOGUE

1 "Teaching Hard History: American Slavery" (Southern Poverty Law Center, 2018), www.splcenter.org.
2 Diana Evans, "*Homegoing* by Yaa Gyasi Review: The Wounds Inflicted by Slavery," *Guardian*, January 13, 2017, www.guardian.com.
3 Tayari Jones, "What Mandela Lost," *New York Times*, July 7, 2018, www.nytimes.com.

INDEX

Abani, Chris: *Becoming Abigail*, 66–68; *GraceLand*, 15, 174, 178, 189–95, 208, 214; *Song for Night*, 73–74, 95–99
Aboke girls, 76–77, 237n21
abolition: contemporary revival, 1–11, 25–28, 35–68; reading and education, 70, 75, 85–89, 135–36, 148–49; sentimentalism, 52–63. *See also* modern abolition; slave narrative; Talking Book
Adichie, Chimamanda Ngozi, 15, 27–28, 171, 175–77, 186, 207
affect: empathy, 33–34; vs. historicism, 110, 139; neo-abolitionist, 2–3, 7, 13, 33, 38, 42, 110, 212; reading, 58–59, 80, 199–201. *See also* sentimentalism
Afro-pessimism, 9–10, 174
Afropolitan: antipathy to, 178, 199; *Beautiful Things That Heaven Bears* (Mengestu), 181; definition, 29, 172, 204–9, 252n54; in fashion, music, art, architecture, 175; *Open City* (Cole), 195–96, 198–204; *We Need New Names* (Bulawayo), 187. *See also* Selasi, Taiye
Akallo, Grace, 69, 77–80
Alexander, Michelle, 43
Allah Is Not Obliged (Kourouma), 74, 99–103
allegory, 1, 173; *GraceLand* (Abani), 192–95; *Open City* (Cole), 201–4; *The Underground Railroad* (Whitehead), 131–39; *We Need New Names* (Bulawayo), 183, 188–89; *What is the What* (Eggers), 59–60
A Long Way Gone (Beah), 26–27, 52, 56, 69–71, 88–89

amanuensis, 17, 37, 40, 47, 51, 56, 59–60
Americanah (Adichie), 15, 175–77, 186, 207
analogy: *Guantanamo Diary* (Slahi), 25; as heuristic, 9–11; to modern slavery, 28, 35–47; refugees and Atlantic slaves, 5–11, 214–15; refusal by Afro-pessimism, 9–10; *The Sellout* (Beatty), 127–31; slavery, 148, 152–67, 174, 203; time of, 10–11; *The Underground Railroad* (Whitehead), 131
Andrews, William, 17–18, 53
antiblackness, 2, 6–7, 65, 173
Arendt, Hanna, 8
Ashe, Bertram, 241n13
Atwood, Margaret, 201–2
autobiography, 16–19, 54, 89–90, 119

Baker, Houston, 18, 147
Baldwin, James, 169–70
Bales, Kevin, 38–41, 43–46, 64
Beah, Ishmael, 51–52, 70; *A Long Way Gone*, 26–27, 69, 73, 84, 88–89; *Radiance of Tomorrow*, 27, 103; on rap music and Talking Book, 238n34
Beasts of No Nation (Iweala), 73, 84, 86–88
Beatty, Paul: *Hokum*, 106, 113; *The Sellout*, 14, 24, 105–6, 114, 124–31, 140, 214
The Beautiful Things That Heaven Bears (Mengestu), 15, 178–81, 207
Becoming Abigail (Abani), 66–68
Beloved (Morrison), 1, 19–20, 22, 109–10, 155, 163, 166–69, 180, 240n60; *Open City*, 197, 203; *Song for Night*, 97–99

253

Berlant, Lauren, 53
Bernstein, Elizabeth, 42
Bernstein, Robin, 91–92
Best Stephen, 19
bildungsroman, 63, 94, 139–40, 172–75, 199–200, 239n48; *Graceland* (Abani), 189–95; *We Need New Names* (Bulawayo), 182–89
The Black Atlantic (Gilroy), 6, 29, 65, 165, 171
blackface minstrelsy, 14, 56; *GraceLand* (Abani), 191–94; literary ventriloquism and, 56, 146; *Othello* (Shakespeare), 164; *The Sellout* (Beatty), 116, 124–25
"black message" in "white envelope": *Desdemona* (Morrison), 162; *Escape from Slavery* (Bok), 49–52; *Guantánamo Diary* (Slahi), 25, 28; slave narrative as, 17, 59–60, 79; *Thirty Girls* (Minot), 26–27, 77, 81–84, 224n24
Blackmon, Douglas, 43
Blight, David, 7
Bok, Francis, 12–13, 47–52
#BringBackOurGirls, 28, 73–84
Bulawayo, NoViolet, 15, 174, 178, 182–89
Butler, Octavia, 1, 20–22, 24, 33–34, 115, 121

Carby, Hazel, 19, 53
Carpio, Glenda, 112
caste, 61, 64, 129
catharsis, 73, 94, 97, 102–3
Chapelle, Dave, 112, 129
Cheah, Pheng, 36
Chibok girls, 13, 73–84
child soldiers, 69–104; as Africanized icon, 84–91, 237n27; as afterlife of slavery, 13, 26–28, 84; Beah and genre of, 69–70; as children, 53, 71, 76, 80, 84–85, 97–99, 181–82, 240n60; critics and figure of, 238n33; *Desdemona* (Morrison), 154, 163–67; gender, 75–84; as genre, 61, 74–75, 85–90; as gothic, 91–95, 97–103; *Open City* (Cole), 198;

Othello as, 154; "Rotten English," 86–87, 95–96, 100, 102, 214, 239n53, 240n61, 237n82; as sentimental object, 71, 73, 239n47
Christianity, 17, 43, 49, 73, 80–81, 91, 188
Chuang, Janie, 45
civil rights era, 13–14, 20, 125–27; post-blackness after, 107–9
Cole, Teju, 15, 35; *Known and Strange Things*, 170; *Open City*, 177–79, 195–204, 214
colonialism, 10, 29, 46, 64, 90, 122, 179, 192–93, 209. *See also* postcolonialism
Comaroff, Jean, 34
Comaroff, John, 34
comedy. *See* humor
Confederate statues, 2
Coundouriotis, Eleni, 97–98
Crawford, Margo, 241n13
Crossing the River (Phillips), 181–82
Crouch, Stanley, 249n77

Dangarembga, Tsitsi, 188
Dante, 180–81
Davis, Angela, 20, 157
Dawes, James, 51
debt bondage, 2, 35, 42–43, 189–90
Deng, Valentino Achak, 47, 54–63
Derrida, Jacques, 223n6
Desdemona (Morrison), 12, 15, 145, 152–67, 224n24
diaspora: from Atlantic to global, 25–30, 37–40; black Atlantic, 5–7, 65, 141–70; migration, 57–59, 171–209; new African diaspora, 171–209; refugees, 5–11, 214–15; slavery, 47–52, 64–68
Dickson-Carr, Darryl, 107, 111, 241n13
double consciousness, 203, 205–6
Douglass, Frederick, 3, 7, 144, 211; abolition, 79, 92, 152; contemporary reinvention, 21–22, 26–28, 113–14, 147, 179; slave narrative, 16–19, 37, 41, 108, 136, 211, 240n61

Doyle, Laura, 92–93
Dubey, Madhu, 244n53

education: Aboke girls, 77–83; boy soldiers, 87–89, 94, 100; Chibok girls, 70–76; sentimental, 50–57, 237n16
Eggers, Dave, 12, 47, 54–63, 234n62, 234n65
empathy: abolition and neo-abolition, 52, 60–61, 84; affect, 3, 8; *Girl Soldier* (Akallo and McDonnell), 78–79; global, 13, 76; literature, 5, 56, 63, 72; rejection of, 66, 95, 100, 121, 188, 200–202; rethinking of, 32–33
Enlightenment, 29, 65, 141–42, 144–45
Equiano, Olaudah, 37–38, 119, 142–43, 152, 206, 214
Escape from Slavery (Bok), 12–13, 47–52, 65
ethics, 2, 29; *Becoming Abigail* (Abani), 66–67; humanitarian, 63; refugees, 7; slave narrative, 4–5; *Song for Night* on, 97–98
Europe, 6, 30, 39–40, 151, 155–59, 169–70
The European Tribe (Phillips), 155–56
Everett, Percival, 106, 112–13, 241n5

Fabian, Johannes, 45
Fassin, Didier, 63
feminism, 21–22, 28, 145, 245n8; Black women in art and, 149–50; carceral, 42; Morrison, 154, 157, 162–66; whiteness, 81–84
Fiedler, Leslie, 69, 91
forced marriage, 2, 35–36
form, 12–16, 30–32. See also bildungsroman; genre; gothic
formalism, 4, 30, 194
Forna, Aminatta, 240n67
Foucault, Michel, 9
Frow, John, 31
Fugitive Slave Act (1850), 133–34

Ganguly, Dejani, 32
Garner, Margaret, 20, 109, 153, 242n22

Gates, Henry Louis, Jr., 17–18, 141–44, 151–52, 226n44
gender, 21–22, 28. See also feminism; masculinity
genocide: *Pym* (Johnson), 122–23; settler colonialism and, 11, 49, 91, 196; *The Underground Railroad* (Whitehead), 132–33
genre: race and, 31–32; transnational, 30. See also bildungsroman; gothic; sentimentalism; slave narrative; Talking Books; ventriloquism; *specific literary works*
Ghosh, Amitav, 64, 147
Gikandi, Simon, 229n90, 252n54
Gilroy, Paul, 6, 29, 65, 165, 171
Girl Soldier (Akallo and McDonnell), 69, 77–79
global: Afropolitan, 29, 206; Anglophone, 4; antiracism, anticolonialism, 29; anti-slavery movements, 35; Atlantic to, 25–32; *The Beautiful Things That Heaven Bears* (Mengestu), 179; "Black Britain" and "African America" in, 155, 157; citizen, 13; comparison, 129, 133; cultural invasion by, 190; definition, 4; diaspora and, 175, 177; empathy and, 12–13; ethical globalism, 5, 28; form, 4, 94; human rights, 36, 49, 64–66; identities as, 198–99; Lagos in, 190–91, 193; migration, 167–69; modern slavery, 43; national histories connections in, 30; Nigeria and, 178; novel, 4, 74, 171–209; postcolonial, 4; sentimental globalism, 12, 35–36; slave narrative, 4, 30; social media campaign, 75; as world beyond borders, 8–9, 44; world literature, 29, 149–51, 178
Global South, 3, 7–9, 30, 33–34, 46–48
Goddu, Teresa, 92
Golden, Thelma, 107
gothic: African, 74, 90–91; American, 91–95, 237n31; Atlantic, 13, 92–93; child soldier genre, 97–103; as genre, 13, 32, 239n46; opacity, 95–99; sentimentalism in, 71–73

GraceLand (Abani), 15, 174, 178, 189–95, 208, 214
Gronniosaw, James, 141, 244n2
Guantánamo Diary (Slahi), 25, 28
Gulliver's Travels (Swift), 133, 135–36

Habila, Helon, 76, 79, 251n27
Haley, Alex, 21
Half of a Yellow Sun (Adichie), 27–28
Hall, Kim F., 153, 247n40
Hartman, Saidiya, 7, 19, 22, 110
Harvey, David, 65
heritage tourism, 24, 171, 227n71
historicism: affect, 110, 139; and *Beloved* (Morrison), 19, 109–10, 166; as melancholic, 19, 197, 204, 213; Phillips invested in, 152; post-black satire, 112–15; rememory, 166, 197–98; *The Underground Railroad* (Whitehead), 131–32
Hitchens, Christopher, 90–91
Hokum (Beatty), 106, 113
horror: from language and form, 102; unspeakable, 19, 144, 164, 167; *We Need New Names* refusing, 188. See also gothic
human rights, 3, 93, 174; abolition based on reading and, 89, 237n16; child legislation on, 84–85; as genre, 236n8; global, 36; *Guantánamo Diary* on, 25, 28; immigrant voices, 5; innocent figure of child and, 84; as legal framework, 240n55; role of narrative, 25–26; scale and proximity in fiction of, 79–80; sentimentalism and, 12, 36, 53; slave narrative in literature of, 12; slavery and abuses of, 2, 36; unthinking conception of, 63–68; as Western constructs, 65–66; world beyond borders as, 8–9, 44; *Zong* galvanizing, 6
human trafficking: abolition of, 35–36; Nigeria and, 232n27; refugee crisis, 8; slavery in, 2; in the US, 44

humor, 105–9, 111–15; *Pym* (Johnson), 116–24; *The Sellout* (Beatty), 124–31. See also post-blackness; satire
Hunt, Lynn, 32

identification: in *Girl Soldier*, 78–80; by reader, 33, 52–53, 73; sympathy and, 82, 84, 239n47
immigrants: Afropolitan, 204–8; Arendt, 8; *The Beautiful Things that Heaven Bears* (Mengestu), 178–81, 207; *Becoming Abigail* (Abani), 66–68; Bok and story of, 12–13, 47–52; child soldier as uneasy, 73, 76, 99; class and mobility of, 206; double consciousness in, 203, 205–6; Douglass as, 7; *European Tribe* (Phillips), 158; identities and allegiances of, 181; legal status and, 183, 187–88; model minority, 40; nation of, 46; new African diaspora, 171–82; *Open City* (Cole), 195–204; plot, 15, 47, 57, 103, 173; reinvention and, 179, 181, 189; relation to Phillips, 182; roles replacing, 180; slavery and undocumented, 2; slavery-based diaspora and, 176; Trump banning Muslim, 7–8, 214; *We Need New Names* (Bulawayo), 182–89; *What is the What* (Eggers), 57–59; from Zimbabwe, 183
Incidents in the Life of a Slave Girl (Jacobs), 18–19, 92, 138–39
India, 2, 35, 42–43, 64–65
Inferno (Dante), 180–81
The Interesting Narrative of the Life of Olaudah Equiano (Equiano), 37, 119, 142
International Labor Organization, 84–85
The Intuitionist (Whitehead), 133
Irr, Caren, 180–81
Islam, 43, 48, 75, 80, 90–91, 143, 152–53
Iweala, Uzodinma, 73, 84–88, 95, 167

Jacobs, Harriet, 41, 108; literary gothic, 92; "loophole of retreat," 50; motherhood

and sexuality, 138–39; reinvention of sentimental genre, 18–19
Jerng, Mark, 31
Jewish history, 148, 154–59, 168, 196, 214–15, 249n77
Jim Crow, 112, 154–55, 169–70
Johnson, Charles, 31, 109
Johnson, Mat, 14, 24, 116–24, 140, 214, 243n40
Judy, Ronald, 144

Keen, John, 147–48
Keen, Suzanne, 32
Keizer, Arlene, 23, 227n70
Key and Peele, 105
Kindred (Butler), 20–22, 24, 115, 121
Kourouma, Ahmadou, 13, 74, 99–103
kunstlerroman, 194–95

labor, 84–85, 147; abolition of bonded, 35–36; modern slavery, 42, 45, 213; in neoliberal world, 179; sex work as, 42
law: African American fugitivity and, 11, 34, 137–39; discrimination, 2, 9, 76, 112, 125, 132, 134, 170, 212; limits, 43–45, 127–28; literature, 230n102; The Sellout (Beatty), 127–28; slavery as incarceration and, 43, 112; war crimes, 38, 127
Laye, Camara, 168
Lerner, Ben, 234n58
Lewis, Robin Coste, 14, 145, 149–51
literacy: abolition, 89, 237n16; canonization, 143–44; child soldier, 95; freedom, 18, 40; *Nature of Blood* (Phillips), 159; race and, 145; slavery, 135–36, 244n53; Talking Book, 141
A Long Way Gone (Beah), 26–27, 52, 56, 69–71, 88–89
Lost Boys of Sudan, 3, 46–47, 54–58, 61
The Lost Child (Phillips), 159–60
Lowe, Lisa, 11

Mabanckou, Alain, 28
Mamdani, Mahmood, 48–49

masculinity, 18, 105, 116, 161, 163–65, 190
Master's words, 146–52
Maus, Derek C., 242n17
McDonnell, Faith, 69, 77–79
Mengestu, Dinaw, 15, 178–81, 207
Middle Passage, 3, 6, 14; Equiano, 143; Morrison, 99, 110, 167–68, 174; new diaspora, 173–74; *Pym* Johnson, 14, 116, 120
migration: modern slavery, 45; new African diaspora, 171–209; *Origin of Others* (Morrison), 167–68; refugees, 5–9; temporality, 32
Minot, Susan, 26–27, 77, 81–84, 224n24, 237n21
modern abolition, 2–5, 12–13, 25–28, 35–68
modern slave narrative: genre of, 2–5, 12–13, 35–68; human rights, 63–68; imperial tropes, 38–39, 44
modern slavery, 35–47, 63–66; *Escape from Slavery* (Bok), 47–52; statistics, 230n5; *What Is the What* (Eggers), 52–63
Moretti, Frano, 95
Morrison, Toni: *Beloved*, 1, 19–20, 22, 109–10, 155, 163, 166–69, 180, 240n60, 242n22; child soldier authors and, 166–67; *Desdemona*, 15, 145, 151–67, 224n24; on freedom, 29; gothic, 74, 92, 99; masculinity, 163–65; on memorials to slavery, 1; on modernity and slavery, 174, 249n8; neo-slave narrative, 19–20, 109–10; *Open City* (Cole), 197, 203; *The Origin of Others*, 167–69; *Othello* (Shakespeare), 156, 160–66; *Playing in the Dark*, 39, 120, 163, 166; on Poe and African Americanism, 120; prizes, 24; on race and literature, 120, 166, 248n62; rememory, 166, 197–98; *Song for Night* (Abani), 97–99, 167; surrogation, 160–67; Talking Book, 14–15, 145, 160–67; trauma and comparison, 155, 163, 180; universalism, 163; "unspeakable thoughts," 50, 94; Western canon and, 157–58; on whiteness, 120, 161–66, 168

Mullen, Harryette, 143
Murray, Derek Conrad, 241n13

The Narrative of Arthur Gordon Pym (Poe), 117–20
Narrative of the Life of Frederick Douglass (Douglass), 3, 16–17, 26–28, 174
The Nature of Blood (Phillips), 145, 148, 152–60, 249n77
Nazer, Mende, 37, 39, 41, 46
Neal, Anthony, 242n14
neo-abolitionism. *See* modern abolition
neoliberalism: African tragedy and American triumph as, 64; Afropolitan as, 178; Deng and privatization of, 58–59; precarious labor in, 179; of racism and competition, 250n12
neo-slave narrative, 19–24, 227n70; as affective or historicist, 139; African American genre as, 13; as afterlife of slavery, 19, 109; agency, choice, selfhood in, 67; anti-sentimental, 53; civil rights and Black Power, 20; critics, 226n54; desire in, 67; exhaustion with, 212; in literature, 1; major book prizes for, 23–24; and post-blackness, 106–8; post-black satire colliding with, 124; postmodernism, 22–23; realism eschewed by, 12; on ripping the veil, 19–24, 49–50; scholarship, 227n71; speculative fiction, 135–36, 244n53. *See also* Butler, Octavia; Cole, Teju; Johnson, Charles; Johnson, Mat; Morrison, Toni; Whitehead, Colson
Nervous Conditions (Dangarembga), 188
Nielsen, Aldon, 242n14
Nigeria, 201, 232n27; #BringBackOurGirls in, 73, 75–84; Chibok girls in, 73–84; as globalized, 178; Lagos as global city, 190–91, 193
Nussbaum, Martha, 32, 56

Obama, Barack, 46–47, 106, 114, 128, 156
ogbanje, 240n60

Olney, James, 16–17, 151–52
Ong, Aihwa, 45
opacity: *Becoming Abigail* (Abani), 67–68; *Beloved* (Morrison), 22; diaspora, 208; gothic, 95
Open City (Cole), 15, 177–79, 195–204, 214
orality, 155, 240n55; textuality and, 98, 142–49, 162; *Zong!*, 149. *See also* Talking Book
Othello (Shakespeare), 151–54, 164; early modern scholarship on race, 247n40

palimpsest, 197, 202, 204
Palumbo-Liu, David, 32, 56
pan-Africanism, 29, 176–78, 205, 207–8
Parable of the Sower (Butler), 1, 33–34
parody, 107, 191–92. *See also* satire
Patterson, Orlando, 26
Philip, M. NourbeSe, 14, 23, 145, 148–49
Phillips, Caryl: critics, 246n34, 248n50; *Crossing the River* by, 181–82; *The European Tribe*, 155–56; historicism in, 152; *The Lost Child*, 159–60; *The Nature of Blood*, 145, 148, 152–60, 249n77; as ventriloquist, 247n36; Western canon, 157–58
Pinto, Samantha, 229n87
Poe, Edgar Allan, 117–20
post-blackness, 105–9, 112–16, 241n13; after civil rights era, 107; genealogies of, 108; improvisation, subversion, parody, comedy, satire in, 107; neo-slave narrative with, 108–9; neo-slavery replaced by, 106; post-civil-rights identity as, 13–14; racial progress and satire of, 112–13
post-black satire, 12–14, 107; in antihistorical vein, 114–15; Beatty, 105–6, 113–14, 124–31, 140, 214; blackness unsettled in, 113; black resistance mocked in, 113–14, 123; commercialized past and, 115–16; Johnson, Mat, 116–24; neo-slave narrative colliding with, 124; racial progress and, 112–13

postcolonialism: African American connections, 150–70; African child soldier fictions, 69–104; Afropolitan, 204–9; allegory and artist of, 194; coalitions in, 10–11; diaspora and, 175, 177; ethics of reading, 2–5, 10–11; form and formalism, 30–32; Global South and, 4; magical realism, 194; migration crisis refiguring, 32; models of trauma, 180–81; new African diaspora narrative, 171–209; revision, 246n20; scholarship, 229n87, 229n90; writing back to empire, 147

postmodernism, 249n8; Eggers and post-, 234n62; metafiction, 51, 59; neo-slave narrative and, 22–23; political agency and, 107, 227n71; satire, 112; *The Underground Railroad* (Whitehead), 137; ventriloquism, 147

post-soul, 106–9, 242n14

poverty porn, 178, 183–85, 189, 204, 207, 251n27

Pratt, Lloyd, 52, 233n52

Pym (Johnson), 116–24, 140, 243n40

queer studies, 239n49

racial capitalism, 2, 6, 46, 65, 122–23, 194

Radiance of the King (Laye), 168

Radiance of Tomorrow (Beah), 27, 103

Ray, Sangeeta, 229n90

realism: African literature, 172, 174; allegory, 132; bad, 194–95; *Beloved* (Morrison), 110; magical, 194; neo-slave narrative eschewing, 12; new African diaspora and, 208; *The Underground Railroad* (Whitehead), 131–33

redemption: afterlife of slavery, 110, 166–67; *Americanah* (Adichie), 209; *Becoming Abigail* (Abani) rejecting, 66; child soldier, 70; gothic terror, 13; *GraceLand* (Abani), 193, 195; immigrant, 171; sentimentalism relying on, 32; Sudan, 46

refugees: African literature, 205; analogy to Atlantic slavery and, 5–9, 167–68, 214–15; Arendt, 8; contemporary lives of, 3; Douglass as, 7; humanitarian storytelling, 50–51, 88; human trafficking helped by, 8; Middle Passage and, 5–9; postcolonial reading, 29–30; slave history and ethics, 7

reinvention: of American dream, 46–47; of form, 1, 12–16; of genres, 47; immigrants and, 179, 181, 189

rememory, 166, 197–98

reparations, 2, 7, 38, 46, 57, 171, 213, 227n71

revisionism: form and genre of, 5, 32; of master's words, 115, 147–51, 154; by Philip, 148–49; postcolonial, 246n20

Rosen, David, 85, 237n27

Rotten English, 82, 86–87, 97, 214, 239n53, 240n61; in *Allah Is Not Obliged* (Kourouma), 100, 102; in *Sozaboy* (Saro-Wiwa), 95–96, 102

Rushdy, Asraf, 23, 227n70

Rwanda, 48–49, 90, 196–97

Saro-Wiwa, Ken, 95–96, 102

satire: absurd used by, 32; African American literature and, 111–16; afterlife of slavery, 110–11; *Allah Is Not Obliged* (Kourouma), 99–101; degenerative, 112; Dickson-Carr on, 107, 111, 241n13; form and genre of, 5; history and historicism, 13–14, 112–15; politics critiqued by, 105–6; post-soul, 242n17; self searching in, 124–25; *The Sellout* (Beatty), 124–31; slave auction block in, 105; slavery revisited as, 105, 120–21; *The Underground Railroad* (Whitehead) as, 133. *See also* post-black satire

segregation, 14, 43, 112, 124, 127

Sekora, John, 17

Selasi, Taiye, 171–75, 204–7

Sellars, Peter, 154, 156–57, 161

The Sellout (Beatty), 14, 24, 105–6, 116, 124–31, 140, 214
sentimentalism: abolition, 12–13, 52–63; child soldiers, 69–104; in modern slavery, 35–68; rejection of, 71, 100, 106, 129, 138–39, 188; slave narrative, 19–20; *Zong* slave ship, 5–6
sex trafficking, 37–38, 40–44; *Becoming Abigail* (Abani), 66–68
Shakespeare, William, 151–70, 203
Sharpe, Christina, 6, 228n71
Sharpe, Jenny, 246n28
The Signifying Monkey (Gates), 141–44
Slahi, Mohamedou Ould, 25, 28
Slaughter, Joseph, 42, 63, 191, 230n102
slave narrative: child soldier fictions, 69–104; contemporary revival, 1–5, 35–68; as genre, 16–19, 225n36; global slave narrative, 25–30; master plan, 17. *See also* gothic; neo-slave narrative; sentimentalism; Talking Book; ventriloquism
Smallwood, Stephanie, 11
Smith, Valerie, 18, 226n44
social death, 3, 22, 25–26, 38
Song for Night (Abani), 73–74, 95–99
Sozaboy (Saro-Wiwa), 95–96, 102, 239n53
Spillers, Hortense, 21–22, 53
Spivak, Gayatri Chakravorty, 28, 97, 229n87
Stauffer, John, 52
Steinem, Gloria, 41
Stepto, Robert, 18
Stoler, Ann, 10–11
Stowe, Harriet Beecher, 52, 119, 147
"Stranger in the Village" (Baldwin), 169–70
subaltern, 67, 95, 97–98
Sudan, 3, 13, 46–49, 54–58, 61
surrogation, 5, 160, 168
Swift, Jonathan, 133, 135–36

Talking Book, 14–15, 18, 136, 141–70, 238n34
textuality, 98, 141–46, 149, 162

Thirty Girls (Minot), 26–27, 77, 81–84, 224n24
time: of analogy, 10–11, 174; and genre, 32; of satire, 111, 113; of slavery (Hartman), 110; timelessness, 87, 99, 155, 167, 203; time travel, 21, 115, 131, 134–38
Todorov, Tzvetan, 31–32
Tompkins, Jane, 52
translation: *Allah Is Not Obliged* (Kourouma), 100; *Desdemona* (Morrison), 161; *The Nature of Blood* (Phillips), 156; *Song for Night* (Abani), 96; world literature, 29
Traoré, Rokia, 157, 161–62
trauma, 3, 23, 184; child soldier fictions, 69–104; comparison, 155; migration, 172–73, 178–82; modern slavery, 47–68; *Open City* (Cole), 195–96, 204; rejection of, 108–16
Trump, Donald J., 7–8, 214

Uganda, 76–77, 237n21
Uncle Tom's Cabin (Stowe), 52, 119, 147
Underground Railroad, 138
The Underground Railroad (Whitehead), 116, 131–40, 243n43, 244n52, 244n53

ventriloquism: archives, 151–60; *Othello* and, 32, 151, 161–63; racial ventriloquism, 14, 32, 144–66, 245n18; slave narrative as literary, 14, 145–46, 152; Talking Book, 14, 141–70; *What Is the What* (Eggers), 56, 60–61
Voyage of the Sable Venus (Lewis), 14, 23, 145, 149–51

war crimes, 38, 127, 154, 164
Warren, Kenneth, 226n54, 241n9
Weheliye, Alexander, 245n8
We Need New Names (Bulawayo), 15, 174, 178, 182–89
What Is the What (Eggers), 12, 47, 54–63
Whitehead, Colson: anti-sentimental, 138–39; *The Intuitionist*, 133; post-

blackness, 106, 132; racial allegory, 131, 137, 140; realism, 131–33; temporality, 134–35, 244n45; *The Underground Railroad*, 14, 116, 131–40, 212, 243n43, 244n52, 244n53

whiteness, 83, 163, 199; in American literature, 165–66; Beatty on, 124, 127–29; blackface and, 146; of humanitarian workers, 40, 44–45, 49, 51, 82, 100, 185–86; Morrison on, 151–56, 160–66, 168; Phillips on, 155–60; *Pym* (Johnson), 14, 118–20; racism and, 117–18; slave narrative and editors of, 3, 16–17, 25, 49–50, 71, 116, 146, 151–52; Underground Railroad and saviors as, 138

"White-Savior Industrial Complex," 199

white supremacy, 2, 108, 128, 211–13, 244n52

Wilderson, Frank B., 10

world literature, 4–5, 29–32, 149–51, 178; *GraceLand* (Abani), 189–95

Wright, Michelle, 243n40

Zeleza, Paul, 205, 250n16

Zimbabwe, 182–87, 189

Zong! (Philip), 14, 23, 145, 148–49

Zong slave ship, 5–6, 23, 148

ABOUT THE AUTHOR

Yogita Goyal is Professor of African American Studies and English at the University of California, Los Angeles. She is the author of *Romance, Diaspora, and Black Atlantic Literature* (2010) and the President of the Association for the Study of the Arts of the Present.

.

www.ingramcontent.com/pod-product-compliance
Lightning Source LLC
Chambersburg PA
CBHW020401080526
44584CB00014B/1120